A Study Guide to
the ISTQB® Foundation Level 2018 Syllabus

Adam Roman

A Study Guide
to the ISTQB® Foundation Level
2018 Syllabus

Test Techniques and Sample Mock Exams

 Springer

Adam Roman
Institute of Computer Science and
Computational Mathematics
Jagiellonian University
Krakow, Poland

ISBN 978-3-319-98739-2   ISBN 978-3-319-98740-8   (eBook)
https://doi.org/10.1007/978-3-319-98740-8

Library of Congress Control Number: 2018952487

This Springer imprint is published by the registered company Springer Nature Switzerland AG
The registered company address is: Gewerbestrasse 11, 6330 Cham, Switzerland

Preface

This book is an excellent, helpful, and up-to-date resource for all the candidates preparing for the ISTQB® Foundation Level certification exam based on a **new Foundation Level 2018 Syllabus**. There are many sample questions and information related to the Foundation Level exam on the web. However, there are two problems with them. First, most of them will be outdated in a while, as the old syllabus and exams will be retracted on June 4, 2019. Second, much of this stuff is of bad quality. Many sample questions that can be found on the web do not follow the strict ISTQB® examination rules. For example:

- They refer to terms that are not defined in the syllabus (so the knowledge of these terms is not required when taking the exam).
- They use the proper names of tools or applications, which a candidate does not need to know about.
- They are incorrectly constructed—for example, a question that should examine some Learning Objective on a K3 level does it only on K1 level, which is a clear violation of the exam question construction rules.

Finally, one can observe a persistent problem with the test techniques. Many explanations of these methods are incorrect, ambiguous, or even wrong. Errors can be found even in the respectable books and official ISTQB® materials. Here are some examples:

- In the book by Black and Mitchell (*Advanced Software Testing* vol. 3), the MC/DC white-box technique is incorrectly explained—the set of test cases given in the example does not achieve the MC/DC coverage.
- In the monograph by Binder (*Testing Object-Oriented Systems*), the technique related to the so-called linearly independent paths is incorrectly interpreted.
- In the official Advanced Level—Test Analyst ISTQB® exam, there is a mistake in one of the questions on state transition testing: the answers do not contain the correct number of 1-switches that need to be covered.

- Another question from the same exam, related to the domain analysis, does not follow the coverage rules described in the syllabus and incorrectly interprets the notion of the boundary.

Below is a list of things that distinguish this book from other ISTQB® exam-related resources:

- **Topicality.** The material in this book complies with the newest version of the Foundation Level Syllabus published in 2018.
- **Quality and originality.** The exam questions in this book are original, not redundant, of high quality, fully aligned with the ISTQB® exam requirements and have never been published before.
- **Huge amount of material.** The book contains five full sample exams (200 questions in total) designed according to the ISTQB® exam rules, with the appropriate distribution of questions regarding the Learning Objectives and K-levels.
- **Well-thought-out sample questions.** Questions are constructed not only to cover the corresponding Learning Objectives in a proper way, but also to show the typical pitfalls usually placed in the exam questions by the respective authors.
- **Diversity.** Questions from different sample exams related to the same Learning Objective are diverse, that is, each of them points out different aspects of a given Learning Objective. This is an excellent method for better and more effective learning and preparing for the exam.
- **Comprehensive, intelligible explanations.** All answers are justified and explained in an exhaustive and detailed way that is easy to understand. We explain not only why a given answer is correct, but also why all the others are wrong. This helps the candidate to understand the way of thinking of a person who designs the exam questions and also helps in better preparation for the exam.
- **A lot of bonus stuff.** The book contains a great bonus pack: the chapters that explain the white-box and black-box test techniques in a detailed way, a set of exercises on test techniques, and the detailed solutions to them. These chapters also discuss some important issues related to the test techniques not mentioned in the syllabus. It is good to be aware of them, as they occur frequently in the exam questions. Another chapter gives some useful tips and tricks that may help the candidate to be more efficient during the preparation and during the exam. Yet another one presents the new version of the Glossary containing terms related to the 2018 Foundation Level Syllabus, as there are some significant changes when compared with the old 2011 syllabus. Finally, the last chapter shows the question numbers in all five sample exam sets, sorted by Learning Objectives. This is very helpful if you want to assess your knowledge related to a specific Learning Objective.

ISTQB® Certification Product Portfolio On January 2016, ISTQB® publicly announced its new product portfolio that constitutes a considerable evolution in ISTQB® go-to-market strategy. The product portfolio architecture has been evolved on the basis of several market studies as well as the outcomes of the ISTQB® Effectiveness Survey. Its main goals are to:

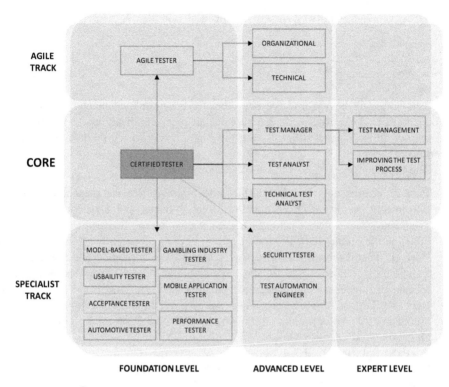

Fig. 1 ISTQB® Certification Portfolio (from May 2018)

- Maintain the mission and vision of ISTQB® and keep the high quality of deliverables that has marked the success of the scheme worldwide.
- Maintain the focus on software testing.
- Maintain the validity of certifications already obtained.
- Extend the coverage of ISTQB® certifications to additional specific topics.
- Make the scheme more modular.
- Make it easier for professionals to obtain the specific certifications they are interested in.
- Provide an overall framework in which existing as well as future modules will fit in a coherent way.

The portfolio is presented in Fig. 1. It follows a matrix approach characterized by two characteristics:

- **Levels**—that identify progressively increasing Learning Objectives

    – Foundation Level
    – Advanced Level
    – Expert Level

- **Streams**—that identify clusters of certification modules

  - Core track
  - Specialist track
  - Agile track

This book will help you to prepare better for the most fundamental certificate: Foundation Level certificate. It is a base for all other certifications: to sit for the exams for all the other certificates, you must be a holder of the Foundation Level certificate.

The book consists of four parts and the appendix:

- **Part I: Foundation Level Syllabus and Exam**—here we present detailed information on the 2018 Foundation Level Syllabus and Foundation Level examination, its structure, and rules. The information in this part of the book is based on the official ISTQB® documents.
- **Part II: Test Techniques**—here we present all the white-box and black-box techniques described in the syllabus. We also give over 30 exercises on these techniques, together with the detailed solutions.
- **Part III: Sample Mock Exams**—here we give five full sets of exam questions (altogether 200 test questions), following the ISTQB® exam rules and covering all the required Learning Objectives.
- **Part IV: Solutions and Answers**—here we give the solutions, extensive justifications, and detailed answers to all the exercises and exam questions from Parts II and III.
- **Appendices**—The Appendices contain the Glossary Terms for the new 2018 version of the Foundation Level Syllabus and the table that shows the distribution of the mock exam questions prepared to fulfill the Learning Objectives, which allows the reader to locate easily all the sample questions that cover a given Learning Objective. This table is very helpful when a reader wants to practice only some particular part of the syllabus material (e.g., the questions on boundary value analysis, the questions on the test process, etc.).

Krakow, Poland   Adam Roman

Contents

About the Author

Adam Roman, (Ph.D., Dr.Sc.), is a member of the Polish ISTQB® Board. He has over 11 years of experience in software testing, both as a researcher and as a teacher. He was a reviewer of the ISTQB® Foundation Level 2018 Syllabus, ISTQB® Model-Based Testing sample exam, as well as the author of many ISTQB® exam questions for both the foundation and advanced levels. He is a member of the ISTQB® Glossary Working Group. He conducted several dozens of trainings, preparing candidates to the Foundation and Advanced Level certification exams.

Adam Roman is a certified tester and a software quality engineer, holding the following certificates:

ASQ (American Society for Quality) Certified Software Quality Engineer
ISTQB® Certified Tester—Foundation Level
ISTQB® Certified Tester—Foundation Extension: Agile Tester
ISTQB® Certified Tester Advanced Level—Test Analyst
ISTQB® Certified Tester Advanced Level—Technical Test Analyst
ISTQB® Certified Tester Advanced Level—Test Manager

He is one of the best recognized testing experts in Poland, mainly because of his 1100 plus page monograph *Software Testing: Models, Techniques and Tools* (published in Polish). He is also the author of the *Thinking Driven Testing*, a book published by Springer, as well as the co-editor of several books on software testing published in Poland (*Software Testing in Practice*—vols. 1 and 2, *Requirements Engineering in Practice*). He is a member of the Polish Committee for Standardization, where he worked on the ISO/IEC/IEEE 29119 Software Testing Standard, which the Foundation Syllabus refers to.

Adam Roman is a professor of computer science at Jagiellonian University. He has published over 40 scientific papers in many peer-reviewed journals. He was a supervisor to more than 40 MSc and PhD students and guided them in writing their theses, including over 10 in the field of software testing. Since 2008, he has given lectures and conducted seminars on software testing at Jagiellonian University. He has also participated in many academic and commercial projects on software testing and quality assurance. He collaborates with many IT companies in Poland in the field of software quality. He was an invited speaker at many software testing conferences and is an expert in the field of test design techniques, mutation testing, and software quality models.

Part I
Foundation Level Syllabus and Exam

Chapter 1
2018 Foundation Syllabus Overview

In this chapter, we briefly introduce the objectives of the ISTQB® certification program and the content of the Foundation Level 2018 syllabus. We also explain what are the Learning Objectives and K-levels, because the exam questions and exam structure are based on these notions. Most of the material in this chapter and Chap. 2 comes from the official ISTQB® documents that can be found on www.istqb.org.

1.1 Background and History of the Foundation Certificate in Software Testing

The independent certification of software testers began in the UK with the British Computer Society's Information Systems Examination Board (ISEB), when a Software Testing Board was set up in 1998 (www.bcs.org.uk/iseb). In 2002, Application Specific Qualification Facility (ASQF) in Germany began to support a German tester qualification scheme (www.asqf.de). The Foundation Level Syllabus is based on the ISEB and ASQF syllabi; it includes reorganized, updated, and additional content, and the emphasis is directed at topics that will provide the most practical help to testers.

The Foundation Certificate does not expire and does not need to be renewed. The date it was awarded is shown on the certificate.

Within each participating country, local aspects are controlled by a national ISTQB®-recognized Software Testing Board. Duties of national boards are specified by the ISTQB® but are implemented within each country. The duties of country boards are expected to include the accreditation of training providers and the setting of exams.

© Springer Nature Switzerland AG 2018
A. Roman, *A Study Guide to the ISTQB® Foundation Level 2018 Syllabus*,
https://doi.org/10.1007/978-3-319-98740-8_1

1.2   Objectives of the Foundation Certificate Qualification

If you bought this book, you probably have already decided to take the ISTQB®
Foundation Level exam. However, if you are still considering the pros and cons of
the certification, in this section, we describe the official objectives of the Foundation
Level Certificate qualification:

- To gain recognition for testing as an essential and professional software engi-
  neering specialization
- To provide a standard framework for the development of testers' careers
- To enable professionally qualified testers to be recognized by employers, cus-
  tomers, and peers and to raise the profile of testers
- To promote consistent and good testing practices within all software engineering
  disciplines
- To identify testing topics that are relevant and of value to industry
- To enable software suppliers to hire certified testers and thereby gain commercial
  advantage over their competitors by advertising their tester recruitment policy
- To provide an opportunity for testers and those with an interest in testing to
  acquire an internationally recognized qualification in the subject

The following list, adapted from the ISTQB® meeting at Sollentuna in November
2001, gives some more general objectives of the international software testing
qualification program. It may be considered as the list of arguments for the certification in software testing:

- To be able to compare testing skills across different countries
- To enable testers to move across country borders more easily
- To enable multinational/international projects to have a common understanding
  of testing issues
- To increase the number of qualified testers worldwide
- To have more impact/value as an internationally based initiative than from any
  country-specific approach
- To develop a common international body of understanding and knowledge about
  testing through the syllabus and terminology and to increase the level of knowl-
  edge about testing for all participants
- To promote testing as a profession in more countries
- To enable testers to gain a recognized qualification in their native language
- To enable sharing of knowledge and resources across countries
- To provide international recognition of testers and this qualification due to
  participation of people from many countries in this qualification scheme

1.3 Syllabus Content

Chapter 1: Fundamentals of Testing The tester learns the basic principles related to testing, the reasons why testing is required, what test objectives are, and the principles of successful testing. The tester understands the test process, the major activities, and work products.

Chapter 2: Testing Throughout the Software Development Life Cycle The tester learns how testing is incorporated in every step of a software development life cycle. The tester learns about the different test levels, test types, and impact analysis when working with maintenance testing.

Chapter 3: Static Techniques The tester learns the various static techniques of testing such as static analysis and reviews (i.e., informal reviews, walkthroughs, technical reviews, and inspections). The tester learns how to apply a review technique to a work product to find defects.

Chapter 4: Test Techniques The tester learns how to apply test techniques to derive test cases from other software work products. Black-box, white-box, and experience-based test techniques are covered.

Chapter 5: Test Management Test management is covered from a perspective where the tester can work with test managers, focusing on risk-based testing, test execution and defect reporting, and handling. The tester learns what could be included in the various test documentation work products, such as test plans and reports. The tester learns to report defects in a clear and understandable way.

Chapter 6: Tool Support for Testing The tester learns to classify tools, the risks and benefits connected with tools, and aspects of selecting and introducing tools.

1.4 Structure of the Syllabus with the Corresponding Learning Objectives

The examinable part of the Foundation Level Syllabus consists of six chapters (described above), divided further into sections. Each section is related to one or more Learning Objectives (LOs; see Sect. 2.1 for a detailed explanation on what the Learning Objectives are). Below we present in detail the examinable part of the syllabus with the corresponding LOs.

Notice that the exam questions will verify your knowledge against the Learning Objectives, not the content of the syllabus or any other source of knowledge! Therefore, when you study the syllabus, pay attention to them. When you learn from a given syllabus section, do it with regard to the Learning Objectives from this section. Learning Objectives are numbered in the form FL-x.y.z, where FL denotes the Foundation Level Syllabus, x denotes the chapter, y denotes the section, and z is the sequence number of the Learning Objectives within a given section.

Chapter 1. Fundamentals of Testing

1.1. What Is Testing?

- FL-1.1.1 (K1) Identify typical objectives of testing.
- FL-1.1.2 (K2) Differentiate testing from debugging.

1.2. Why Is Testing Necessary?

- FL-1.2.1 (K2) Give examples of why testing is necessary.
- FL-1.2.2 (K2) Describe the relationship between testing and quality assurance and give examples of how testing contributes to higher quality.
- FL-1.2.3 (K2) Distinguish between error, defect, and failure.
- FL-1.2.4 (K2) Distinguish between the root cause of a defect and its effects.

1.3. Seven Testing Principles

- FL-1.3.1 (K2) Explain the seven testing principles.

1.4. Test Process

- FL-1.4.1 (K2) Explain the impact of context on the test process.
- FL-1.4.2 (K2) Describe the test activities and respective tasks within the test process.
- FL-1.4.3 (K2) Differentiate the work products that support the test process.
- FL-1.4.4 (K2) Explain the value of maintaining traceability between the test basis and test work products.

1.5. The Psychology of Testing

- FL-1.5.1 (K1) Identify the psychological factors that influence the success of testing.
- FL-1.5.2 (K2) Explain the difference between the mindset required for testing activities and the mindset required for development activities.

Chapter 2. Testing Throughout the Software Development Life Cycle

2.1. Software Development Life Cycle Models

- FL-2.1.1 (K2) Explain the relationships between software development activities and test activities in the software development life cycle.
- FL-2.1.2 (K1) Identify reasons why software development life cycle models must be adapted to the context of project and product characteristics.

2.2. Test Levels

- FL-2.2.1 (K2) Compare the different test levels from the perspective of objectives, test basis, test objects, typical defects and failures, and approaches and responsibilities.

2.3. Test Types

- FL-2.3.1 (K2) Compare functional, nonfunctional, and white-box testing.
- FL-2.3.2 (K1) Recognize that functional, nonfunctional, and white-box tests occur at any test level.
- FL-2.3.3 (K2) Compare the purposes of confirmation testing and regression testing.

2.4. Maintenance Testing

- FL-2.4.1 (K2) Summarize triggers for maintenance testing.
- FL-2.4.2 (K2) Describe the role of impact analysis in maintenance testing.

Chapter 3. Static Testing

3.1. Static Testing Basics

- FL-3.1.1 (K1) Recognize types of software work products that can be examined by the different static testing techniques.
- FL-3.1.2 (K2) Use examples to describe the value of static testing.
- FL-3.1.3 (K2) Explain the difference between static and dynamic techniques, considering objectives, types of defects to be identified, and the role of these techniques within the software life cycle.

3.2. Review Process

- FL-3.2.1 (K2) Summarize the activities of the work product review process.
- FL-3.2.2 (K1) Recognize the different roles and responsibilities in a formal review.
- FL-3.2.3 (K2) Explain the differences between different review types: informal review, walkthrough, technical review, and inspection.
- FL-3.2.4 (K3) Apply a review technique to a work product to find defects.
- FL-3.2.5 (K2) Explain the factors that contribute to a successful review.

Chapter 4. Test Techniques

4.1. Categories of Test Techniques

- FL-4.1.1 (K2) Explain the characteristics, commonalities, and differences between black-box test techniques, white-box test techniques, and experience-based test techniques.

4.2. Black-Box Test Techniques

- FL-4.2.1 (K3) Apply equivalence partitioning to derive test cases from given requirements.
- FL-4.2.2 (K3) Apply boundary value analysis to derive test cases from given requirements.
- FL-4.2.3 (K3) Apply decision table testing to derive test cases from given requirements.
- FL-4.2.4 (K3) Apply state transition testing to derive test cases from given requirements.
- FL-4.2.5 (K2) Explain how to derive test cases from a use case.

4.3. White-Box Test Techniques

- FL-4.3.1 (K2) Explain statement coverage.
- FL-4.3.2 (K2) Explain decision coverage.
- FL-4.3.3 (K2) Explain the value of statement and decision coverage.

4.4. Experience-Based Test Techniques

- FL-4.4.1 (K2) Explain error guessing.
- FL-4.4.2 (K2) Explain exploratory testing.
- FL-4.4.3 (K2) Explain checklist-based testing.

Chapter 5. Test Management

5.1. Test Organization

- FL-5.1.1 (K2) Explain the benefits and drawbacks of independent testing.
- FL-5.1.2 (K1) Identify the tasks of a test manager and tester.

5.2. Test Planning and Estimation

- FL-5.2.1 (K2) Summarize the purpose and content of a test plan.
- FL-5.2.2 (K2) Differentiate between various test strategies.
- FL-5.2.3 (K2) Give examples of potential entry and exit criteria.
- FL-5.2.4 (K3) Apply knowledge of prioritization, and technical and logical dependencies to schedule test execution for a given set of test cases.
- FL-5.2.5 (K1) Identify factors that influence the effort related to testing.
- FL-5.2.6 (K2) Explain the difference between two estimation techniques: the metrics-based technique and the expert-based technique.

5.3. Test Monitoring and Control

- FL-5.3.1 (K1) Recall metrics used for testing.
- FL-5.3.2 (K2) Summarize the purposes, contents, and audiences for test reports.

5.4. Configuration Management

- FL-5.4.1 (K2) Summarize how configuration management supports testing.

5.5. Risks and Testing

- FL-5.5.1 (K1) Define risk level by using likelihood and impact.
- FL-5.5.2 (K2) Distinguish between project and product risks.
- FL-5.5.3 (K2) Describe, by using examples, how product risk analysis may influence the thoroughness and scope of testing.

5.6. Defect Management

- FL-5.6.1 (K3) Write a defect report, covering defects found during testing.

Chapter 6. Tool Support for Testing

6.1. Test tool considerations

- FL-6.1.1 (K2) Classify test tools according to their purpose and the test activities they support.
- FL-6.1.2 (K1) Identify benefits and risks of test automation.
- FL-6.1.3 (K1) Remember special considerations for test execution and test management tools.

6.2. Effective use of tools

- FL-6.2.1 (K1) Identify the main principles for selecting a tool.
- FL-6.2.2 (K1) Recall the objectives for using pilot projects to introduce tools.
- FL-6.2.3 (K1) Identify the success factors for evaluation, implementation, deployment, and on-going support of test tools in an organization.

In total there are 62 Learning Objectives in the syllabus:

- 15 K1 Learning Objectives
- 40 K2 Learning Objectives
- 7 K3 Learning Objectives

The exam consists of 40 questions, so it will cover ca. 40 of them (some questions may cover more than one Learning Objective; also, one of the FL-4.2.1 and FL-4.2.2 will be covered by two questions).

1.5   Business Outcomes

Table 1.1 presents the Business Outcomes expected of a candidate who has achieved the Foundation Level certification. Business Outcomes represent the skills that a certified tester should have.

Table 1.1 Business Outcomes for the Foundation Level certificate

FL-BO1	Promote efficient and effective communication by using a common vocabulary for software testing.
FL-BO2	Understand fundamental concepts of software testing.
FL-BO3	Demonstrate understanding of how different development and testing practices, and different constraints on testing, may apply in optimizing testing to different contexts.
FL-BO4	Contribute effectively in reviews.
FL-BO5	Use established techniques for designing tests at all test levels.
FL-BO6	Interpret and execute tests from given test specifications. Report on test results.
FL-BO7	Understand test management principles for resources, strategies, planning, project control, and risk management.
FL-BO8	Write and communicate clear and understandable defect reports.
FL-BO9	Understand the project factors that drive the test priorities and the test approach.
FL-BO10	Understand the value that software testing brings to stakeholders.
FL-BO11	Appreciate how testing activities and work products align with project objectives, measures, and targets.
FL-BO12	Assist in the selection and implementation process of testing tools.

1.6 Changes in the New Version of the Syllabus

ISTQB® Foundation syllabus 2018 is a major update and rewrite of the 2011 release. For this reason, the ISTQB® did not publish a detailed release note per chapter and section, but a separate Release Note document where all changes can be viewed on Learning Objective level. In the separate Release Note document, there is traceability from all Learning Objectives in 2011 to 2018, which have been added, updated, or removed.

In the 2018 version, all Learning Objectives have been edited to make them atomic and to create a 1 on 1 traceability from Learning Objectives to content, and not having content without also having a Learning Objective.

The goal has been to make this version easier to read, understand, learn, and translate while also focus on increasing the practical usefulness and the balance between knowledge and skills.

This major release has made the following changes:

- Fewer K1 Learning Objectives in general: 15 in 2017 compared with 27 in 2011.
- Less focus on Chapter 5 Test Management: 15 Learning Objectives in 2017 compared with 24 in 2011.
- More emphasis on review, a K3 Learning Objective has been added to Chapter 3.
  - Static Analysis by Tools sections is removed, and will be covered in other syllabi.
- More emphasis on test techniques in Chapter 4.
  - Section 4.1 of 2011 moved and merged with Section 1.4 of Chapter 1.

- Agile is mentioned in the content of the syllabus but not included in wording of any Learning Objective.
- White box techniques downgraded.
  - K3 and K4 removed—they will be covered in other syllabi.

Additional changes made to the 2018 Foundation syllabus are the following:

- ISO/IEC/IEEE 29119 is now used for reference instead of IEEE 829 standard.
- ISO/IEC 25010 is now used for reference instead of ISO 9126 standard.
- ISO/IEC 20246 is now used for reference instead of IEEE 1028.
- The Code of Ethics has been moved from Chapter 1 to the istqb.org web page.

Chapter 2
ISTQB® Foundation Level Exam Structure and Rules

In this chapter we give a detailed information on the Foundation Level exam structure and the rules it follows. The Foundation Level examinations are based on the Foundation Level Syllabus. Answers to examination questions may require the use of material from more than one section of the syllabus. All Learning Objectives (on cognitive level K1–K3) in the syllabus are examinable. All keywords in the syllabus are examinable for their definition (K1). Each exam question *must* be related to one or more Learning Objectives or Glossary term. You cannot be asked about things that go outside the scope of the syllabus. Therefore, it is important to study the Learning Objectives for all chapters—you will better know what to expect during the exam.

2.1 Learning Objectives and K-Levels

The Learning Objectives support the Business Outcomes and are used to create the examination for achieving the Certified Tester Foundation Level. Each Learning Objective is examinable at a certain level, expressed in terms of the so-called cognitive levels (K levels). These cognitive levels come from the so-called Bloom's Taxonomy[1]—a framework for categorizing educational goals. The original taxonomy consists of six categories: Knowledge, Comprehension, Application, Analysis, Synthesis, and Evaluation. In 2001, the taxonomy was revised[2] by a group of cognitive psychologists. It points to a more dynamic concept of classification by describing the cognitive levels by verbs and gerunds rather than nouns of the original

---

[1]Bloom, B.S., Engelhart, M.D., Furst E.J., Hill, W.H., Krathwohl, D.R., Taxonomy of educational objectives: The classification of educational goals. Handbook 1: Cognitive domain, New York: David McKay (1956).

[2]Anderson, L.W., Krathwohl, D.R., et al., A taxonomy for learning, teaching and assessing: a revision of Bloom's taxonomy of educational objectives, New York: Longman (2001).

© Springer Nature Switzerland AG 2018
A. Roman, *A Study Guide to the ISTQB® Foundation Level 2018 Syllabus*,
https://doi.org/10.1007/978-3-319-98740-8_2

taxonomy. The six levels of the revised taxonomy are: Remember, Understand, Apply, Analyze, Evaluate, and Create.

The Foundation Level Syllabus uses only first three of them. The specific Learning Objectives levels are shown at the beginning of each chapter and classified as follows:

- K1: Remember
- K2: Understand
- K3: Apply

The Foundation Level Certificate examination is based on the syllabus. Answers to examination questions may require the use of material based on more than one section of this syllabus. All sections of the syllabus are examinable.

In general, all parts of the syllabus are examinable at a K1 level. That is, the candidate will recognize, remember, and recall a term or concept. This is also true regarding the definitions of terms required to be known by the candidate. On the official ISTQB® web page, www.istqb.org, you can download the Glossary for the Foundation Level and get familiar with the required vocabulary. The Glossary can be also found in the Appendix A.

The following Learning Objectives are defined as applying to the Foundation Level syllabus. Each topic in the syllabus will be examined according to the Learning Objective for it.

Level 1: Remember (K1): Recall Facts and Basic Concepts The candidate will recognize, remember, and recall a term or concept.

Keywords: identify, remember, retrieve, recall, recognize, know

Example: Can recognize the definition of "failure" as:

- "Nondelivery of service to an end user or any other stakeholder"
- "Actual deviation of the component or system from its expected delivery, service or result"

Level 2: Understand (K2): Explain Ideas or Concepts The candidate can select the reasons or explanations for statements related to the topic and can summarize, compare, classify, categorize, and give examples for the testing concept.

Keywords: summarize, generalize, abstract, classify, compare, map, contrast, exemplify, interpret, translate, represent, infer, conclude, categorize, construct models

Example: Can explain the reason why test analysis and design should occur as early as possible:

- To find defects when they are cheaper to remove
- To find the most important defects first

Example: Can explain the similarities and differences between integration and system testing:

- Similarities: The test objects for both integration testing and system testing include more than one component, and both integration testing and system testing can include nonfunctional test types.

- Differences: Integration testing concentrates on interfaces and interactions, and system testing concentrates on whole-system aspects, such as end-to-end processing.

Level 3: Apply (K3): Use Information in New Situation   The candidate can select the correct application of a concept or technique and apply it to a given context.

Keywords: implement, execute, use, follow a procedure, apply a procedure

Example: Can identify boundary values for valid and invalid partitions.

Example: Can select test cases from a given state transition diagram in order to cover all transitions.

2.2   Entry Requirements

The Foundation Level qualification is suitable for anyone who is involved as well as interested in software testing. This includes people in roles such as testers, test analysts, test engineers, test consultants, test managers, user acceptance testers, and software developers. This Foundation Level qualification is also appropriate for anyone who wants a basic understanding of software testing, such as project managers, quality managers, software development managers, business analysts, IT directors, and management consultants.

The entry criterion for taking the ISTQB® Certified Tester Foundation Level Software Testing exam is that candidates have an interest in software testing. However, it is strongly recommended (although not necessary) that candidates also:

- Have at least a minimal background in either software development or software testing, such as 6-month experience as a system or user acceptance tester or as a software developer
- Take a course that has been accredited to ISTQB® standards (by one of the ISTQB®-recognized member boards)

Exams may be taken as part of an accredited training course or taken independently (e.g., at an examination center or in a public exam). Completion of an accredited training course is not a prerequisite for the exam.

2.3   The Exam

General Information About the Exam

The Certified Tester Foundation Level examination is based solely on the Certified Tester Foundation Level Syllabus. Answers to examination questions may require the use of material from more than one section of the syllabus. All Learning

Objectives (on cognitive levels K1–K3) in the syllabus are examinable. Also, all keywords in the syllabus are examinable for their definition (K1).

Foundation Level Exam Structure

The examination comprises 40 multiple-choice questions. Each correct answer has a value of one point. Hence, the maximum possible score for each examination is 40. There are no negative points (so, giving the wrong answer results in 0 points). The time allowed for the examination is 60 minutes, if given in the candidate's native language. If the candidate's native language is not the examination language, the time allowed is 75 minutes.

Each question is a multiple-choice question. The most typical (and recommended) question type has four possible answers, from which exactly one is correct. However, there *may* be questions with five possible answers, from which you will have to choose one or two correct answers. In such a case, you will always be informed about the number of correct answers that you need to choose. Since such "one-out-of-five" or "two-out-of-five" questions are considered to be more difficult than "one-out-of-four" questions, but are still worth one point, it is not recommended to use them in the Foundation Level exams.

Passing Score

A score of at least 65% is required to pass. This means that a candidate must answer correctly at least 26 out of 40 questions.

Question Distribution

Exam questions are distributed based on the cognitive level as follows:

- 20% of each exam is K1 level questions
- 60% of each exam is K2 level questions
- 20% of each exam is K3 level questions (Table 2.1)

The exam questions will be also distributed per chapter, as shown in Table 2.2. Each question must cover a different Learning Objective, except one K3 question from Chapter 4.

Real exam questions may not be arranged by chapters: their order may be random.

Table 2.1 Exam question distribution and timing based on cognitive levels

Cognitive level	Number of questions	Question timing (approximate)	Total time by K level
K1	8	1 minute per question	8 min
K2	24	1 minute per question	24 min
K3	8	3 minutes per question	24 min
Total	40		56 min

Table 2.2 Exam question distribution per chapter

Chapter	# of "keyword" questions	# of K1 questions	# of K2 questions	# of K3 questions	Total
1	1	**1** from: FL-1.1.1, FL-1.5.1	**6** from: FL-1.1.2, FL-1.2.1, FL-1.2.2, FL-1.2.3, FL-1.2.4, FL-1.3.1, FL-1.4.1, FL-1.4.2, FL-1.4.3, FL-1.4.4, FL-1.5.2	**0**	**8** K1 = 2 K2 = 6 K3 = 0
2	0	**1** from: FL-2.1.2, FL-2.3.2	**4** from: FL-2.1.1, FL-2.2.1, FL-2.3.1, FL-2.3.3, FL-2.4.1, FL-2.4.2	**0**	**5** K1 = 1 K2 = 4 K3 = 0
3	0	**1** from: FL-3.1.1, FL-3.2.2	**3** from: FL-3.1.2, FL-3.1.3, FL-3.2.1, FL-3.2.3, FL-3.2.5	**1** from: FL-3.2.4	**5** K1 = 1 K2 = 3 K3 = 1
4	1	**0**	**5** from: FL-4.1.1, FL-4.2.5, FL-4.3.1, FL-4.3.2, FL-4.3.3, FL-4.4.1, FL-4.4.2, FL-4.4.3	**5** from: FL-4.2.1, FL-4.2.2, FL-4.2.3, FL-4.2.4 (the fifth question must be based either on FL-4.2.1 or FL-4.2.2)	**11** K1 = 1 K2 = 5 K3 = 5
5	0	**2** from: FL-5.1.2, FL-5.2.5, FL-5.3.1, FL-5.5.1	**5** from: FL-5.1.1, FL-5.2.1, FL-5.2.2, FL-5.2.3, FL-5.2.6, FL-5.3.2, FL-5.4.1, FL-5.5.2, FL-5.5.3	**2** from: FL-5.2.4, FL-5.6.1	**9** K1 = 2 K2 = 5 K3 = 2
6	0	**1** from: FL-6.1.2, FL-6.1.3, FL-6.2.1, FL-6.2.2, FL-6.2.3	**1** from: FL-6.1.1	**0**	**2** K1 = 1 K2 = 1 K3 = 0
Total	2	6	24	8	40

2.4   Exam Tips and Tricks

In this section, we give some tips and tricks for better exam preparation.

Before the Exam

The best way to increase your chances to pass the exam is to study and to learn. **Reading the Syllabus and the Glossary is a must**. Remember that all the exam questions are based strictly on the syllabus. Each of them covers a certain Learning Objective. Some questions even contain the phrases copied from the syllabus. If you read it before, during the exam you will recall these sentences. This will make answering the questions much easier. The knowledge of the Foundation Level–related Glossary terms is mandatory. Make sure that you know and understand all these terms.

Taking a training is also an option. If you are completely new to testing, this is a recommended step. A good, professional trainer will explain to you all the ambiguities and places in the syllabus that may seem to be unclear to you. Also, during the training, the candidates typically solve some mock exams or sample exam questions. For each K3 Learning Objective, there is also a requirement to solve, during the training, an exercise that covers this Learning Objective. No matter whether you take a training or not, you should definitely solve some sample exams. You can find them on the ISTQB® official webpage, and also on the web pages of the national boards. The national boards usually translate them to the national languages. Some boards (like the American board, ASTQB) prepare their own versions of the mock exams. Of course, you can also verify your knowledge using the mock exams from this book. When solving the sample mock exams, read carefully not only the questions and the answers, but also the justifications for the answers: they will show you clearly how the questions are constructed and what are the intentions of the authors who framed these questions.

If you are new to testing and you decide to take a training, it is recommended to take the exam a few days after the training. Taking it immediately after the training is not a good idea. You will need time to get used to dozens of new terms, definitions, concepts, and techniques. However, you should not wait too long: otherwise, you will forget what you have learned. The maximal reasonable period between the training and the exam is 1–2 weeks.

During the Exam

Here are some useful hints, which you can apply during the exam:

Read the questions carefully: Sometimes one word in the stem or in the question completely changes the meaning of the questions and hence—the correct answer.

Pay attention to the keywords: These words and phrases (like Glossary terms, SDLC names, keywords, specific formulations, etc.) are usually very important indicators for the correct answer. For example, if the question says that in your project there is a high *time pressure*, the documentation is *poor*, and the testers are *experienced*, this clearly indicates that the preferable test strategy is the exploratory testing.

Match the question with the corresponding Learning Objective: If you know what Learning Objective the question is related with, it will be easier to answer the question, because you will know the question author's intention.

Watch out for the "negative" questions: These questions are formed with the negative words, like "which of the following is NOT ...," "which of the following is FALSE," "which of the following will NEVER ...," and so on. In these questions, three answers will be correct and you need to find and mark the incorrect one.

Choose the option that directly answers the question: Sometimes more than one option will be true, but only one of them will be the direct answer to the question.

If you don't know the answer, just guess: Do not leave the question unanswered. There are no negative points for choosing the incorrect answer.

The answers with strong statements are *usually* false: If the answer contains such strong statements as "always," "never," "you must ...," they are probably false. Notice that this is just a heuristic method—sometimes, these answers may be correct!

The answers with "weak" statements are *usually* true: If the answer contains words like "usually," "it should," "often ...," they are probably candidates for the correct answer. But, as in the above remark, this is not always true.

For the questions with lot of text in the steam, don't read the stem first: In such questions read the question first, then the answers, and *then* the question stem. This way, you will be aware what are you asked about and you will be able to read the stem with better understanding, paying attention to things that are important.

Don't waste too much time on hard questions: Just leave them and go to the next one. After the first iteration, when you go through all the questions, you will probably know the answer for most of them. When you go back to the unanswered questions, the ideas will start coming to your mind and you will be able to solve most of them. However, there will probably be two or three questions for which you won't know the correct answer. Don't worry—this is typical. In such situations, don't panic and just make a guess. Don't leave the questions unanswered—there are no negative points for the wrong answers.

Trust your intuition: Usually, your first answer is the correct one. This is because the first impression comes from our subconsciousness. The next ones are the product of the "conscious mind," which may be distracted or biased and hence may prompt you to take the the wrong decision.

The "roman questions" are the easiest: In a roman question, you are given a set of options and you are asked to select some subset of these options that fulfills a certain criterion. There is a nice strategy that allows you not to waste too much time on this type of questions. Below, we give an example. Suppose you are asked the following question:

Which of the following answers reflect when regression testing should normally be performed?

I. Every week
II. After the software has changed
III. On the same day each year
IV. When the environment has changed
V. Before the code has been written

Answers:

A. II & IV are true; I, III, & V are false.
B. I &II are true; III, IV, & V are false.
C. II, III, & IV are true; I & V are false.
D. II is true; I, III, IV, & V are false.

First, don't think about each of the five options whether it is true or false—this is a waste of time. Identify an option that is true in two answers and false in two others. For example, IV is true in A and C and false in B and D. Look at option IV: "when the environment has changed." This is a situation when the regression testing should definitely be performed, so the correct answer will be either A or C. Then, compare these two answers and identify the differences. In our case, the only difference between these two answers is III—in A, it is false and in C, it is true. III says: "on the same day each year," which is obviously false. Hence, we have identified the correct answer: A.

Notice that we had to analyze only two out of the five presented options. Of course, when we identify the correct answer, we can check whether it makes sense regarding the other options (in our case, I, II, and V).

Part II
Test Techniques

Chapter 3
Test Techniques and Exercises

Test techniques constitute over 25% of the exam questions and, according to the ISTQB® guidelines, the training should spend over one-third of the time for explaining them. However, the syllabus describes the test techniques very roughly and gives no examples of using them in practice. Therefore, in this part of the book, we describe them in more detail. We give some remarks about the techniques that may be helpful during the exam. We also present some extra exercises on test techniques so that you can practice them better. This is the best way to learn and to master these techniques.

The Foundation syllabus introduces three types of test techniques (see Fig. 3.1):

- **Black-box test techniques** (also called behavioral or specification-based techniques)—based on an analysis of the appropriate test basis, for example: requirements specification, use cases, user stories, business processes, or even the customer knowledge or common sense. Black-box test techniques concentrate on the behavior of the system under test, that is, on the inputs and outputs of the test object, without reference to its internal structure.
- **White-box test techniques** (also called structural or structure-based techniques)—based on an analysis of the architecture, design, internal structure, or the code of the test object. They concentrate on the processing within the test object. The analysis of the internal structure of the test object is used to design test cases.
- **Experience-based test techniques**—utilize the knowledge and experience of developers, testers, and users to determine what should be tested. These techniques are often combined with black-box and white-box test techniques.

The description of the test techniques, as well as the corresponding coverage measures, can be found in the standard ISO/IEC/IEEE 29119-4.

© Springer Nature Switzerland AG 2018
A. Roman, *A Study Guide to the ISTQB® Foundation Level 2018 Syllabus*,
https://doi.org/10.1007/978-3-319-98740-8_3

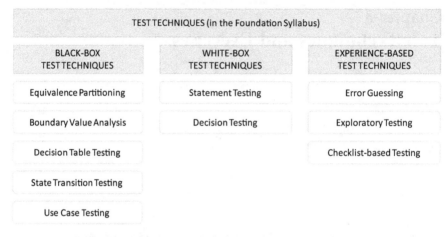

Fig. 3.1 Test techniques introduced in the Foundation syllabus

The syllabus introduces five black-box, two white-box, and three experience-based test techniques. In the following chapters, we will discuss in detail the black-box and white-box techniques. These chapters contain also the exercises that will allow you to understand better the techniques.

Chapter 4
Black-Box Testing Techniques

The common characteristics of the black-box techniques, according to the syllabus, are as follows:

- Test conditions, test cases, and test data are derived from a test basis that may include software requirements, specifications, use cases, and user stories.
- Test cases may be used to detect gaps between the requirements and the implementation of the requirements, as well as deviations from the requirements.
- Coverage is measured based on the items tested in the test basis and the technique applied to the test basis.

Each of the black-box techniques is based on a particular model of the system under test. These models abstract from nonimportant things, and each of them focuses on a certain aspect of the tested system. Such an approach allows us to systematically derive test conditions from the model. It also allows us to detect certain types of defects in the software. Table 4.1 summarizes the black-box techniques, the models related to them, and the typical defects that can be found using these techniques.

4.1 Equivalence Partitioning

4.1.1 Technique Description

Equivalence partitioning (EP) is a domain-oriented technique. Given a domain of some variable, a tester divides it into a finite number of nonempty subsets called *equivalence classes* (or equivalence partitions, or just partitions). The idea is that the partitioning should be done in a way that for any two values from the same equivalence class, the system under test behaves in a similar way. In particular, this means that if for one of these values the system fails, it should also fail for the

© Springer Nature Switzerland AG 2018
A. Roman, *A Study Guide to the ISTQB® Foundation Level 2018 Syllabus*,
https://doi.org/10.1007/978-3-319-98740-8_4

Table 4.1 Summary of the black-box techniques in the Foundation syllabus

Technique	Model	Typical defects that can be found using this technique
Equivalence partitioning	Domain model	Wrong handling of data/domain values
Boundary value analysis	Domain model	Wrong handling of data on the domain boundaries
Decision table testing	Decision logic model	Wrong handling of the business rules
State transition testing	Behavioral model	Wrong handling of transitions between states
Use case testing	Business process model	Wrong handling of the business processing

other one. After partitioning the domain, it is enough to choose to test only one value from each partition.

The EP technique tries—in some sense—to overcome one of the fundamental principles of testing, saying that "exhaustive testing is impossible": from the potentially infinite number of possible inputs, outputs, or internal variables, we derive a finite number of test cases. The test suite size is equal to the number of equivalence classes.

Here are some important considerations about equivalence partitioning:

- It can be used to *any* nonempty domain—it does not need to be a numerical domain, it may be any ordered or unordered set of values, finite or infinite, discrete or continuous, for example: {2, 4, f, d, aa}, an interval [0, 1], an infinite set {0, 1, 2, ...} of nonnegative integers etc.
- The proper partitioning requires that each domain element belongs to exactly one partition and that all partitions are nonempty.
- Equivalence partitioning can be performed not only for the input variables, but also for output ones or any other kind of variables — each domain can be subject to this technique.
- There are two types of partitions: valid and invalid. Valid partitions represent correct, expected values, and incorrect partitions represent incorrect, unexpected values.
- The coverage is computed as the number of different classes from which we picked the elements and tested them, divided by the number of all partitions.
- Taking more than one element from one partition to the test suite does not increase the coverage.

Figure 4.1 shows two different partitionings of the same 7-element set {A, B, C, D, E, F, G}. Each partition is denoted by a gray ellipse. The partition on the left is correct: each element belongs to exactly one partition and there are no empty partitions: the partitions are {A, B}, {C, D, E}, and {F, G}. The partition on the right is incorrect. There are three problems with it:

Fig. 4.1 An example of good and wrong equivalence partitioning. (**a**) Correct partitioning, (**b**) incorrect partitioning

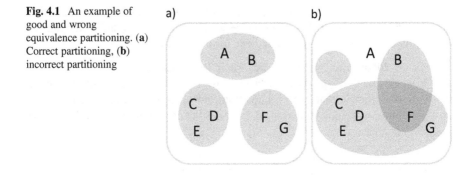

1. There is an empty partition.
2. Element A does not belong to any partition.
3. Element F belongs to two different partitions.

Valid partitions are usually easy to construct—their structure comes from the specification. The more difficult part is to construct the incorrect partitions, because there may be many ways of doing that. For example, assume that the correct partitions are $\{1, 2, \ldots, 10\}$ and $\{11, 12, \ldots, 20\}$. Should we put all values lower than 1 and greater than 20 to one invalid partition or should we create two such partitions, one for the number lower than 1 and another for the numbers greater than 20? What about noninteger numbers? Should they be included in one incorrect partition or to two or more? What about nonnumeric characters, like strings, etc.? And so on. Some exam questions may tell you explicitly that you should consider only valid equivalence classes. Usually, it should be clear from the question what kind of partitions should be considered.

The coverage is calculated as the number of class from which we selected the elements to tests, divided by the total number of all identified equivalence classes. For example, for a partitioning $p_1 = \{1, 2, 3\}$, $p_2 = \{4, 5, 6\}$, $p_3 = \{7, 8\}$, and a set $\{1, 4\}$ of test input values, the coverage is $2/3 \approx 66\%$, because we covered only p_1 and p_2. If we add 2 as the third test input value, we don't increase the coverage, because 2 belongs to the same class as 1, which is already in our test set. On the other hand, if we add a test with the input value 8, the set $\{1, 4, 8\}$ of test values achieves 100% coverage, as we covered all the equivalence classes.

4.1.2 Exercises

Exercise 1: Partitions
Consider the domain $\{1, 2, 3, 4\}$.

(a) Write down all possible partitionings of this domain.

(b) Suppose that some system accepts a value from this set and the following action depends on whether the input value is odd or even. Which equivalence partitioning is the most reasonable one for this problem?

Exercise 2: Identifying Variables and Their Domains

The program TriangleType accepts three positive integers a, b, c as input and returns the type of a triangle that can be built from the sections of lengths a, b, c. The possible outputs are equilateral triangle, isosceles but not equilateral triangle, scalene triangle, not a triangle.

(a) Identify the possible variables and their domains.
(b) What are the reasonable partitionings of these domains?
(c) One of the possible output is "isosceles but not equilateral." Why can't we just write "isosceles"?

Exercise 3: Identifying Partitions from the Specification

During the account registration process, a user chooses his status from a drop-down list. The possible options are: child, student, adult. The system behavior depends on which option will be selected. Suppose you analyze this variable with respect to the equivalence partitioning. What is the domain and how should its partitioning look like?

Exercise 4: One Partition with Many Classes

A system classifies a car according to its age given as the integer input value. The system uses the business rules according to the following algorithm:

```
INPUT CarAge
IF CarAge is incorrect
   THEN Return 'error' and terminate
IF CarAge< 6
   THEN Classify car as 'new'
ELSE IF CarAge ≤ 12
   THEN Classify car as 'used'
ELSE
   Classify car as 'old'
```

Identify valid and invalid equivalence classes. Design the smallest set of test cases that achieves 100% equivalence partition coverage.

Exercise 5: Many Equivalence Partitionings

A BMI calculator calculates the BMI (body mass index) taking as the input two variables: height (in m, with two digit precision) and weight (in kg—an integer value). Valid height is between 1.0 and 2.5 m. Valid weight is between 20 and 300 kg. A test input is a pair (height, weight). If a given variable's value is too low (resp. too high), the system gives a warning message "X too low" (resp. "X too high"), where X denotes height or weight. Design the test cases that cover all valid and invalid equivalence classes for both input variables. Use the following strategy, considered as a good practice:

- First try to cover as many valid equivalence classes as you can.
- Then, provide one test case for each invalid partition (all other data inputs should belong to the valid partitions).

Exercise 6: Hidden Variables
You test a function *CalcSquareArea()*, which takes a side length as an input (which is a nonnegative integer) and returns one out of three possible decisions, according to the area of the square of a given length:

- If area is less than 100, it returns "square too small."
- If area is between 100 and 400, it returns "square OK."
- If area exceeds 400, it returns "square too big."

You want to apply an equivalence partitioning to the output value. Design the test cases.

4.2   Boundary Value Analysis

4.2.1   Technique Description

Boundary value analysis (BVA) is, like EP, also a domain-oriented technique. It is built upon the equivalence partitioning method. The first step in applying the BVA is to perform the equivalence partitioning of a given domain. The difference between EP and BVA lies in the way in which we choose class representants to tests. In the case of EP, we had to take one arbitrary element from each class. In the case of BVA, we take only the so-called *boundary values* of the identified classes. The idea of this method is that the defects are often found on the boundary values of the domains.

The boundary values of a given equivalence class are the minimal and maximal elements from this class. Notice, that this property requires that the elements are *ordered*, and that we can compare them using the relational operators ($<$, $>$, $\leq$, $\geq$, $=$).[1] For example, a set of natural numbers is ordered, because for every two natural numbers, we can say which one is greater and which one is smaller. On the other hand, we cannot apply the BVA to the domain {Linux, Windows, iOS} representing operating systems, because we cannot compare them. It makes no sense to say that, for example, Windows is greater than or equal to Linux.

---

[1]The old, 2011 version of the syllabus claimed that the BVA technique "can only be used when the partition consists of numeric, sequential data," but it is possible to apply this technique to *any* ordered set. For example, we can use it for a set of alphabet letters with a natural, lexicographic order: $a < b < c \ldots < x < y < z$.

There is one more important thing about the equivalence classes that are used in the BVA. Every class needs to be "compact." Formally, this means that if any two values a, b belong to a certain class, then necessarily all elements x, such that $a < x < b$, must also belong to this class. Informally, we can say that the classes cannot have "holes."

As the BVA is based on the EP technique, in the case of the BVA, we also have valid and invalid equivalence classes. The boundary values of the valid classes are called the valid boundary values, and the boundary values of the invalid classes are called the invalid boundary values.

Once we have a proper partitioning, we need to identify the boundary values and select the test values corresponding to them. There are two variants of the BVA method: 2-value and 3-value. In a 2-value version, for each identified equivalence class, the test values are:

- The boundary values of this class (i.e., the minimal and maximal elements)
- The element just below the minimal one
- The element just above the maximal one

Notice that the two last elements are also the boundary values for the adjoining equivalence classes. Hence, if we want to achieve 100% BVA coverage in the 2-value version, we just have to identify all boundary values for all identified classes and take them as the test inputs.

In a 3-value version, for each identified equivalence class, the test values are:

- The boundary values of this class (i.e., the minimal and maximal elements)
- The elements just below and just above the minimal one
- The elements just below and just above the maximal one

Notice that in this case, some test values will not be the boundary values, but the values from the inside of the partitions. Let us see in practice how these two versions work.

Suppose we have a domain {1, 2, ..., 15, 16}, which is split into three valid equivalence classes: {1, ..., 6}, {7, ..., 13}, and {14, ..., 16} (see Fig. 4.2a). The

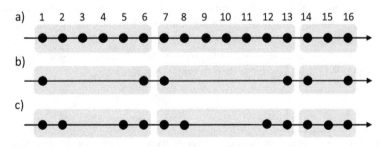

Fig. 4.2 2-value and 3-value versions of the BVA. (**a**) Equivalence partitioning, (**b**) boundary values (and at the same time the test elements for the 2-value version of the BVA), (**c**) test elements for the 3-value version of BVA

domain is ordered and the classes are with no holes. Therefore, we may apply the BVA technique. First, let us identify the boundary values:

- For the class {1, 2, 3, 4, 5, 6}, the boundary values are 1 and 6.
- For the class {7, 8, 9, 10, 11, 12, 13}, the boundary values are 7 and 13.
- For the class {14, 15, 16}, the boundary values are 14 and 16.

In total, we have identified six boundary values for all partitions: 1, 6, 7, 13, 14, 16 (see Fig. 4.2b). As all three classes are valid, these values are the valid boundary values. Which values are selected as test inputs? In the 2-value version, we take the boundary values and their neighbors from other classes. For example, for a boundary value 7 of the second class, we take 7 and its neighbor from other class (in our case 6). Notice that there is a kind of symmetry here: for the boundary value 6 of the first class, we take 6 and 7—the same values. For 13, we take 13 and 14, for 14—we take 14 and 13 and so on. So, if we want to cover all the boundary values for the 2-value version of the BVA, it is enough to identify all the boundary values and take them as the test inputs.

Now consider the smallest and the largest values in our domain, that is, 1 and 16. Which values should be taken as the test inputs in these cases? It depends. If the interface allows us to input values lower than 1, we should definitely have a test with the test input 0. If the interface allows us to input values greater than 16, we should also take the test input 17. In such a case, 0 and 17 are called the invalid boundary values. Otherwise, for example, if the input value can be chosen from a drop-down list and it is impossible to select a value other than the one from the set {1, ..., 16}, we take only 1 and 16.

Hence, the final set of the test values is equal to the set of all the boundary values: 0 (if possible), 1, 6, 7, 13, 14, 16, 17 (if possible).

In the 3-value version for each boundary value x, we take three test inputs: x, the value just below x and the value just above x, no matter which partitions these values belong to. In our example (see Fig. 4.2c), these are

- For the boundary value 1: 0 (if possible), 1, 2
- For the boundary value 6: 5, 6, 7
- For the boundary value 7: 6, 7, 8
- For the boundary value 13: 12, 13, 14
- For the boundary value 14: 13, 14, 15
- For the boundary value 16: 15, 16, 17 (if possible)

Hence, the values to test are: 0 (if possible), 1, 2, 5, 6, 7, 8, 12, 13, 14, 15, 16, 17 (if possible).

Notice that the 3-value version is stronger than the 2-value version, as it requires more elements to cover. The example below shows that sometimes, the 2-value method is not enough to detect a failure.

Suppose that the code should contain the following decision (assume x and y are integers):

```
if (x ≥ 15) then y := 0
```

The program sets y to 0 if and only if x is greater or equal 15. Suppose that this case is of interest to us. When applying the BVA technique to the x value, we see that the natural valid partition is $\{15, 16, 17, \ldots\}$. Suppose that the above-mentioned line of the code was incorrectly implemented as

```
if (x = 15) then y := 0
```

The developer used an equality operator instead of the relational one. In the 2-value version of the BVA, we test the boundary $(x \geq 15)$, so the boundary values are 14 and 15. In case of 14, we see that the outcomes of both correct and incorrect implementations of the predicate are FALSE, because it is not true that $14 \geq 15$, and it is also not true that $14 = 15$. In case of 15 also, both implementations give the same logical value (TRUE): it is true that $15 \geq 15$ and it is also true that $15 = 15$. Hence, neither the test 14, nor 15, detected the fault—in both cases, the expected and actual results are the same!

If we use the 3-value version of the BVA, we need to test not only 14 and 15, but also 16. In case of 16, the condition $(x \geq 15)$ is true (because $16 \geq 15$), but the outcome of the faulty implementation is false, since it is not true that $16 = 15$. Hence, we detected the fault: the expected result (true) is different from the actual one (false).

In case of continuous domains, there is a problem: suppose we have a set of real numbers from 0 to 1 inclusively. The boundary values of this class are obviously 0 and 1, but what are the neighbors from the adjoining classes? For example, what is the value *just above* 1? Is it 2? Or 1.01? Or may be 1.0001? In fact, for every such value, we can find some smaller one, but still greater than 1.

It is because the set of real numbers is *dense*. In practice, this problem is easy to solve: the smallest increment is defined either by the nature of the problem, or by the way the numbers are represented in the computer memory. For example, if we test an e-shop application and the considered variable stores some price in dollars, it is obvious that the smallest increment is $0.01 (one cent). In this case, the boundary values for the set [0, 1] will be -0.01 and 1.01 dollars. If the variable represents some physical value (like the rocket velocity), the precision is defined by the way the value is represented in the memory. The tester may also define other greater, reasonable increment.

What about one-element equivalence classes in case of the 2-value version of the BVA? Suppose that we want to apply it to the class $\{5\}$ for the following partition: $\{1, 2, 3, 4\}, \{5\}, \{6, 7, 8, 9\}$. In such a case, the boundary value 5 should be treated as both the minimal and maximal values in its class. Hence, for 5 as the minimal value, we take 4 and 5 as the test values, and for 5 as the maximal one, we take 5 and 6 as the test values. Altogether, for a boundary value 5 in a 2-value version of the BVA, we need to test the values 4, 5, and 6.

The coverage for the BVA is defined as the number of test values tested divided by the total number of test values identified. Let us consider once again the example from Fig. 4.2 and suppose we can only select the values from the set $\{1, 2, ..., 15, 16\}$. Suppose we chose the following four values to be tested: 5, 6, 10, 14. In case of the 2-value BVA version, the boundary values are 1, 6, 7, 13, 14, 16 and we covered only two of them (6 and 14), so the coverage is $2/6 \approx 33\%$. In this case, the values 5 and 6 do not impact the coverage, as they are not the boundary values.

In the case of the 3-value BVA version, the full set of the test values is $\{1, 2, 5, 6, 7, 8, 12, 13, 14, 15, 16\}$—it has 11 elements. Our four tests covered only 3 of them (5, 6, and 14), so the coverage is $3/11 \approx 27\%$.

4.2.2 Exercises

Exercise 7: Identifying Boundary Values

A system automatically designs the positions of the tiles so that a certain pattern is formed. There are two types of tiles: white and black. The tiles have to be ordered in a sequence, to form a pattern according to the following rules:

- The pattern starts and ends with a sequence of one, two, or three white tiles; the number of initial and final white tiles must be the same.
- Between the initial and final sequences, the pattern forms a repetitive sequence of black and white fragments, starting and ending with the black one; the black fragments consist of three consecutive black tiles and the white ones—of one, two, or three white tiles; all the white fragments must consist of the same number of tiles (1, 2, or 3).
- There must be at least two black fragments in the sequence.

As the input the system takes the integer number $n > 0$ of tiles to be placed. As the output, it returns the positions of the tiles or returns the error message, if the tiles cannot be positioned. You want to apply the BVA technique to verify whether the system works correctly. Identify two adjoining boundary values that verify whether the system returns the correct answer (tiles positions or error message).

Exercise 8: Two- and Three-Point Boundary Value Methods

You test the automatic school grading system. It takes the number of marks collected by a student and automatically returns the final grade for the student according to the following rules:

A student can get a score between 0 and 100. A score is an integer number. The mapping of points to grades is as follows:

- More than 90 points: A
- More than 75 points: B
- More than 60 points: C
- More than 49 points: D
- Else: F

Assuming that the input can be in range 0–100, identify equivalence classes and boundary values for both two- and three-point boundary value methods.

Exercise 9: Boundary Values and Equivalence Partitioning

(a) A system accepts the year of birth (an integer number). The valid years are between 1900 and 2020. Which of the following is the minimal set of test values that achieves both boundary value and equivalence partition coverage?

  (A) 2003
  (B) 1900, 2020
  (C) 1900, 2003, 2020
  (D) 1899, 1900, 2020, 2021
  (E) 1899, 1900, 2003, 2020, 2021

(b) A temperature change detection system accepts an integer number denoting the difference between the actual and the former temperature measurements. For example, if two last measurements are -2 and 3, the system detects the change by $+5$ degrees; for 5 and 2 degrees, the system detects the change by -3 degrees, and so on. Consider the following piece of code that realizes the system logic:

```
1 INPUT PresentTemp, FormerTemp
2 Change := PresentTemp - FormerTemp
3 IF (Change = 0) THEN
4    Do nothing
ELSE
5    Light the diode 'Change detected' for 1 second
END IF
```

You want to apply a 3-value boundary value analysis for the domain of the Change variable. Which of the following is the set of values that should be tested?

(A) 0
(B) -1, 1
(C) -1, 0, 1
(D) -2, -1, 0, 1, 2

Exercise 10: Rounding
You test a system that calculates the final ski jumper score based on the novel scoring rules. Four notes are given by four judges. Each judge gives a note 1, 2, 3, 4, or 5. The system averages the values and returns the final note, which is this average value rounded up to the closest integer (e.g., 1.25 is rounded to 1, 3.5 is rounded to 4, etc.). A ski jumper is qualified to the next round if and only if his final grade is at least 3. Assume the test case is a set of four notes given by the four judges. Identify the example set of test cases that cover the boundary values of the averaged note before rounding.

Exercise 11: Deriving Classes from Boundary Values
Infer the partitions (if possible) of the domains of the integer variables, for which the sets of *all* their boundary values are

(a) 3, 4, 8, 9
(b) 2, 3, 4, 5
(c) −5, −4, 1, 2, 3, 6, 7
(d) 4, 7
(e) 3

Exercise 12: Limits of the BVA Method
For which of the following variables, the application of the BVA method is possible?

(a) The set of integer numbers
(b) The set of real numbers
(c) The set {5, 6, 7}
(d) The set of all strings of length 1, 2 or 3
(e) The set {Linux, Windows, MacOS}

4.3   Decision Table Testing

4.3.1   Technique Description

Decision tables are the models used in the test deign when we want to test the business logic. Each column of the decision table represents a single *decision rule* in a form:

IF (conditions) **THEN** (actions)

The process of deriving the test cases from the decision tables is as follows:

1. Identify all possible *conditions*.
2. Identify all the corresponding *actions* that may occur in the system.
3. Generate all possible combinations of conditions; each single combination forms a separate column in the decision table.

4. For each combination of conditions, identify which actions should hold and which should not; fill the corresponding fields in a given column below the corresponding combination of conditions.
5. For each column design a test case in which a given combination of conditions hold; the test should verify if the corresponding actions hold.

Having constructed the decision table, we may derive test cases. The standard, minimal decision table coverage is one test for each column. When designing test cases with the use of decision tables, it often happens that a tester finds some ambiguities or contradictions in the requirement specification. This is a good example of how the test *design* process acts as a kind of the requirement document review.

Let us see on a practical example how the decision tables work. Suppose we have a system that checks if a candidate for a driving license fulfills all requirements to receive the license. The requirement specification describes the above mentioned business rules as follows:

The operator enters the following information to the system:

- The result of the theory exam (an integer value in the range 0–100 points)
- The result of the practice exam (an integer value greater or equal to zero, representing the number of errors done by the candidate during the practice exam)

A candidate receives the driving license, if she gained at least 85 marks (out of 100) from the theory exam and if she made at most 2 errors during the practice exam. In case of failing on one of these criteria, the candidate is eligible to retake the exam. In case of failing in both parts, the candidate is required to retake the driving lessons.

Let us go through the process described above to derive test cases for this problem.

1. **Identify all possible conditions.** The possible conditions on which the system's decisions depend are obviously:

   - The result of the theory exam (number of points)
   - The result of the practice exam (number of errors)

   The decisions will depend on the results of these exams. From the specification we know that the theory exam is passed when a candidate receives at least 85 points. The practice exam is passed, when the number of mistakes is 2 or less.

2. **Identify all the corresponding actions that may occur in the system.** The system may take the following decisions:

   - Should a candidate receive the driving license? (possible values: YES or NO)
   - Should a candidate retake the theory exam? (possible values: YES or NO)

- Should a candidate retake the practice exam? (possible values: YES or NO)
- Should a candidate retake the driving lessons? (possible values: YES or NO)

In the decision tables, the logical value of "true" is usually denoted by "T", "Y" (yes) or "1," and of "false"—by "F," "N" (no) or "0". The actions that should happen can be also denoted by "X." The irrelevant values are usually denoted by a dash symbol "–" or by "N/A" (not applicable).

3. **Generate all possible combinations of conditions; each single combination forms a separate column in the decision table.** Each condition has two possible values, so we have $2 \times 2 = 4$ possible combinations of conditions (and, hence, four columns in the decision table):

   - Points ≥ 85 and errors ≤ 2.
   - Points ≥ 85 and errors > 2.
   - Points < 85 and errors ≤ 2.
   - Points < 85 and errors > 2.

   As for now, our decision table looks like the one in Table 4.2.

4. **For each combination of conditions identify which actions should hold and which should not; fill the corresponding fields in the given column below the corresponding combination of conditions.** Now we go through the columns one by one and for each of them, we identify the expected behavior of the system:

   - Column 1: points ≥ 85, errors ≤ 2. This means that the candidate passed both exams, so she should get her driving license. There is no need to retake exams or the driving lessons. Hence, the four corresponding actions in the column 1 should be respectively YES, NO, NO, NO.
   - Column 2: points ≥ 85, errors > 2. This means that the candidate failed the practice exam. She cannot receive the driving license and she should retake the practice exam. Hence, the corresponding actions in the column 2 are respectively NO, NO, YES, NO.
   - Column 3: points < 85, errors ≤ 2. The candidate failed the theory exam. She cannot receive the driving license and she should retake the theory exam. Hence, the corresponding actions in the column 3 are respectively NO, YES, NO, NO.

Table 4.2 Decision table after identifying the conditions and their possible combinations

CONDITIONS ↓ RULES →	1	2	3	4
Points ≥ 85?	YES	YES	NO	NO
Errors ≤ 2?	YES	NO	YES	NO
ACTIONS ↓				
Grant the license?				
Retake theory?				
Retake practice?				
Retake driving lessons?				

Table 4.3 The complete decision table for the driving license problem

CONDITIONS ↓ RULES →	1	2	3	4
Points ≥ 85?	YES	YES	NO	NO
Errors ≤2?	YES	NO	YES	NO
ACTIONS ↓				
Grant the license?	YES	NO	NO	NO
Retake theory?	NO	NO	YES	YES
Retake practice?	NO	YES	NO	YES
Retake driving lessons?	NO	NO	NO	YES

- Column 4: points < 85, errors >2. The candidate failed both exam. She cannot receive the license and should retake the driving lessons.

When deriving the corresponding actions for the column 4, we see a problem: for sure, the candidate cannot receive the driving license and should retake the driving lessons, but what about exams? The specification does not tell anything about this. As the testers, we should clarify this with the client although it makes sense to require the candidate to retake the exams. Suppose the client says so, the corresponding actions for the column 4 are NO, YES, YES, YES. The complete decision table is shown in Table 4.3.

5. **For each column, design a test case in which a given combination of conditions holds; the test should verify if the corresponding actions hold.**

For each column, we need to design a test case. A test case needs to have the concrete input values. In our case, this will be the number of points and the number of errors. The corresponding test cases for our four columns in the decision table might look like as follows:

Test case	Input Points	Errors	Expected output
1	85	0	Grant the license, does not require the candidate to retake any exam or lessons
2	95	2	Requires the candidate only to retake the practice exam
3	84	5	Requires the candidate only to retake the theory exam
4	11	3	Requires the candidate to retake both exams and the driving lessons

Notice that when providing the input values, we also took opportunity and tested the boundary values for both exam points (85, 86) and number of errors (0, 2, 3). Although it is not required, it is a common practice when providing the concrete input values for the test cases being designed.

* * *

The values in the decision table do not need to be logical. They may represent, for example, the equivalence classes, or any other sets of values. For example, consider

Table 4.4 Decision table with nonlogical values

CONDITIONS ↓ RULES →	1	2	3	4	5	6
Points	0–50	0–50	51–84	51–84	85–100	85–100
Errors	≤2	>2	≤2	>2	≤2	>2
ACTIONS ↓						
Grant the license?	NO	NO	NO	NO	YES	NO
What to retake?	T	T, P, D	T	T, P	Nothing	P

T = theory exam, P = practice exam, D = driving lessons

the decision table from Table 4.4, which presents some more complicated business rules for the driving license problem.

In this table, we can see both rules and actions that have nonlogical values. The "Points" rule has now three possible values: 0–50, 51–84, and 85–100. The "Errors" rule has two possible, mutually exclusive values, so it might be represented by a logical value (as in Table 4.3). Here we have a slightly different (but equivalent!) representation.

Instead of the three different actions referring to the three different "retakes," we have only one action, which describes what should be retaken. For example, in Column 2, we see that when a candidate fails in both exams, she needs to retake both exams and driving lessons as well.

Here is another example. Suppose that we test a discount system in some e-shop. The system can send a loyalty card to a client and admit a discount of 0% (no discount), 5%, or 10% according to the following rules (we assume the values are used with the precision of one dollar):

- "No discount" is the default discount option.
- A nonregistered user has 0% discount by definition.
- If a registered user spent more than $1000 in the previous shopping sessions, and there were 19 or less shopping sessions, admit 5% discount.
- If a registered user spent more than $1000 in the previous shopping sessions and there were at least 20 shopping sessions, admit 10% discount.
- A loyalty card is sent only to registered customers who spent more than $1000 or had at least 20 shopping sessions.

From the specification above, we can derive the following conditions:

- C1: user is registered (possible values: True, False)
- C2: user spent more than $1000 (possible values: True, False)
- C3: user had at least 20 shopping sessions (possible values: True, False)

and the following actions:

- A1: admit discount (possible values: 0%, 5%, 10%)
- A2: send a loyalty card (possible values: YES, NO)

The decision table for this problem can look like the one in Table 4.5.

Table 4.5 Decision table for the e-shop

Conditions	1	2	3	4	5	6	7	8
C1: registered user?	T	T	T	T	F	F	F	F
C2: user spent more than $1000	T	T	F	F	T	T	F	F
C3: user had at least 20 shopping sessions	T	F	T	F	T	F	T	F
Actions								
A1: discount	10%	5%	0%	0%	0%	0%	0%	0%
A2: send a loyalty card?	YES	YES	YES	NO	NO	NO	NO	NO

Table 4.6 Collapsed decision table for the e-shop

Conditions	1	2	3	4	5
C1: registered user?	T	T	T	T	F
C2: user spent more than $1000	T	T	F	F	–
C3: user had at least 20 shopping sessions	T	F	T	F	–
Actions					
A1: discount	10%	5%	0%	0%	0%
A2: send a loyalty card?	YES	YES	YES	NO	NO

Notice an interesting fact, regarding columns 5–8. If a user is not registered (C1 = False), no matter what the combination of the other conditions C2 and C3 is, the actions will always be the same: give no discount and do not send a loyalty card. In such situations—when for a fixed values of some conditions and *all possible combinations* of *all other* conditions the corresponding actions are the same, we can minimize the table. In our example, we can "collapse" columns 5, 6, 7, 8 into one column implementing the following rule:

IF (registered user = False) **THEN** (discount = 0% **AND** do not send a loyalty card)

The collapsed decision table is presented in Table 4.6. The "–" sign should be interpreted as "don't care."

Collapsing (or minimization) the decision table allows us to reduce the number of columns and, hence, the number of test cases to be derived. Of course, there is a risk that by doing this, we may not detect the incorrect program behavior. In our example (Table 4.6), this might happen for a certain combination of C2 and C3, because we provide only one test case for column 5.

When we design decision tables, we usually generate columns for all possible combinations of conditions. However, sometimes some combinations are impossible—either from logical or business reasons. For example, if we have two conditions:

- age > 18
- age ≤ 18

one of them will always be true and the other one will be false. It is impossible that both of them hold (or not hold) together. Hence, instead of four combinations of these two conditions, we have only two combinations:

- (age > 18) = True **AND** (age ≤ 18) = False
- (age > 18) = False **AND** (age ≤ 18) = True

There may be also a business reason that makes some combinations of conditions infeasible. For example, consider the following three conditions:

- C1: a user agreed to take medical tests (possible values: True or False)
- C2: a user took the blood pressure test (possible values: True or False)
- C3: a user took the USG test (possible values: True or False)

Theoretically, we have three binary conditions, so the number of all combinations of these three conditions is $2 \times 2 \times 2 = 8$. However, in case a user does not agree to take any medical tests (C1 = False), it makes the two other conditions irrelevant. In this case, the only possible combinations of conditions are:

#1. C1 = False, C2 and C3 irrelevant
#2. C1 = True, C2 = True, C3 = True
#3. C1 = True, C2 = True, C3 = False
#4. C1 = True, C2 = False, C3 = True
#5. C1 = True, C2 = False, C3 = False

It is important to remember that the coverage is defined with respect to the *number of columns*, not the number of all theoretical possible combinations of conditions! In the example with the medical tests (assuming that these are the only conditions in the decision table), we have only 5 columns to cover with test cases, not 8. For example, a set of three tests:

- (combination #1) a user did not agree to take any medical test
- (combination #3) a user agreed to take medical tests and took only blood pressure test
- (combination #5) a user agreed to take medical tests but did not take any of them

achieves $3/5 = 60\%$ coverage, not $3/8 = 37.5\%$!

4.3.2   Exercises

Exercise 13: Reading the Full and Collapsed Decision Table
Consider the decision table shown in Table 4.7 and used by the LoanAssistant application for assessing the loan maximal value and the related risk.

(a) What is the maximal loan value and the risk value for a 32-year-old man with a gros annual salary of $11,000 who does not have any other loans?

Table 4.7 Decision table for the LoanAssistant

Conditions	1	2	3	4	5
Age> 21?	FALSE	TRUE	TRUE	TRUE	TRUE
Gross annual salary ≥ $36,000?	–	FALSE	FALSE	TRUE	TRUE
Has other loans?	–	TRUE	FALSE	TRUE	FALSE
Actions					
Maximal loan value	$0	$1000	$1000	$3000	$5000
Risk	N/A	High	Medium	Medium	Low

(b) What is the maximal loan value and the risk value for a 21-year-old man with a monthly salary of $1200 who has 1 other loan.

(c) Assuming the test case is a triple (age, gross annual salary, number of other loans), give an example of a test case for which the maximal loan value is (1) low, (2) medium, (3) high.

Exercise 14: Building the Table from Requirements
Consider the following piece of requirement specification:

A system takes as an input the results of the three vocational examinations and returns the total exam result and the type of entitlements granted. For each exam, the possible grade is 0, 1, or 2 points. If a candidate receives 0 for at least one of them, the total result is 0 and the entitlements are not granted. Otherwise, the total result is the sum of the three grades and if it exceeds 4, the full entitlements are granted; otherwise, the partial entitlements are granted.

(a) From the above specification derive: the conditions, the actions, and their values.

(b) What number of columns would have a full decision table for this problem?

(c) Write down the collapsed decision table for this problem.

Exercise 15: Unfeasible Combinations
You are designing a decision table for the problem with the following conditions:

• condition 1: age < 18 (YES or NO)
• condition 2: age between 18 and 35 (YES or NO)
• condition 3: age > 35 (YES or NO)
• condition 4: type of payment (credit card, cash)
• condition 5: PIN correct (YES or NO)
• condition 6: payment value (<$100, $100, or more)

Moreover, the PIN correctness is relevant only in case of credit card payment. How many columns will have the corresponding decision table that has only feasible combinations of conditions? Write down all these combinations.

Exercise 16: Collapsing the Decision Table
Collapse the table shown in Table 4.8. T and F denote TRUE and FALSE respectively. A, B, and C are the three possible variants of C2.

Table 4.8 Decision table to be collapsed

Conditions	1	2	3	4	5	6	7	8	9	10	11	12
C1	T	T	T	T	T	T	F	F	F	F	F	F
C2	A	A	B	B	C	C	A	A	B	B	C	C
C3	T	F	T	F	T	F	T	F	T	F	T	F
Actions												
A1	F	T	T	T	F	F	F	T	T	T	F	F
A2	T	T	F	F	F	F	T	T	F	F	F	T

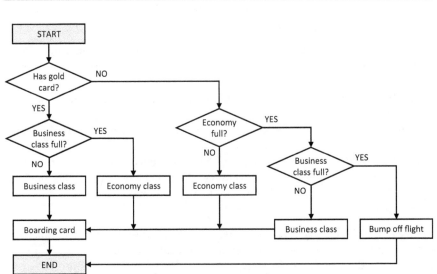

Fig. 4.3 Control flow diagram for flight check-in

Exercise 17: Using Decision Table to Detect Defects in Requirements

Consider the flight check-in control flow presented in Fig. 4.3.

You want to transform this problem into the decision table to make sure that you will systematically cover all possible process flows with the appropriate test cases. You have identified the following conditions and actions:

- Condition1: has gold card? (possible values: YES, NO),
- Condition2: is economy full? (possible values: YES, NO),
- Condition3: is business class full? (possible values: YES, NO),
- Action1: assign to economy class? (possible values: YES, NO),
- Action2: assign to business class? (possible values: YES, NO),
- Action3: final decision (possible values: print boarding card, bump off flight).

Construct the full decision table and identify the proper actions using the control flow from Fig. 4.3. Did you notice any flaw in the requirements? If so, how can it be fixed?

4.4   State Transition Testing

4.4.1   Technique Description

State transition testing is used when we want to check the *behavioral* aspect of the system, that is—its behavior in time. The model for such tests is a finite state machine, called a *state transition diagram* in the syllabus. This model presents the next possible system's behavior depending on its history (which is represented by the machine's current state) and occurring event.

The state transition diagram consists of:

- **States**—they represent the possible conditions in which the system can be.
- **Transitions**—they represent the possible machine changes from one state to another.
- **Events**—they represent the external things that may happen and trigger the state change.
- **Actions**—they represent the possible activities done by the machine when changing the state.
- **Guard conditions**—they represent the additional conditions for the transitions that need to be fulfilled in order to trigger the transition; in particular, they are used if there is more than one possible transition from the same state under the same event.

States, transitions, and events are the typical components of a state diagram. Actions and guard conditions are optional. Figure 4.4 presents graphically an example of a state transition diagram.

It consists of four *states*: S0, S1, S2, and S3. At any given moment of time, the machine is always in one particular state. At the beginning, it is in the *initial state* (in our example S0). The machine ends its computations when it reaches the *final state*

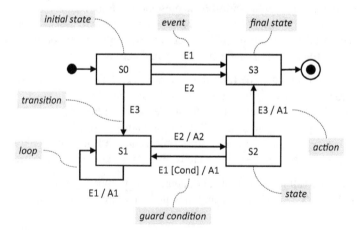

Fig. 4.4 An example of a state transition diagram

(in our example S3). There are several ways to present the initial and final states. One of them is shown graphically in Fig. 4.4: the initial state is denoted by a small circle incoming to this state, and the final one with the outgoing, bordered circle. In the exam question, the initial and final states may not be denoted in the picture. The information on which state is initial and which is final may be given in the question stem.

Possible changes between states are modeled by the *transitions*—these are the arrows between states. For example, from S1, we may go to S2 or we can stay in S1 (the latter one is modeled by the transition that goes to the same state—such a transition is called a *loop*). From S2, we can move to S1 or S3, and so on. Transitions are triggered by *events*, which the transitions are labeled with. The transition may be also labeled by the corresponding *action* and/or *guard condition*. For example, when the machine from Fig. 4.4 is in state S2 and the event E1 happens, the machine moves to S1 only if the condition Cond is true. While moving from S2 to S1, the machine additionally performs the action A1.

When we model the system with a state transition diagram, it is often problematic to differentiate states from events. States are the conditions that span in time, for example, when a system shows a login screen, waiting for a user to log in, we may represent this situation as being in state "Login screen." Events can be viewed as situations that take place in a quick, immediate manner. In our example, the event might be "Pressing the Login button."

State transition diagrams can be represented in different ways. Look at the Fig. 4.5. It shows a diagram that models the life cycle of a defect. A defect can be in one of the four states: New, Fixing, Verifying, Closed. Figure 4.5a shows this diagram in a graphical form. Figure 4.5b is the equivalent way of presenting it in a tabular form, called the state transition table. The rows (resp. columns) represent states (resp. events). The cell at the intersection of state S and event E represents the target state to which the system should move if, being in state S, the event E occurred.

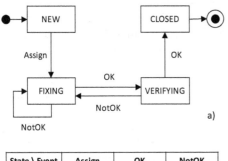

State	Event	NextState
NEW	Assign	FIXING
NEW	OK	(undef)
NEW	NotOK	(undef)
FIXING	Assign	(undef)
FIXING	OK	VERIFYING
FIXING	NotOK	FIXING
VERIFYING	Assign	(undef)
VERIFYING	OK	CLOSED
VERIFYING	NotOK	FIXING
CLOSED	Assign	(undef)
CLOSED	OK	(undef)
CLOSED	NotOK	(undef)

State \ Event	Assign	OK	NotOK
NEW	FIXING		
FIXING		VERIFYING	FIXING
VERIFYING		CLOSED	FIXING
CLOSED			

b)   c)

Fig. 4.5 Different representations of a state transition diagram

Finally, Fig. 4.5c shows another way to model the same system. This table is called a *full transition table*. The rows of this table represent all possible combinations of states and events. For each such combination, the last column contains the target state. In case there is no transition for a given combination of a state and an event, there is no next state—such transition is called *invalid* (in our table, it is represented by the word "(undef)"). The number of rows in a full transition table equals the number of states multiplied by the number of *different* events defined in the machine. For example, for a machine in Fig. 4.5a, we have four states (New, Fixing, Verifying, Closed) and 5 transitions in total, but they are labeled only by 3 different events (Assign, OK, Not OK). Hence, the full transition table will have $5 \times 3 = 15$ rows. An example of the invalid transition may be the transition from state Fixing in case the event Action occures: in this case, the machine behavior is undefined.

In case of some coverage criteria, which will be described later, it is important to count the number of *valid transitions*, that is—the transitions represented by the arrows (in case of the graphical representation), filled cells (in case of the state transition table), or the rows with no "(undef)" string (in case of the full transition table). Be careful when you have to count the valid transitions, because sometimes, one arrow may represent more than one transition!

Look at the left part of Fig. 4.6. Its upper part shows a single arrow between states, but it is labeled by the two different events. This means that there are really two parallel transitions from Fixing to Verifying, as shown in the bottom part.

The events, actions, and guards can be presented in different ways. The right part of Fig. 4.6 shows some examples. From top to bottom: a transition labeled only by the event (OK); a transition labeled by the event (OK) and the corresponding action (PrintMsg); another way of presenting the same transition; the transition labeled by the event (OK), action (PrintMsg), and guard condition ($x > 0$).

In case of state transition diagrams, we have the whole family of the coverage criteria. When we design tests, we derive them from the state transition model so that a given coverage criterion is fulfilled. A test is a sequence of states going from the initial state along the transitions and ending in a final state. A test may also end earlier, for example, when we try to force an invalid transition. Every test derived to

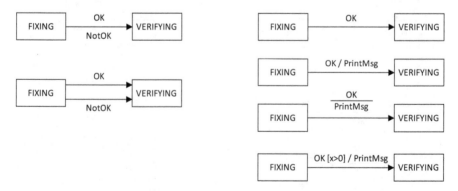

Fig. 4.6 Different ways of representing transitions and their labeling

cover one or more test conditions checks if a given sequence of transitions in a system under test is executed properly, according to the behavior modeled by the state transition diagram.

The classical coverage criteria for the state transition diagrams are as follows:

- **State coverage**—the weakest coverage criterion; requires that every state should be visited at least once in at least one test; the test conditions are all the states.
- **Transition coverage** (called also the 0-switch coverage)—requires that every valid transition should be executed at least once in at least one test; the test conditions are all the transitions.
- **Invalid transition coverage**—requires that we should try to execute every invalid transition in our test suite; the test conditions are all the invalid transitions.

The syllabus says that tests can also be designed to exercise **specific sequences of transitions**. There is a special type of such coverage criteria, called the n-switch coverage. An n-switch is a sequence of states such that there are exactly n states between the first and the last one in this sequence (excluding the first and the last one).

Figure 4.7 shows some examples. A 0-switch is a sequence from some state to another one with no (zero) states between them. This is exactly a single transition between the two states. Hence, the 0-switch coverage and the transition coverage are synonyms. Figure 4.7 also shows the examples of 1-switch and 2-switch.

The coverage metric is calculated as the number of test conditions covered by our tests divided by the number of all possible test conditions to be covered.

Let us give an example of how to derive test cases in order to achieve a given type of coverage. We will use the state transition diagram shown in Fig. 4.4 as the working example.

State Coverage In order to achieve the state coverage, we need to exercise every state at least once. Notice that we may do this with only one test (hereinafter, the notation S1 → (E) → S2 denotes the transition between states S1 and S2 triggered by the event E):

S0 → (E3) → S1 → (E1) → S2 → (E3) → S3

Notice that we didn't exercise all the possible transitions (e.g., we did not go from S1 to S1, which is triggered by the E1 event). The coverage criterion required to exercise only the states, not the transitions.

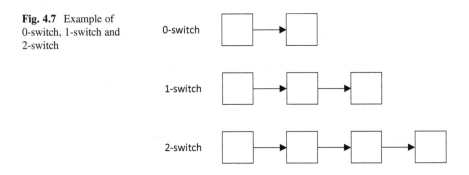

Fig. 4.7 Example of 0-switch, 1-switch and 2-switch

Table 4.9 Minimal set of test cases for achieving the 0-switch coverage

#	Test	0-switches covered
1	S0 → (E1) → S3	(1)
2	S0 → (E2) → S3	(2)
3	S0 → (E3) → S1 → (E1) → S1 → (E2) → S2 → (E1) [Cond] → S1 → (E2) → S2 → (E3) → S3	(3), (4), (5), (6), (7), (8)

Transition (0-Switch) Coverage In order to achieve the coverage, we need first to identify all the 0-switches in the diagram, that is—all the valid transitions. These are

(1) S0 → (E1) → S3
(2) S0 → (E2) → S3
(3) S0 → (E3) → S1
(4) S1 → (E1) → S1
(5) S1 → (E2) → S2
(6) S2 → (E1) [Cond] → S1
(7) S2 → (E3) → S3

We need to cover all these seven transitions. Notice that when we cover the transition (1) or (2), the test case must end, as we reach the final state. Hence, we need two test cases that cover these two 0-switches. All the other 0-switches can be covered with a single test. Hence, we need three test cases to achieve the 0-switch coverage. They are shown in Table 4.9.

Notice that when implementing and executing the tests, exercising the transition from S2 so S1 requires not only the occurrence of the event E1, but also that the condition Cond holds.

1-Switch Coverage In order to achieve the 1-switch coverage, we need first to identify all 1-switches. It is a little bit harder than in case of 0-switches, but there is a simple, systematic method for doing that. We start with identifying all 0-switches. Next, we analyze them, one by one. For each such 0-switch, we identify all possible "one step" extensions of these paths. This results in 1-switch, because 1-switch is created by "gluing" two 0-switches together.

This concept is shown in Table 4.10. For the sake of simplicity, we omit the conditions and consider only the events. In the first column, we write down all the 0-switches. In the second one, for each 0-switch, we write down all possible continuations. The last column presents these two 0-switches "glued" in the form of the 1-switches. Altogether we obtain eight 1-switches. They can be covered by two test cases:

S0→(E3)→S1→(E1)→S1→(E1)→S1→(E2)→S2→(E1)→S1→(E1)→S1→ (E2) → S2 → (E3) → S3, which covers (1), (3), (4), (5), (6), (7), and

S0 → (E3) → S1 → (E2) → S2 → (E1) → S1 → (E2) → S2 → (E3) → S3, which additionally covers (2), (8).

Notice that these two tests did not cover two 0-switches: S0 → (E1) → S3 and S0 → (E2) → S3. It is a common practice to require that *n*-switch coverage should

Table 4.10 A systematic way to derive all 1-switches

0-Switch	Possible continuations	Resulting 1-switches	1-Switch label
S0 → (E1) → S3	No possible continuations	–	
S0 → (E2) → S3	No possible continuations	–	
S0 → (E3) → S1	S1 → (E1) → S1	S0 → (E3) → S1 → (E1) → S1	(1)
	S1 → (E2) → S2	S0 → (E3) → S1 → (E2) → S2	(2)
S1 → (E1) → S1	S1 → (E1) → S1	S1 → (E1) → S1 → (E1) → S1	(3)
	S1 → (E2) → S2	S1 → (E1) → S1 → (E2) → S2	(4)
S1 → (E2) → S2	S2 → (E1) → S1	S1 → (E2) → S2 → (E1) → S1	(5)
	S2 → (E3) → S3	S1 → (E2) → S2 → (E3) → S3	(6)
S2 → (E1) → S1	S1 → (E1) → S1	S2 → (E1) → S1 → (E1) → S1	(7)
	S1 → (E2) → S2	S2 → (E1) → S1 → (E2) → S2	(8)
S2 → (E3) → S3	No possible continuations		

cover not only all n-switches, but also all k-switches for $k < n$. If we do so, the n-switch coverage subsumes all the k-switch coverages for $k < n$. Recall that a criterion A subsumes a criterion B if any set of tests that achieves 100% coverage for A achieves also 100% coverage for B. In our example, if we use the modified definition of the n-switch coverage, we need to add two tests to our test suite: S0 → (E1) → S3 and S0 → (E2) → S3.

In the ISTQB® exams, the usual thing we are asked about is to provide the *minimal* set of test cases that achieves a given criterion. As in case of state transition diagrams, one test usually covers more than one test condition, in order to construct the minimal number of test cases, each new test should exercise as many yet uncovered elements as possible. However, this refers only to the positive test cases.

Invalid Transitions Coverage   In case of this criterion, one test should cover only one invalid transition. This is because in the negative testing, we want to test only one "bad" thing at once to avoid the so-called defect masking. In our example, we have five invalid transitions:

(1) S1 → (E3) →?
(2) S2 → (E2) →?
(3) S3 → (E1) →?
(4) S3 → (E2) →?
(5) S3 → (E3) →?

Hence, we need five test cases. In each of them, we *try* to invoke a specific, invalid sequence of states. For example, in case of (2), we need to first arrive to S2 and then try to invoke the event E2. So, the test could look like this: S0 → (E3) → S1 → (E2) → S2 → (E2) →?

If it is not possible to invoke (E2) when being in S2, everything is OK. If it is possible, but nothing happens, it may be OK, but we might ask if it is normal that it's possible to invoke an event, which is not defined in the model—so this test may be considered as a failed one. Finally, if it is possible and the system crashes, or goes to some other state, we definitely consider such a test as a failed one, since the model does not allow such a behavior (we assume that the model is correct!).

4.4.2 Exercises

Exercise 18: Identifying the Correct Behavior of a State Machine
Figure 4.8 presents a state transition diagram modeling the ordering process in some
e-shop.

Which of the following are the expected behaviors of the system modeled with
this diagram?

(a) When the system shows the client's basket, the client can make payment.
(b) Being in the checkout, the client can go back to his basket.
(c) When paying, if error occurs, the system goes back to the checkout screen.

Exercise 19: Identifying Correct Sequences
Refer to the state machine from Fig. 4.8. Which of the following sequences of events
are valid?

(A) AddItem, Finalize, GoBack, Finalize
(B) ToCatalog, AddItem, Finalize, Payment
(C) GoBack, ToCatalog
(D) ToCatalog, ToCatalog, Finalize, Payment, TransactionConfirmed
(E) AddItem, Payment, TransactionConfirmed
(F) ToCatalog, AddItem, ToCatalog, AddItem, Finalize, GoBack, Finalize,
    Payment

Exercise 20: Working with Different Representations of a State Machine
Table 4.11 presents the actions of a state machine for a certain part of the HVAC
control system (Heating, Ventilation, and Air Conditioning). "Idle" is the initial
state.

(a) How many states and how many different events are in this state machine?
(b) Give an example of the invalid transition.
(c) Draw the graphical representation of the state machine.
(d) Assuming we start from the initial state, in which state the machine will be after
    the following sequence of events: tooCold, atTemp, tooCold, tooHot, tooCold?

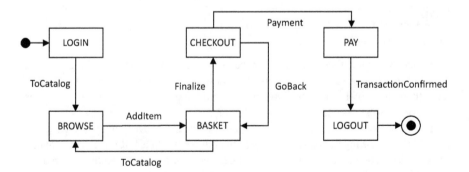

Fig. 4.8 An e-shop ordering process

Table 4.11 State transition
table for a HVAC controller

State/Event	atTemp	tooCold	tooHot
Idle		Heating	Cooling
Cooling	Idle	Heating	
Heating	Idle		Cooling

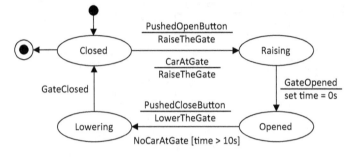

Fig. 4.9 State machine for gate controller

Exercise 21: Identifying and Counting 0-Switches and 1-Switches

Figure 4.9 presents a state machine for a gate controller. A gate can be in one out of
four possible states: closed, raising, open, lowering. The gate can be opened either
manually (by pushing the "OPEN" button) or when a sensor detects that a car is at
gate. After the gate fully opens, it can be closed by pushing the "CLOSE" button. It
can be also closed after 10 seconds from being fully opened, but only if there is no
car at gate.

(a) How many 0-switches are there in the machine?
(b) Consider the following scenario: a car arrives at gate and the gate starts raising.
    During this process, the car drives away, before the system reaches the state
    "Opened." What should happen next according to the state machine model?
(c) What should happen, according to the state machine model, when a user presses
    the "CLOSE" button when the gate is being raised?
(d) How many 1-switches starting from the state "Raising" are there in the machine?

Exercise 22: Designing Tests for Achieving Different Types of Coverage

Refer to the machine from the previous exercise shown in Fig. 4.9. Assuming that
each test ends when arriving to the state "Closed," what is the minimal number of
test cases that achieve:

(a) 0-switch coverage?
(b) 1-switch coverage?
(c) State coverage?

In each case, write down the test cases.

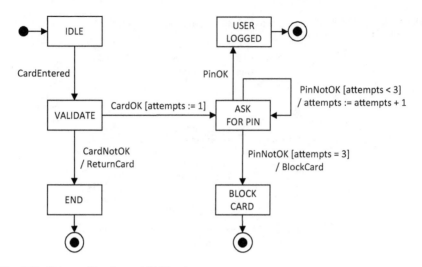

Fig. 4.10 State machine for an ATM logging process

Exercise 23: Automata with Guarded Transitions

Figure 4.10 presents the state transition diagram describing the logging process for an ATM machine.

(a) How many 1-switches are in the machine?
(b) Suppose that a certain test case goes along the following path: IDLE (CardEntered) VALIDATE (CardOK) ASK FOR PIN (PinNotOK) ASK FOR PIN. In this moment, what is the value of the variable *attempts*? What will happen if the next action is PinNotOK?
(c) Is it possible to cover all 1-switches with the test cases? Explain.

Exercise 24: Building a State Machine and Deriving Test Cases

Figure 4.11 presents the ticket machine selling two types of tickets: normal and reduced. In one session, a user can buy 1 or 2 tickets (but all of the same type—normal or reduced). First, a user selects the type and number of tickets by pressing the corresponding button once or twice. When she inserts the first coin, the option of adding new tickets is blocked. The machine expects the user to enter the correct amount of money. If the total amount is equal or greater than the requested value, the machine prints the ticket(s), dispenses a change (if needed), and returns to the initial state. At any moment, a user can push the "Cancel" button. In such cases, all the inserted coins are returned and the machine returns to its initial state. Once the machine arrives to the WAIT state, we assume it reached its final state.

(a) Design a state machine that models the ticket machine behavior described above, using the following states, events, and actions:

States:

- WAIT—welcome screen (the initial and the final state)
- R1—1 reduced ticket selected

Fig. 4.11 A ticket machine

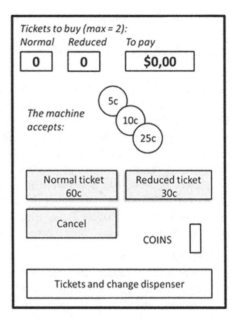

- R2—2 reduced tickets selected
- N1—1 normal ticket selected
- N2—2 normal tickets selected
- PAY_LOW—waiting for the payment; the current amount is too low

Events:

- RED—"Reduced ticket" button pushed
- NORM—"Normal ticket" button pushed
- CANCEL—"Cancel" button pushed
- INS—coin inserted; total amount still too low
- INS_LAST—coin inserted; the amount equals or is greater than the expected amount

Actions:

- RET—return inserted coins
- PRINT—print the ticket(s), dispense the change

(b) What is the minimal number of test cases to achieve 0-switch coverage for the machine you have just designed? Write down these test cases.

(c) Suppose the machine can also accept a 50c coin. Will this have any impact on the state machine design?

(d) Use a common sense to describe other, valid situations nondefined above that may happen during the machine operation. Add the corresponding transitions to the model.

4.5   Use Case Testing

4.5.1   *Technique Description*

A use case specifies the behavior of a system that interacts with one or more actors resulting in an observable result of value to the actors. An actor is typically a user, but it might be as well the other system. Well-structured use cases denote essential system or subsystem behaviors only, and are neither overly general nor too specific.[2]

There is no standard way to write the test cases. Below we give the "fully dressed" use case template. In practice, the use cases may have their structure simplified, because not always the full level of detail is required. Figure 4.12 shows the "fully dressed" structure of a use case, according to Cockburn[3]:

According to the ISTQB® Foundation 2018 Syllabus, the use case should consist of (in the brackets we give the corresponding item from the Cockburn's list)

- Preconditions (optional)
- Post-conditions (observable results) [success guarantees]
- Only one main path (sometimes called the happy path) [main success scenario]
- Alternate paths (0 or more) [technology & data variation list]
- Exception paths (0 or more) [extensions]

- **use case name, identifier** and **version number** – the name should be the goal as a short active verb phrase
- **context of use** – a longer statement of the goal; if needed, its normal occurrence conditions
- **scope** – design scope, what system is being considered black-box under design
- **level** – one of: summary, user-goal, subfunction
- **primary actor** – a role name for the primary actor or description
- **stakeholders and interests** – list of stakeholders and key interests in the use case
- **precondition** – what we expect is already the state of the world
- **minimal guarantees** – how the interests are protected under all exits
- **success guarantees** – the state of the world if goal succeeds
- **trigger** – what starts the use case, may be time event
- **main success scenario** – the steps of the scenario from trigger to goal delivery and any cleanup after
  - **step # – action description**
  - ...
- **extensions** – extensions, one at a time, each referring to the step of the main scenario
  - **step altered – condition – action** or **sub use case**
  - ...
- **technology & data variation list** – the variations that will cause eventual bifurcation in the scenario
  - **step** or **variation #** – list of variations
  - ...
- **related information** – whatever your project needs for additional informations

---

Fig. 4.12   A full use case template according to Cockburn

---

[2]G. Booch, J. Rumbaugh, I. Jacobson, The Unified Modeling Language User Guide.

[3]A. Cockburn, Writing Effective Use Cases, Addison-Wesley, 2001.

The alternative paths allow the user to achieve her goal by executing an alternate path, which is usually longer than the main scenario. For example, in a use case for withdrawing the money, a user enters the PIN number incorrectly and the use case flow may require the user to enter the PIN again. When the user selects the PIN correctly second time and withdraws the money, she achieves her goal, but with an alternative (longer) path.

The exceptions are the unexpected situations that usually lead to the abnormal termination of the use case. For example:

- A user cancels her operation
- A system lost the connection with the server
- There is not enough money in the machine (in case of the ATM money withdrawing example)

Figure 4.13 shows an example of a use case from the Cockburn's book. We see that there is one main path, described in the "Main success scenario" section. We have three exceptions ("Extensions" section)—one of them may happen during the step 2, and two others—during the step 4. We also have three alternative paths ("Variations" section):

Use case #001: Register arrival of a box
RA means "Receiving Agent".
RO means "Registration Operator"
Primary Actor: RA
Scope: Nightime Receiving Registry Software
Level: user goal
Main success scenario:
    1. RA receives and opens box (box id, bags with bag ids) from TransportCompany TC
    2. RA validates box id with TC registered ids.
    3. RA maybe signs paper form for delivery person
    4. RA registers arrival into system, which stores:
        RA id
        date, time
        box id
        TransportCompany
        <Person name?>
        # bags (?with bag ids)
        <estimated value?>
    5. RA removes bags from box, puts onto cart, takes to RO.
Extensions:
    2a. box id does not match transport company
    4a. fire alarm goes off and interrupts registration
    4b. computer goes down
        leave the money on the desk and wait for computer to come back up.
Variations:
    4'. with and without Person id
    4''. with and without estimated value
    5'. RA leaves bags in box

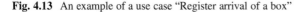

Fig. 4.13 An example of a use case "Register arrival of a box"

- In step 4, a person's id may or may not be registered.
- In step 4, an estimated value of the box may or may not be registered.
- In step 5, the bags may or may not be removed from the box.

There is no commonly accepted definition of the use case coverage. The ISTQB[®] Foundation 2018 Syllabus says that "the coverage is usually measured by the number of use case paths tested divided by the total number of use case paths." By "paths" the syllabus means all possible sequences of actions that go through all possible exceptions and alternate paths. Hence, to cover the use case, we need

- One test case to cover the main scenario
- One separate test case for *each* exception
- One separate test case for *each* alternative

In the example from Fig. 4.13 we need seven-test cases shown in Table 4.12 to cover the use case. In this case, we assume that in the main path, in step 4, an operator must fill in all the fields mentioned in this step.

In the context of calculating the coverage, it is important to count properly the total number of paths to be covered. Look at Fig. 4.14. It presents the same use case

Table 4.12 Test cases that cover the use case "Register arrival of a box"

TC #	Path covered
1	(main path): 1, 2, 3, 4, 5
2	(exception 2a): 1, 2a
3	(exception 4a): 1, 2, 3, 4a
4	(exception 4b): 1, 2, 3, 4b
5	(alternative path 4′): 1, 2, 3, 4 (without person id), 5
6	(alternative path 4″): 1, 2, 3, 4 (without estimated value), 5
7	(alternative path 5′): 1, 2, 3, 4, 5 (with bags left in the box)

Fig. 4.14 Two ways of annotating exceptions in a use case

Use case ...

...

Step 1 ...
Step 2 ... (E1)
Step 3 ...
Step 4 ... (E1, E2)
Step 5 ... (E3)

...

Exceptions:
E1: ...
E2: ...
E3: ...

Use case ...

...

Step 1 ...
Step 2 ...
Step 3 ...
Step 4 ...
Step 5 ...

...

Exceptions:
2a: ...
4a: ...
4b: ...
5a: ...

with two different ways of annotating the exceptions. On the left, the exceptions are put inside the steps description. The detailed description of the exceptions is given below the scenario. In the use case shown on the right all exceptions are put under the use case and their numbering refers to the use case steps in which these exceptions occur.

When looking at the use case on the left, it may seem that we need three use cases to cover the exception paths, because there are three exceptions: E1, E2, and E3. However, the exception E1 occurs twice in the use case—once in step 2 and the second time in step 4. Hence, we need two test cases to cover this exception—one path should be 1, 2 (E1), and the other: 1, 2, 3, 4 (E1). Altogether, we need not three, but four test cases to cover these exceptions. For the use case on the right counting the number of the exception paths is easier—it is equal to the number of the exceptions shown below the scenario.

Finally, we give a few good practices that should be applied when designing use cases and test cases based on them:

- Do not use "if" statements in the scenario—the main path should be a single sequence of steps and should contain no logic (no bifurcations).
- Using the UML use case diagram is not enough to properly define the use cases—the UML use case diagram is not a notation for capturing use cases; it only shows the packaging and decomposition of the use cases, not their content.
- When deriving test cases from the use case, it is a good practice to combine the use case–based technique with other black-box techniques; for example, when we go through a step "a user enters the number of products," we may apply the boundary value analysis and, in the test case, we may require that the user enters the boundary value (e.g., 1 or the maximal allowed value); the alternatives/exceptions should also be invoked with the boundary values (e.g., 0 products or maximal allowed plus one).

4.5.2   Exercises

Exercise 25: Analyzing a Use Case
Consider the following excerpt from the use case "Order a soda from a soda machine":

Pre-conditions: The machine is in the initial state, showing a welcome screen
Main scenario steps:

1. A user selects the "Soda-1" type of a beverage.
2. The machine shows the price of the Soda-1 (80 cents).
3. A user enters 80 cents into the coin slot.

(continued)

4. The machine returns the Soda-1 beverage.

Alternative paths:

3a. A user inserts more than 80 cents (the machine returns change in step 4).
3b. A user cancels the operation (the machine returns the money and goes back to the welcome screen).

Exceptions:

2. There are no "Soda-1" beverages in the machine

Consider also the following test cases.

TC1. Preconditions: the machine is in the initial state and shows the welcome screen; there is at least one can of each soda type in the machine

#	Test step	Expected result
1	the user selects "Soda-2" beverage	the machine asks for 80c
2	the user enters 80c	the machine returns the soda

TC2. Preconditions: the machine is in the initial state and shows the welcome screen; there is at least one can of each soda type in the machine

#	Test step	Expected result
1	the user selects "Soda-1" beverage	the machine asks for 80c
2	the user enters $1 (2*50 cents)	the machine returns the soda and 20c change

TC3. Preconditions: the machine is in the initial state and shows the welcome screen; there is at least one can of each soda type in the machine

#	Test step	Expected result
1	the user selects "Soda-1" beverage	the machine asks for 80c
2	the user enters 50c and then pushes the "Cancel" button	the machine returns 50c and goes back to the welcome screen

TC4. Preconditions: the machine is in the initial state and shows the welcome screen; there are no "Soda-1" cans in the machine

#	Test step	Expected result
1	the user selects "Soda-1" beverage	the machine displays the error message "This beverage cannot be selected" and returns to the welcome screen

(a) How many test cases are required to cover the use case?
(b) What coverage is achieved by the four test cases shown above?
(c) Which of the test cases TC1–TC4 covers the alternative path 3b?

Exercise 26: Designing the Test Cases from a Use Case

Consider the following use case "The order of a premium class client" for an e-shop.

Use case UC-002—shopping done by a premium class client with a 5% discount

Precondition: a registered client is logged in the system; the basket is empty

Main scenario:

1. The system calculates the total value of the previous shoppings done by the client and verifies that this value exceeds $1000.

   Exception: the system cannot connect to the shopping database.
   Exception: the total value is less than or equal $1000.

2. The system informs the client that she is the "premium class" client and has a 5% discount.

3. The client inserts the product X of price $200 into the basket.

   Exception: there are no products X in the stockroom.

4. The system shows the total price $200 before the discount.

5. The client selects the "Pay" button.

   Exception: the client cancels the operation.

6. The system shows the price $190 after the discount.

   Exception: the discount is calculated incorrectly.

7. The client accepts the transaction, enters the credit card details, and approves the transaction.

   Exception: the credit card is invalid.
   Exception: the transaction was rejected by a bank.
   Exception: the client cancels the transaction.

8. The system confirms the transaction correctness and generates the shipment ordering using the registered client's address

Post-conditions: The client's credit card is charged for $190 and the shipment ordering is generated.

(a) Provide a test case that covers the main path scenario for this use case. The test case should contain preconditions, test steps, and expected results after each test step.

(b) How many test cases are required to achieve the use case coverage for this use case?

Exercise 27: Exceptions and Alternate Flows

You have just designed the main path scenario for a use case "Student's registration to a course." The present form of the use case looks as follows:

Use case 001: A student's registration to a course
Preconditions: A registered student is logged in the system
Steps:

1. The user clicks on the "Show the available courses" link.
2. The system shows the list of all the available courses with a checkbox next to each course.
3. The user selects one checkbox and clicks "Submit."
4. The system confirms that the user is registered to the selected course.

Think about the examples of alternative paths and of exceptions that could happen in this use case. Write them down.

Chapter 5
White-Box Test Techniques

White-box testing is based on the structure of the software of the system. It is commonly used at the component testing level (so-called unit testing), but it may as well be applied at any other test level using the different white-box models of the software, for example,

- Call graphs at the integration level
- Business processes at the system level
- Menu structures at the acceptance testing level

At the component testing level, the model is usually a source code. At first glance, it seems weird, as the code cannot be the oracle for itself. However, the code does not serve as the source of truth—it is used only to design test cases that cover some structural elements of the code (statements, decisions, etc.). The expected result of such a test must be of course defined based on the external source, such as requirements specification or other kinds of documentation.

Common characteristics of white-box test techniques include the following:

- Test conditions, test cases, and test data are derived from a test basis that may include code, software architecture, detailed design, or any other source of information regarding the structure of the software.
- Coverage is measured based on the items tested within a selected structure (e.g., the code or interfaces).
- Specifications are often used as an additional source of information to determine the expected outcome of the test cases.

The syllabus introduces two common code-related white-box techniques:

- Statement coverage
- Decision coverage

© Springer Nature Switzerland AG 2018
A. Roman, *A Study Guide to the ISTQB® Foundation Level 2018 Syllabus*,
https://doi.org/10.1007/978-3-319-98740-8_5

There are many other stronger white-box techniques not discussed in the syllabus, such as:

- Condition testing
- Condition/decision (C/D) testing
- Modified condition/decision coverage (MC/DC)
- Multiple condition testing
- Path testing, and so on

The knowledge of these methods is not required on the foundation level.

Although the white-box techniques will be exercised on the K2 cognitive level (understand), it may happen that some questions contain the source code. The code in the exam questions related to the white-box techniques can be represented in two ways: either as a listing in the pseudocode or as the control flow graph (CFG). We now briefly discuss both these notations.

The pseudocode is a convenient way of describing the algorithm. The most important algorithmic constructions used to define the control flow are as follows:

- Basic blocks—the blocks of the instructions executed one by one (so either all the instructions in the basic block are executed, or none of them is executed)
- IF or IF-ELSE statement—which allows to take one out of two or more ways depending on the condition(s)
- WHILE loop—which allows to repeat some sequence of instructions as long as a certain condition holds

Let us consider the example shown in Fig. 5.1. The executable lines are numbered.

In line 1, a system takes as an input a number x. Then, in line 2, it is checked if $x > 0$. If it is true, the body of IF is executed, that is, lines 3 and 4, in which a message is displayed and the x variable is set to 0 and then the control flow jumps at the end of the IF-ELSE statement (line 6). However, if in line 2, $x \leq 0$ (the decision is false), the system jumps to the ELSE block (line 5) and, after its execution, the control flow jumps at the end of the IF-ELSE statement (line 6).

The indentations (like the one in lines 3 and 4) are used to denote the blocks of code to convey program structure. Let us consider some more complicated examples shown in Fig. 5.2.

Here, if $x > 0$ in line 2, the whole IF block is executed (lines 3–8). This block begins with the WHILE loop: the lines 4 and 5 are executed until the condition $x > 0$ in line 3 is not true anymore. Then the control flow goes after the WHILE loop, to the line 6, where the decision $y > 0$ is checked. If true (resp. false), line

```
1. INPUT x
2. IF (x>0) THEN
3.    PRINT 'The entered number is a positive number'
4.    x := 0
   ELSE
5.    PRINT 'x is negative or 0'
6.END PROGRAM
```

Fig. 5.1 A simple piece of code

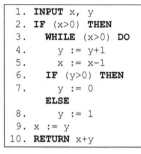

```
 1. INPUT x, y
 2. IF (x>0) THEN
 3.    WHILE (x>0) DO
 4.       y := y+1
 5.       x := x-1
 6.    IF (y>0) THEN
 7.       y := 0
       ELSE
 8.       y := 1
 9. x := y
10. RETURN x+y
```

Fig. 5.2 A more complicated piece of code

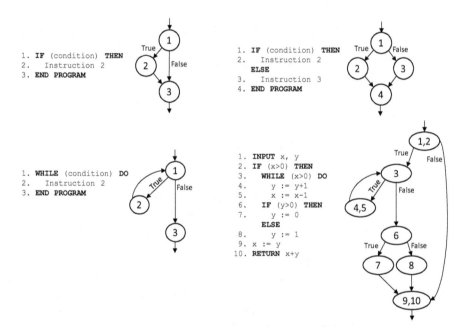

Fig. 5.3 Some algorithms and the corresponding control flow graphs

7 (resp. line 8) is executed. After that the control flow exits the IF block (lines 3–8), so it moves to the first line after this block, that is, line 9 and then line 10.

Control flow graph is a graphical way to represent the code. In the CFG, the nodes represent the instructions (or basic blocks of instructions) and the arrows—the possible ways the control flow can take. For example, Fig. 5.3 shows the CFGs of the basic algorithmic constructions, the algorithm from Fig. 5.2, and the control flow graphs related to them.

5.1   Statement Testing and Coverage

Statement testing coverage requires that each executable statement is exercised at least once by at least one test. The coverage is defined as the number of executable statements exercised divided by the total number of the executable statements.

Let us look at the CFG of the 10-line code from Fig. 5.3. The minimal number of test cases that achieve the (100%) statement coverage is 2, because lines 7 and 8 cannot be executed within one test. So the two sample test cases may, for example, go along the following paths:

- Test 1: 1, 2, 3, 4, 5, 3, 6, 7, 9, 10
- Test 2: 1, 2, 3, 6, 8, 9, 10

If our test suite contains only the first test, this suite would achieve 90% statement coverage, as the test exercises 9 out of 10 executable statements. In case of the test 2, this would be 70%. These two tests together exercise all the executable statements, so together, they achieve the 100% statement coverage.

5.2   Decision Testing and Coverage

Notice that the tests from the previous paragraph exercise all nodes of the CFG, but they do not exercise all arrows—for example, they do not exercise the arrow $(1, 2) \rightarrow (9, 10)$. The program may fail when going through this flow, so it would be wise to test all the possible control flows between the statements. The decision coverage is a criterion that requires it.

Decision coverage requires that every decision outcome (both TRUE and FALSE) should be exercised at least once by at least one of our tests. For example, in the code from the previous paragraph, we have three decision points—these are the nodes: (1, 2), (3), and (6). Each of them has two outgoing transitions; hence altogether, we have six test conditions to cover:

1. Decision (1, 2) outcome to TRUE
2. Decision (1, 2) outcome to FALSE
3. Decision (3) outcome to TRUE
4. Decision (3) outcome to FALSE
5. Decision (6) outcome to TRUE
6. Decision (6) outcome to FALSE

The minimal number of test cases achieving the decision coverage in this example is 3. For example,

- Test 1: 1, 2, 9, 10 (covers the test condition 2)
- Test 2: 1, 2, 3, 4, 5, 3, 6, 7, 9, 10 (covers the test conditions 1, 3, 4, and 5)
- Test 3: 1, 2, 3, 6, 8, 9, 10 (covers the test conditions 1, 4, and 6)

The minimal number of test cases in this case is 3, because no two of the test conditions (decision outcomes) 2, 5, and 6 can be exercised in one test case. Notice that we were able to cover both the test conditions 3 and 4 in one test case, taking advantage of the fact that there is a loop in the code, so we can cover the test condition 3, return, and then, in the next loop iteration, we cover the test condition 4.

5.3   Exercises for White-Box Techniques

The difficulty level of the following exercises is usually higher than the one required for the exam. Some of the exercises are on the K3 level, not the required K2 level. However, if you go through these exercises, you will have a better understanding of the white-box techniques. The syllabus describes them in a very general way. The exercises will allow you to see some more practical aspect of the techniques.

Exercise 28: Transforming the Code into the Control Flow Graph
Consider the following code.

```
1. INPUT x, y
2. WHILE (x>0) DO
3.   WHILE (y>0) DO
4.     y := y-1
5.     x := x+1
6. x := x-1
7. IF (x>y) THEN
8.   RETURN x
   ELSE
9.   RETURN y
```

Transform it to the equivalent control flow graph.

Exercise 29: Calculating the Coverage
Consider the CFG shown in Fig. 5.4.

(a) How many decisions are in this CFG? Name them.
(b) Consider the following set of test cases:

- A, B, F, G
- A, C, E, C, E, C, E, G
- A, C, E, G

   What is the statement and decision coverage for this test suite?
(c) Construct the minimal set of test cases that achieve the statement coverage.
(d) Construct the minimal set of test cases that achieve the decision coverage.

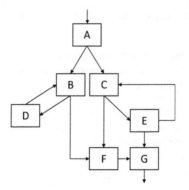

Fig. 5.4 A sample control flow graph with seven nodes

```
1.  IF NumberOfTransactions > 10 THEN
2.     IF TotalAmountSpent > $500 THEN
3.        discount := 5%
       ELSE
4.        discount := 2%
    ELSE
5.     discount := 0%
```

Fig. 5.5 Discount admission process

Exercise 30: Designing the Test Cases to Achieve the Given Coverage Level

The system for discount calculation takes as the input two values: *NumberOfTransactions* (representing the total number of transactions for a given client) and *TotalAmountSpent* (representing the total amount spent by this client during these transactions). Assume that each test case input is a pair (*NumberOfTransactions*, *TotalAmountSpent*). Consider the code shown in Fig. 5.5 describing the business rules for this system.

(a) Give an example of the test case that should result in admitting the 5% discount.
(b) What is the statement coverage for the following test suite: (9, $600), (10, $200)?
(c) What is the decision coverage for the following test suite: (15, $50), (20, $750)?
(d) Design the set of test cases that achieves the statement coverage.
(e) Design the set of test cases that achieves the decision coverage.

Exercise 31: Analyze Code with Respect to the Coverage Criteria

Suppose the code from the previous exercise was modified: at the end the line was added that prints the message to the client. Now the code looks as in Fig. 5.6.

Consider your test suite from the Exercise 35 (e). What is the number of tests that should be added to this suite so that both the statement and decision coverage will be achieved for the modified code?

Exercise 32: Coverage Criteria Subsumption

This exercise is a little bit advanced and requires a deep understanding of the white-box techniques. It goes beyond the requirements for the Foundation Level certificate.

```
1. IF NumberOfTransactions > 10 THEN
2.    IF TotalAmountSpent > $500 THEN
3.       discount := 5%
      ELSE
4.       discount := 2%
   ELSE
5.    discount := 0%
6. PRINT 'Your discount equals' + discount
```

Fig. 5.6 Discount admission process after modifications

The syllabus says that 100% decision coverage guarantees 100% statement coverage, but not vice versa. This property is called a criterion *subsumption*. In our case, decision coverage subsumes statement coverage. However, this property holds only for code with at least one decision (the syllabus does not say about that).

(a) Give an example of the code and the test suite that achieves 100% statement coverage, but does not achieve 100% decision coverage.
(b) Prove that for code with at least one decision, 100% decision coverage implies 100% statement coverage.
(c) Why it is important that there must be at least one decision in the code in order to decision coverage subsumes statement coverage?

Exercise 33: Provide Test Cases to Achieve a Given Coverage
Consider the following piece of code:

```
INPUT x, y
WHILE (x > 0)
   WHILE (y > 0)
      y := y - 1
      print 'something happened!'
   END WHILE
   x := x - 1
   y := y + x
END WHILE
```

What is the minimal number of test cases to achieve statement coverage of this code?

(A). 2.
(B). 3.
(C). 1.
(D). It is impossible to achieve statement coverage, since there are loops in the code.

Part III
Sample Mock Exams

Chapter 6
Sample Exam: Question Set 1

Question 1.

During the test process of an Internet of Things software, a defect was discovered, but it was not corrected due to the release deadline. After the release, it has not yet caused a failure. A test team decides to fix this defect. Which trigger for maintenance is described in this scenario?

(A) Upgrade of the software
(B) Migration
(C) Corrective change
(D) Introduction of completely new or modified thing into the system

Question 2.

Consider the following activities:

  (i) Implementing an automated test case
 (ii) Performing the review of the architectural design
(iii) Checking grammar and spelling of a user manual
(iv) Planning test activities
 (v) Designing a test case

    Select all the activities that are part of the testing process.

(A) (i), (iv), and (v)
(B) (ii) and (v)
(C) (i), (iii), and (iv)
(D) (i), (ii), (iii), (iv), (v)

© Springer Nature Switzerland AG 2018

A. Roman, *A Study Guide to the ISTQB® Foundation Level 2018 Syllabus*,
https://doi.org/10.1007/978-3-319-98740-8_6

Question 3.

Consider the following piece of code:

```
1 INPUT NumberOfValues
2 i := 1
3 sum := 0
4 WHILE (i <= NumberOfValues)
5   PRINT 'Enter the value number i'
6   INPUT value
7   sum := sum + value
8   i := i + 1
  END WHILE
9 RETURN sum
```

You executed a predefined set of test cases for this code. Which of the following guarantees that in at least one of these test cases, the *while* loop was executed at least once?

(A) A set of test cases achieved 50% decision coverage.
(B) A set of test cases achieved 100% statement coverage.
(C) One of these tests executes the code with NumberOfValues = 0.
(D) There are at least two test cases in the test suite.

Question 4.

You test the autopilot system for the airplanes. You want to perform the tests that check the correctness of the communication between two modules of this system: geolocalization module and engine controller. Which of the following would be the best example of a test basis for designing your tests?

(A) Detailed design of the geolocalization module
(B) Architectural design
(C) Risk analysis reports
(D) Legal regulations in the field of avionics

Question 5.

Choose the correct sequence of events.

(A) A mistake results in defect, which in turn may result in a failure.
(B) A defect results in mistake, which in turn may result in a failure.
(C) A failure results in a mistake, which in turn may result in a defect.
(D) A defect results in failure, which in turn may result in a mistake.

Question 6.

You test a system that computes the pass/fail result for a student who attends a lecture on software testing. The lecture consists of laboratories and exam. For each of these two parts, a student can get from 0 to 50 points (it is always an integer number). The final evaluation is based on the following rule:

> Let L be the number of points achieved by the student during the labs.
> Let E be the number of points achieved by the student during the exam.
> Final Result: $= L + E$.
> If (FinalResult > 50), then decision := StudentPassed.
>   else decision := StudentFailed.

You want to apply the equivalence partitioning technique to a FinalResult variable. Assume that each test is a pair (L, E). Which set of test cases covers all valid equivalence classes?

(A) (1, 50); (50, 50)
(B) (39, 19); (28, 23)
(C) (0, 50); (50, 0)
(D) (35, 15); (40, 20)

Question 7.

You work as a tester in a software house and you concurrently work on two projects. One of them is an internal tool for on-line room reservation, done within an agile life cycle. The other one is a commercial software for managing hospital patients' data, conducted in the waterfall model. In onemonth, new versions of both systems will be released. You don't have time to perform all the planned tests for both systems. You decide to focus on testing the commercial system. Select the correct answer.

(A) This is a good decision, because the commercial software is much more important for the company than the internal system.
(B) This is a bad decision, because critical defects can occur in both systems, and one of them will not be tested.
(C) This is a bad decision, because testing commercial project will be much more expensive than testing the internal one.
(D) This is a good decision, because the waterfall model requires testing during the end of the project.

Question 8.
Figure 6.1 presents the set of test cases you want to execute. An arrow from a test case A to B indicates logical dependencies between these test cases: the execution of B is possible only after the execution of A. The numbers in parentheses represent the priorities of test cases (1 = the highest, 5 = the lowest). In your strategy, you want to prioritize the execution sequence regarding the test priority.

Which test case should be executed as the fifth one?

(A) TC2
(B) TC7
(C) TC5
(D) TC6

Question 9.
Consider the collapsed decision table presented in Table 6.1 that describes the business rules for admitting a free bus ticket.

Assume that a test consists of three Boolean values corresponding to three conditions. Which of the following tests demonstrates that the business rules described in the table are *contradictory*?

(A) (member of parliament = TRUE, disabled = FALSE, student = TRUE)
(B) (member of parliament = TRUE, disabled = TRUE, student = FALSE)
(C) (member of parliament = FALSE, disabled = FALSE, student = TRUE)
(D) (member of parliament = FALSE, disabled = FALSE, student = FALSE)

Fig. 6.1 Dependencies between test cases

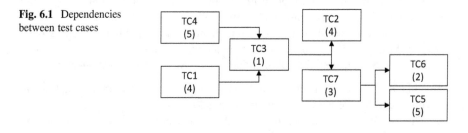

Table 6.1 Decision table with contradictory rules

	T1	T2	T3
Conditions			
Member of Parliament?	TRUE	–	–
Disabled person?	–	TRUE	–
Student?	–	–	TRUE
Action			
Free ride?	TRUE	TRUE	FALSE

Question 10.
You test a system that produces very big output files. Their structure must follow some set of predefined rules. The expected result of a test case is the file that follows these rules. You want to execute a set of test cases. Suppose you have a tool that takes two files as an input and returns TRUE if they are identical and FALSE otherwise. What would be the type of this tool in this case?

(A) A test oracle
(B) A comparator
(C) A test data generator
(D) A monitoring tool

Question 11.
Match the actions with the corresponding work product review activities.

Action 1—Distribution of the work product
Action 2—Noting questions and recommendations about the work product
Action 3—Allocating roles

Activity a—Individual review
Activity b—Planning
Activity c—Initiating the review

    (A) 1b, 2a, 3c
    (B) 1c, 2a, 3b
    (C) 1a, 2b, 3c
    (D) 1b, 2c, 3a

Question 12.
A tester, together with a developer, architect, and test manager, participates in the inspection of an architectural design of a component. The design was done by the architect. During the inspection, the test manager finds an error in the design. After the inspection, the tester creates the new, corrected version of the design. Using the new design, the developer implements the component.
    Who performed the debugging?

(A) Tester
(B) Developer
(C) Architect
(D) Test manager

Question 13.
If there are n binary decisions in the code, and there are no other decisions apart form these ones, what is the total number of coverage elements for the decision coverage?

(A) $2n$
(B) 2^n
(C) n
(D) n^2

Question 14.

The client of a system under test is interested primarily in a high availability of this system. One of his requirements is as follows: "The system may be unavailable no more often than 1 hour per week." You prepare a test report designed specifically for the client, regarding the above-mentioned requirement. The report covers the data from the period of last week. Which information should contain this report?

(A) Number of test cases executed, number of test cases that failed, number of test cases that passed
(B) Number of defects found, number of defects fixed
(C) Total repairing time
(D) Mean time between failures, number of failures

Question 15.

You work as a tester in a project for a dedicated client. You have a set of automated test cases, which are traced back to the functional requirements and to the software components. Each functional requirement is traced back to one or more risk items. Suppose that in a certain moment, risk level of one of the risk items has changed. Using the impact analysis, what can we infer from this fact?

 (i) Which requirements may be affected by this change?
 (ii) Which test cases may be affected by this change?
(iii) Which software components may be affected by this change?

(A) We can infer about (i); we cannot infer about (ii) and (iii).
(B) We can infer about (i), (ii), and (iii).
(C) We can infer about (i) and (ii); we cannot infer about (iii).
(D) We can infer about (iii); we cannot infer about (i) and (ii).

Question 16.

Which of the below information affects the testing effort and at the same time is the outcome of the testing itself?

(A) The size of the product
(B) The number of testers
(C) The client requirements
(D) The number of defects found

Question 17.

A moderator was asked to organize a code review (walkthrough) of a component X for a group of developers. He organized an inspection and invited an author of X and a team of testers. Based on this scenario, which type(s) of the success factors for reviews are missing?

(A) Neither organizational nor people-related success factors are missing.
(B) Only a certain people-related success factor is missing.
(C) Only a certain organizational success factor is missing.
(D) Both organizational and people-related success factors are missing.

Question 18.

You test the program that takes a sequence of numbers as the input and returns these numbers sorted. Before you start your testing, you get the idea (without referring to any documentation) to check what happens, if you enter the empty set of numbers as the input. This is an example of which technique?

(A) Black-box testing
(B) White-box testing
(C) Error guessing
(D) Checklist-based testing

Question 19.

Which of the following gives the best description of a decision table testing?

(A) A technique for representing complex business rules, by identifying conditions and the resulting actions
(B) A technique for representing a behavior of a test item depending on current conditions or previous history
(C) A technique for representing a sequence of decisions undertaken by a subject in collaboration with one or more actors
(D) A technique for deriving test cases that exercise the decisions in the code and for testing the code that is executed based on the decision outcomes

Question 20.

Which sentence explains correctly the importance of performing regression tests regarding the SDLC model chosen?

(A) Regression testing is important in incremental models, because after adding an increment, we need to check if it did not cause problems in other, already developed, parts of the system.
(B) Regression testing is important during the system testing, because regression testing is usually performed on a system that allows end-to-end testing, no matter which SDLC model is chosen.
(C) Regression testing is important in a waterfall model, because in the sequential models, testing is performed in the late phases, when the system is already implemented, so the testing effort will be usually bigger than in case of incremental models.
(D) Regression testing is important in the iterative SDLC models, because these models put a strong emphasis on the constant interaction between end users, testers, and developers.

Question 21.

Software development models must be adapted to

(A) Testing model
(B) User requirements
(C) Testing process
(D) Context of the project

Question 22.
A system calculates the bonus for airplane pilots. The bonus is based on the total number of flying hours, which is the sum of the number of hours on a flight simulator and the number of hours on regular flights. The business rules R1–R5 for admitting the bonus are presented in the following decision table.

	R1	R2	R3	R4	R5
Simulator hours	<100	$101 - 200$	$101 - 200$	>200	>200
Flight hours	–	<200	≥ 201	<100	≥ 101
Bonus	0%	10%	20%	20%	25%

Which of the following sets of test inputs is a minimal set that achieves the equivalence partitioning coverage for the output value? Assume each test input is a pair (s, f), where s denotes the simulator hours and f—flight hours.

(A) (25, 300), (200, 199), (150, 345), (350, 0), (227, 101)
(B) (0, 0), (101, 0), (200, 207), (200, 99), (205, 210)
(C) (90, 0), (120, 90), (210, 80), (200, 201)
(D) (0, 300), (200, 50), (300, 50), (300, 300)

Question 23.
Recently, your organization outsourced the test team for conducting the performance testing. You talk with a developer, who told you that it was a very good idea, because now they—developers—do not need to care so much about the performance issues, as they will be found by the test team. This is an example of

(A) Benefit of test independence, as developers may focus on other activities
(B) Benefit of test independence, as the outsourced testing team may see other and different defects and is unbiased
(C) Drawback of test independence, as the outsourced team is isolated from the developers
(D) Drawback of test independence, as some of the team members may lose a sense of responsibility for quality

Question 24.
Which of the following can be the root cause of the fact that a developer implemented an ineffective algorithm?

(A) Poor performance of the system
(B) Acceptance testing done by testers in the client's location, not by client
(C) Developer's lack of education in the area of algorithms and complexity
(D) Memory leaks that occurred after a long time of the software operation

Question 25.
Which of the following is an example of the analytical test strategy?

(A) Designing software models and then deriving test cases from these models
(B) Prioritizing the test execution with respect to the related risk levels
(C) Performing fault attacks with the use of predesigned checklist containing the types of defects that had occurred in the past in other projects
(D) Automating extensively functional regression tests

Question 26.
Select the right relation between quality assurance, quality control, and testing.

(A) Testing is a synonym of quality assurance, which is a part of quality control.
(B) Testing is a form of quality control, which is a part of quality assurance.
(C) Quality control is a form of quality assurance, which is a synonym for testing.
(D) Quality control is a synonym of quality assurance, which is a part of testing.

Question 27.
Your company has recently published an official document describing how to perform static analysis of a source code. Can this document be a subject to static analysis?

(A) Yes, because every software work product can be examined using static techniques.
(B) No, because we would have to apply the rules described in the document to themselves.
(C) No, because the document describes how to perform a static analysis of a source code, but the document itself is not a source code.
(D) No, because static analysis can be performed only for specifications and source code.

Question 28.
Which of the following is the benefit of using the checklist-based testing?

(A) It allows us to appreciate the nonfunctional testing, which is often underestimated.
(B) It allows us to test effectively in absence of formal requirements.
(C) It allows us to take advantage of the tester's expert knowledge.
(D) It allows us to test in a more consistent way.

Question 29.
Risk level is characterized by:

(A) Likelihood and priority
(B) Probability and impact
(C) Severity and priority
(D) Product risks and project risks

Table 6.2 Valid transitions
of a state machine

State	Event	Next state
Initial	GoToLogin	LoginPage
LoginPage	LoginOK	WelcomePage
LoginPage	LoginNotOK	Initial
WelcomePage	LogOut	Initial

Question 30.

Table 6.2 shows all the valid transitions of some state machines with three states: Initial, LoginPage, and WelcomePage.

Assuming there are only four possible events in the system: GoToLogin, LoginOK, LoginNotOK, LogOut, how many *invalid* transitions are in this state machine?

(A) 8
(B) 0
(C) 4
(D) 12

Question 31.

Which of the following are the examples of the metrics-based approach and which are the examples of the expert based approach?

  (i) planning poker
 (ii) Wideband Delphi
(iii) burndown chart
(iv) software reliability model

(A) (i) and (ii) are metric based; (iii) and (iv) are expert based.
(B) (i), (iii) and (iv) are metric based; (iv) is expert based.
(C) (iii) and (iv) are metric based; (i) and (ii) are expert based.
(D) (ii) is metric based; (i), (iii), and (iv) are expert based.

Question 32.

Testers may test the software more efficient than developers, because:

(A) Testers may have programming skills.
(B) Testers usually do not have programming skills.
(C) Developers' responsibility is to write code, not to test it.
(D) Developers have the emotional attitude to their code.

Question 33.

You test the online reservation system for a hotel chain. Consider the following artifact:

ID 003. Normal reservation.
Precondition: user exists in the database.

1. Choose "make a reservation."
2. Fill up the form with the valid data.
3. Click "submit." The site should redirect the user into the payment page.
4. Perform the payment with the valid card. The system should go back to the reservation site and show a message with payment confirmation and that the reservation is done correctly.
5. Log out.

Postcondition: a new record in the Orders database; user bank account balance decreased by the amount of payment.

This artifact is an example of:

(A) Test suite
(B) Low-level test case
(C) Test condition
(D) High-level test case

Question 34.

You perform an ad-hoc review of the model of a process that realizes the following business requirement: "User can send any file of size at most 1 GB through a web form. If the file size exceeds this bound, the system should reject the file, clear the form, and return to the initial state. Otherwise, the system accepts the file."

The model under review is presented in Fig. 6.2.

What type of defect in the model can you uncover during the review?

(A) Wrong design, because there is a potentially infinite loop.
(B) Inconsistency with the requirement regarding the business rule.
(C) Ambiguity, because the model does not say what file types are accepted.
(D) There are no defects—the model conforms to the business requirement.

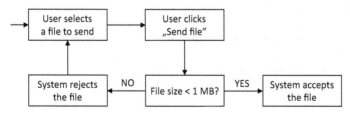

Fig. 6.2 A model of business flow

Table 6.3 Business rules for calculating a discount

Total price (rounded)	Discount
Less than $100	No discount
$100–$299	5%
$300 or more	10%

Question 35.

A shopping discount system takes as an input the total price T (a positive integer with precision of 1 cent), rounds it to the nearest integer value (in dollars), and basing on this value calculates a discount using the rules presented in Table 6.3.

You want to test if the system correctly calculates the discount for a given total price T. Which of the following is a set of boundary values for one of the equivalence classes of a variable T? Assume that you follow 2-point boundary value analysis.

(A) $0.01, $99.49
(B) $0, $100
(C) $100, $299
(D) $299.49, $299.50

Question 36.

Which of the following is a clear advantage of static testing over dynamic testing?

(A) Static techniques can locate defects other than dynamic techniques.
(B) Static techniques are cheaper than dynamic techniques.
(C) Static techniques can detect defects earlier than dynamic techniques.
(D) Static techniques can detect failures, while dynamic techniques are only able to find defects.

Question 37.

You write a defect report with an intention to provide developers a sufficient information to reproduce defect as quick as possible. The current form of your report looks as follows:

"When leaving the (optional!) field for postal code empty, after clicking 'Submit' button, a pop-up 'Unknown error' appears."

Which additional information in the defect report will be the most beneficial in this scenario?

(A) Your name and date of the defect occurrence
(B) Information about the form name and system version
(C) Information that you suspect that there is a problem with the database, which fails to write a record when a postal code is empty
(D) Information about defect priority and severity

Question 38.
Consider the following use case describing the course enrollment.

USE CASE UC-4.33.001—Course enrollment

Actors: Student, System
Preconditions: Student is logged in the EnrollmentSystem application

Steps:

1. Student selects the "Browse course catalog" option.
2. System describes the list of all active courses (E1).
3. Student selects a course.
4. System describes information about the course and asks to confirm the enrollment (E1).
5. Student clicks "Enroll."
6. System checks that a Student is allowed to enroll, enrolls the Student, and displays the confirmation message (E2).

Exceptions:

E1—System cannot connect to the course database and shows a message "Connection error." A use case ends.
E2—Student is already enrolled to the course. System shows a message "Enrollment not allowed." A use case ends.
Also, at any moment, Student can resign from the enrollment. In such case, a use case ends.

What is the minimal number of test cases to achieve the standard use-case coverage defined in the Foundation Level Syllabus?

(A) 3
(B) 4
(C) 7
(D) 10

Question 39.
Which of the following is an example of how configuration management supports testing, when a user reports the field bug?

(A) A tester can search for the similar issues that might have happened before and look up for the potential solution.
(B) A tester can reproduce the test cases related to the client's version of the software.
(C) The bug can be identified, version controlled, and tracked for changes by a tester.
(D) Configuration management supports the development activities, not testing activities.

Question 40.

Your manager asked you to participate in a tool selection process. What task you may be given?

(A) To assess the organizational maturity and decide whether the tool acquisition will be beneficial to the organization
(B) To decide on standard ways of using the tool across the organization
(C) To evaluate how well the tool fits with existing processes and practices
(D) To perform a pilot project.

Chapter 7
Sample Exam: Question Set 2

Question 1.
In which moment of a project's life cycle should the test planning occur?

(A) At the beginning. All further activities should be done according to that plan.
(B) It is a continuous activity, as feedback from different test activities may impact the plans and force us to change them.
(C) During the test analysis phase, because planning is an analytical activity.
(D) In sequential models, planning should occur through the whole project's life cycle, while in the iterative models, planning should be generally avoided.

Question 2.
To overcome the pesticide paradox, we should:

(A) Use test techniques to derive a finite number of test cases for a potentially infinite number of combinations of input values.
(B) Start testing activities as early as possible.
(C) Align the test strategy to the context.
(D) Review and update tests on a regular basis.

Question 3.
Choose the correct sentence about defects, failures, and errors.

(A) A failure is caused by one or more errors, which are caused by one or more defects.
(B) Code review can reveal a failure.
(C) Executing a defect in code during testing may result in actual result being equal to the expected result.
(D) A root cause of every failure is one or more human errors.

© Springer Nature Switzerland AG 2018
A. Roman, *A Study Guide to the ISTQB® Foundation Level 2018 Syllabus*,
https://doi.org/10.1007/978-3-319-98740-8_7

Question 4.
Consider the following criterion: "there are no failures with high severity." What type of a criterion can it be?

(A) Entry criterion for the "test design" phase
(B) Entry criterion for the "test implementation" phase
(C) Exit criterion for the "test execution" phase
(D) Exit criterion for the "test completion" phase

Question 5.
Traceability between test cases and risk items can allow the testers to:

(A) Perform the impact analysis in terms of the effort needed to change the test cases in case a functional requirement is changed.
(B) Calculate statement and decision coverage achieved by the executed tests.
(C) Calculate the risk level by analyzing the test results for each test case.
(D) Implement effective monitoring in terms of calculating the residual risk.

Question 6.
Choose an example of a white-box test technique.

(A) Designing tests based on the architectural design
(B) Designing tests based on the functional requirements
(C) Designing tests by generating random inputs
(D) Designing tests based on the tester's knowledge and experience.

Question 7.
Which type of testing cannot be planned in advance?

(A) Regression testing
(B) Operational acceptance testing
(C) User acceptance testing
(D) Confirmation testing

Question 8.
Which of the following is *not* a typical tester's task according to Foundation Level Syllabus?

(A) Preparing test data
(B) Automating the tests
(C) Supporting the selection of test tools
(D) Reviewing and contributing to test plans

Question 9.
A source to determine expected results to compare with the actual results of the system under test is called:

(A) Comparator
(B) Test oracle
(C) Test specification
(D) Test basis

Question 10.
You are testing a Customer Relationship Management (CRM) system and you have
prepared the following test cases:

TC1: Precondition: CRM database contains at least two client records.
Steps: Clear the whole CRM client database by removing all records.
Expected result: The database is empty.

TC2: Precondition: No preconditions.
Steps: Create a new client record that does not exist in the database.
Expected result: Record correctly added in the database.

TC3: Precondition: Database contains at least one client record.
Steps: Try to create a new client record that is already present in the
database.
Expected result: System does not allow to duplicate the record.

At the beginning, the CRM database is empty. The execution of each test lasts
5 minutes. You want to execute all three test cases, but in the shortest possible time.
What is the reasonable test execution schedule in this situation?

(A) TC2, TC3, TC1
(B) TC2, TC2, TC3, TC1
(C) TC2, TC2, TC1, TC2, TC3
(D) TC2, TC1, TC3

Question 11.
Your project follows a V-model as the life cycle model. It is currently in the
"Requirements" phase. What kind of test activities can you perform at this phase?

(A) No test activity is allowed, as V-model is a sequential process. We need to wait
till the "Testing" phase.
(B) Design of the integration tests.
(C) Design of the acceptance tests.
(D) Code review.

Question 12.
Figure 7.1 presents the state machine for a part of a CRM (Customer Relationship
Management) system. The operator is able to print reports, create records for new
customers, and modify records for already existing customers.
What is the number of transitions (0-switches) in this state machine and what is
the minimal number of test cases that achieve 0-switch coverage? By a test case, we
understand a sequence of events starting from the initial state (S1).

(A) 7 0-switches; 1 test case
(B) 6 0-switches; 2 test cases
(C) 5 0-switches; 2 test cases
(D) 6 0-switches; 1 test case

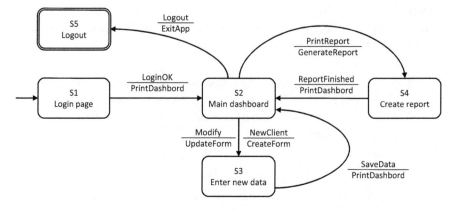

Fig. 7.1 A state machine for a data-oriented application

Question 13.
You are working as a tester in the project in which the following documents are available:

- Requirements specification
- 50 automated test scripts
- Test plan

Which of these documents *cannot* be examined during the review and why?

(A) 50 automated test scripts, because it is impractical to perform a manual review for such a big number of the work products.
(B) Test plan, because it is a high level document that cannot be modified by testers.
(C) Requirement specification, because it is a test basis, which may play the role of a test oracle.
(D) All these documents can be subject to a review.

Question 14.
A word processor can be classified as which type of tool, assuming the classification is done according to the testing activities the tools support?

(A) Test specification tool.
(B) Test execution tool.
(C) Test monitoring tool.
(D) A word processor cannot be classified this way, as this is not a test tool.

Question 15.

You are testing the automatic gate controller. The following use case presents the situation of a standard car passing through the gate.

Use case UC-001: standard passing through the gate
Preconditions:
    1. Gate is in the "bottom" position.
    2. There is no car before the gate.

Car	System
1. A car approaches the gate.	2. System recognizes the car before the gate and starts raising the gate (E1).
	3. The gate is raised to the "top" position.
4. The car passes through the gate.	
	5. System recognizes the car passed through the gate.
	6. The system starts to lower the gate (E2).
	7. The gate is lowered to the "bottom" position.

Exceptions:
E1—The car passes through the gate before it reaches the "top" position. System starts lowering the gate immediately, and the use case continues in Step 5.
E2—A new car approaches the gate. System starts raising the gate immediately—a use case ends and a new use case UC-001 starts immediately in Step 2.

You want to cover this test case, according to the standard use case coverage proposed by the Foundation Level Syllabus. Which of the following test cases should NOT be included in the test suite?

(A) Step 1, Step 2 with exception E1, Step 5, Step 6 with exception E2.
(B) Step 1, Step 2, Step 3, Step 4, Step 5, Step 6 with exception E2.
(C) Step 1, Step 2 with exception E1, Step 5, Step 6, Step 7.
(D) Step 1, Step 2, Step 3, Step 4, Step 5, Step 6, Step 7.

Question 16.

Consider the variable DayOfWeek, whose domain is {Mon, Tue, Wed, Thu, Fri, Sat, Sun}. Which of the following is not a correct equivalence partitioning of this domain, no matter what error hypothesis is considered by a tester? Assume that each class is denoted by the curly brackets { ... }.

(A) {Mon}, {Tue}, {Wed}, {Thu}, {Fri}, {Sat}, {Sun}
(B) {Mon, Tue, Wed, Thu, Fri, Sat, Sun}
(C) {Mon, Tue, Wed}, {Mon, Thu, Fri}, {Tue, Sat, Sun}
(D) {Mon, Tue, Sat}, {Sun, Thu}, {Wed, Fri}

Question 17.

What is the direct consequence of communicating defects by a tester to other team members in an unconstructive way?

(A) Decreasing the team effectiveness
(B) Conflict in the team
(C) Increasing the team effectiveness
(D) Losing a sense of responsibility for quality

Question 18.
Who uses the test charters?

(A) Developer
(B) Client
(C) User
(D) Tester

Question 19.
You are asked to perform a review of the user interface prototype for the web-based e-banking application. The interface will be used by the bank clients only. As the application will be used by many different clients, your team has defined the so-called personas that represent different, but typical client types:

- A teenager with no income except from the pocket money, experienced with the web technologies
- A businessman with high salary and many different accounts, moderately experienced with the web technologies
- An old women that has sight problems, inexperienced in the web technologies

Your team will conduct the review of the interface from the point of view of these customer types. Which review technique will be the most useful in this case?

(A) Role-based review
(B) Perspective-based review
(C) Checklist-based review
(D) Scenarios and dry runs

Question 20.
Which of the following is an organizational success factor for reviews?

(A) A culture of learning and process improvement is promoted.
(B) Participants have adequate time to prepare.
(C) The review is conducted in an atmosphere of trust.
(D) Defects found are acknowledged, appreciated, and handled objectively.

Question 21.
The role of the impact analysis is to

(A) Estimate the coverage of a given test suite in order to predict its effectiveness.
(B) Calculate the risk level using the information about its likelihood and impact.
(C) Assess the impact of a risk related to a given test case during the test analysis phase.
(D) Identify the possible side effects of a planned or actual change.

Question 22.
Structural testing can be performed:

(A) Only by developers, because developers know and have access to the code they write.
(B) Only by testers, because structural testing is a testing, not developing activity.
(C) Only by clients, because they define the structure of the software that is going to be implemented, so only they can verify its correctness.
(D) By anyone, since it can be applied to all test levels: developers can perform component and integration white-box testing, testers—white-box system testing and clients—white-box acceptance testing.

Question 23.
Which of the following test techniques is an extension of the equivalence partitioning?

(A) Exploratory testing
(B) Boundary value analysis
(C) Decision table testing
(D) Equivalence classes testing

Question 24.
A user defines her password according to several rules. The rules are:

• The password must have at least six characters.
• The password must contain at least one numerical character (0, 1, . . ., 9).
• The password must contain at least one capital letter.

Assume that each rule defines a separate equivalence partitioning on the set of all strings. Each rule defines one valid and one invalid equivalence class. Each test case can cover only one invalid equivalence class. Which set of input values is the smallest set that achieves the equivalence partitioning coverage?

(A) ABC123, AB1, ABCDEF, 123456
(B) Abc1234, abcdef, 123, ABC
(C) Abc1234, Abc, ab1, AB1
(D) Abc12, Abc123, Ab1, ab1234, abc

Question 25.
The RiskEvaluator application assesses the risk of admitting a loan for a customer. It makes the decision upon four conditions, chosen by a client from the drop-down lists. The conditions are

• age—possible answers:
  – under 18
  – between 18 and 35
  – between 36 and 65
  – over 65

- education—possible answers:
  - elementary or high school
  - undergraduate
  - graduate
- place of living—possible answers:
  - city
  - village

If a client selects age "under 18," the field "education" is automatically filled with "elementary or high school" and the client is not able to change this value. The output can be one of the following:

- Low risk
- Medium risk
- High risk

How many columns will have the decision table for this problem assuming that it contains only the feasible combinations of conditions?

(A) 22
(B) 24
(C) 7
(D) 20

Question 26.
Which of the following is an example of a product risk?

(A) Good performance
(B) Poor reliability
(C) Test environment not ready on time
(D) Low quality of the requirements

Question 27.
Your team follows the sequential model with three phases: requirements, design, code, and testing. Your team uses the following approach to estimate the number of defects detected in the testing phase.

Input: d_{REQ} = number of defects found in the requirement phase
         d_{DES} = number of defects found in the design phase
         d_{COD} = number of defects found in the coding phase

Output: d_{TES} = estimated number of defects that escaped to the testing phase
         E = estimated effort (in man-hours) needed to fix the defects found in the testing phase

Estimations: $d_{TES} = 0.2 \cdot d_{COD} + 0.1 \cdot d_{DES} + 0.06 \cdot d_{REQ}$
               $E = 0.85 \cdot d_{TES} \cdot 1.3$ man-hours

The constants in the formulas come from the previous experience of your team in the similar projects.

The approach described above is an example of what test estimation technique?

(A) Expert-based approach, because it utilizes the team's knowledge about the previous projects.
(B) Risk-based approach, because it takes into account a certain phase-containment parameters, expressed in the constants used in the formulas.
(C) Metric-based approach, because it uses a statistical modeling involving metrics.
(D) Methodical approach, because it uses some predefined set of test conditions.

Question 28.
Which of the following is an example of how product risk analysis may influence the thoroughness and scope of testing?

(A) From the risk analysis, it follows that there may be very serious delays when the potential tool vendor fails with the tool delivery, so the team decides to perform a thorough and detailed tool selection process.
(B) The team analyzed all the identified risks and prepared a contingency plan for the high level risks.
(C) The team performed a detailed functional testing, according to the results of the risk analysis phase.
(D) 70% of the identified high level risks are related to security issues, so the team decides to outsource the security testing to professional penetration testers.

Question 29.
Analyzing defects in order to propose preventive actions so that this defect's reoccurrence can be avoided is a process that is called:

(A) Root cause analysis
(B) Debugging
(C) Review
(D) Dynamic testing

Question 30.
What should be taken into account when we plan to use a keyword-driven approach?

(A) The keyword-driven tool needs to interface with other tools or spreadsheets in order to produce useful information in a format that fits the needs of the organization.
(B) In order to introduce a keyword-driven approach we need to have a well-defined inspection process.
(C) In order to introduce a keyword-driven approach, we need to have a technical expertise in scripting language.
(D) We have to transform our SDLC model to the V-model.

Question 31.

You are preparing to perform the acceptance testing of an invoice management system. Which of the following is the best test basis for this task?

(A) Architectural design of the application at system level
(B) Documentation about communication interfaces of the application
(C) Legal regulations describing how invoices should be constructed and processed
(D) Source code of the application

Question 32.

Why is it a good reason to collect test metrics?

(A) They help us in defining the test process.
(B) They help us in monitoring and reporting test activities.
(C) They can be collected in an automatic way.
(D) They improve communication between testers and other team members.

Question 33.

Evaluating testability of the test basis and test items takes place during which phase of the testing process?

(A) Test design
(B) Test planning, monitoring, and control
(C) Test analysis
(D) Test implementation

Question 34.

You need to decide which version of the architectural design will be used in your project. Which type of review would be the most appropriate for discussing this issue?

(A) Informal review
(B) Walkthrough
(C) Technical review
(D) Inspection

Question 35.

You test one of the on-line banking system functions that verifies the correctness of the PIN for a credit card. A valid PIN:

- Must contain at least 4 and at most 6 digits
- Must contain at least 2 different digits

You want to apply a 2-point boundary value analysis for checking that the system follows the two above rules. A test case consists of a PIN number. Which set of test cases covers all the boundary values that you need to test?

(A) 123, 1234, 123456, 1234567
(B) 949, 0011, 33333, 123123, 6667778
(C) 123, 1111, 123456, 1234567
(D) 777, 8888, 999999, 4444444

Question 36.

Which action is done by a moderator during the "review initiation" step of a formal review?

(A) Sending an e-mail to the participants explaining what is the goal of the review, with an attachment of a document to be reviewed
(B) Defining the review criteria and checking entry criteria
(C) Allocating roles
(D) Preparing for the review meeting by reviewing the documents

Question 37.

A tester wrote the following defect report regarding the financial application, which grants loans up to $10,000.

> **Defect report:** wrong calculation of interest rate for the LoanSystem ver. 2.1.
> **Status:** new.
> **Configuration id:** LS-348-33, operating system: Win7.
> **Symptom:** after entering in the TotalLoanValue field a value greater than $10,000, interest rate is calculated as 0%.
> **Steps to reproduce:**
> 1. Log in to the system. A main menu appears.
> 2. Choose "Request for a new loan." A "New loan" form appears.
> 3. Enter "10,001" in the field "TotalLoanValue".
> 4. Interest rate is shown as 0% instead of 12%. A system asks for confirmation.
> 5. Click "Enter new loan value".
> 6. Enter "10,000" in the field "TotalLoanValue".
> 7. Interest rate is shown as 12%, as expected. A system asks for confirmation.
> 8. Confirm. The loan is granted.

What is wrong with this defect report?

(A) Expected result is wrong in one step.
(B) Expected result is missing in one step.
(C) Defect status is missing.
(D) Nothing is wrong with this report.

Question 38.

Suppose you have three test cases:

- Test 1 gives you 20% decision coverage.
- Test 2 gives you 30% decision coverage.
- Test 3 gives you 30% decision coverage.

What is the possible decision coverage that can be achieved by a test suite consisted only of these three tests?

(A) 82%
(B) 50%
(C) 25%
(D) 1.8%

Question 39.

What can we be sure about, if we achieved 100% statement coverage of a given code?

(A) That our tests executed all executable statements in the code
(B) That we tested any possible behavior of the code
(C) That our tests achieved 100% decision coverage as well
(D) That there are no decision points in the code

Question 40.

Choose a good example of why testing is necessary.

(A) It allows software development process to be aligned with the testing process.
(B) It fixes defects detected in software.
(C) It allows to detect and prevent from contradictions in the requirements.
(D) It allows to manage better the testing process.

Chapter 8
Sample Exam: Question Set 3

Question 1.
Which of the following sets of test techniques contains only the examples of black-box techniques?

(A) Statement coverage testing, state transition testing, error guessing
(B) Use-case based testing, decision table testing, boundary value analysis
(C) Exploratory testing, equivalence partitioning testing, system testing
(D) Integration testing, acceptance testing, defect-based testing

Question 2.
You test a function that takes two positive integers: width and height as an input and checks if it is possible to print on a canvas these two dimensions. Both width and height cannot be too small, but the canvas area, calculated as the product of width and height, cannot be too large. The function follows the process described in a figure (Fig. 8.1).

Assume that each test case is a triple (width, height, expected result), where "expected result" can be accepted or rejected. Which of the following is the minimal set of test cases that covers boundary values for width, height, and area and all of them have correct expected results defined? Assume you follow the 2-point version of the boundary value analysis.

(A) (4, 9, reject), (5, 4, reject), (7, 5, accept), (6, 6, reject).
(B) (4, 9, reject), (6, 4, accept), (5, 5, accept), (7, 5, accept), (6, 6, reject).
(C) (4, 9, reject), (5, 4, reject), (5, 5, accept), (6, 6, reject).
(D) (4, 9, accept), (7, 5, accept), (5, 4, reject).

© Springer Nature Switzerland AG 2018
A. Roman, *A Study Guide to the ISTQB® Foundation Level 2018 Syllabus*,
https://doi.org/10.1007/978-3-319-98740-8_8

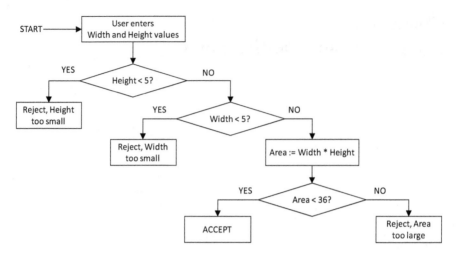

Fig. 8.1 Process flow for calculating the canvas area

Question 3.
Why are the validation activities examples of a positive role of testing?

(A) They help to detect defects in the early phases of the software life cycle.
(B) They help to prevent ambiguities in requirements.
(C) They help to reduce the risk of logic or calculation errors within the code and
    test cases, because they enforce testers to work closely with developers.
(D) They help to ensure that the system meets the client's expectations.

Question 4.
From the following, choose the set of the iterative SDLC models.

(A) Waterfall, Boehm spiral model, Rational Unified Process
(B) Test Maturity Model, Rapid Application Development, V-model
(C) Scrum, Kanban, Lean
(D) Extreme Programming, Fundamental Test Process, Capability Maturity Model

Question 5.
A support in setting up adequate configuration management of testware for traceability is the responsibility of which project role?

(A) Tester
(B) Test automation engineer
(C) Developer
(D) Test manager

Question 6.
Confirmation by examination and through provision of objective evidence that specified requirements have been fulfilled is called:

(A) Validation
(B) Debugging
(C) Verification
(D) Root cause analysis

Question 7.
Table 8.1 presents the set of regression test cases available to you. Recently, the software under test was modified to make some performance improvements. Now your manager wants you to perform the full regression testing restricted to the performance area only, following a descending priority order for the corresponding tests.
    Which test case should be executed as the last one?

(A) TC4
(B) TC6
(C) TC3
(D) TC7

Question 8.
Which role is responsible for leading a review?

(A) Manager
(B) Facilitator
(C) Author
(D) Reviewer

Question 9.
What is the minimal number of columns for the collapsed version of the full decision table with eight columns presented in Table 8.2?

(A) 4
(B) 5
(C) 6
(D) 7

Table 8.1 A set of available test cases to execute

Test case id	Area	Priority	Dependent on
TC1	Functionality	High	TC7
TC2	Performance	High	TC3
TC3	Performance	High	TC5
TC4	Functionality	Low	
TC5	Security	High	TC1
TC6	Performance	Low	TC1, TC7
TC7	Functionality	Low	

Table 8.2 A full decision table

	1	2	3	4	5	6	7	8
Condition 1: Registered user?	F	F	F	F	T	T	T	T
Condition 2: Premium user?	F	F	T	T	F	F	T	T
Condition 3: Account active?	F	T	F	T	F	T	F	T
Action 1: Show error message "You are not registered."	T	T	T	T	F	F	F	F
Action 2: Allow user to log in to the system.	F	F	F	F	F	T	F	T
Action 3: Assign a discount.	F	F	F	F	F	F	F	T

Question 10.
Which of the following tool types can be used during the dynamic tests execution phase?

A) Test data preparation tool
B) Coverage measurement tool
C) Configuration management tool
D) Modeling tool

Question 11.
A tester performed a code analysis and noticed that the cyclomatic complexity of a certain component is very high. This information was passed to developers, and they refactored this code, making it more readable and more testable. This example shows a benefit from what?

(A) Dynamic testing
(B) Static technique
(C) Test management
(D) Using formal test technique

Question 12.
A system you are currently testing calculates a discount for the clients that do shopping through an e-commerce system. A discount is valid for one shopping session. There are three types of clients:

- New (he does shopping in our system for the first time)—receives 20% discount
- Typical (he is not a new client, but the total amount he spent in our shop does not exceed $5000)—receives 5% discount
- Regular (he is not a new client and the total amount he spent in our shop is at least $5000)—receives 10% discount

Each test case is a single shopping session. You have the following test cases prepared for execution:

TC1—a new client who will spend $1
TC2—a new client who will spend $5500
TC3—a typical client who has already spent $1000 and now will spend $3999
TC4—a typical client who has already spent $4500 and now will spend $1000
TC5—a regular client who has already spent $5000 and now will spend $1
TC6—a regular client who has already spent $9000 and now will spend $5000

Which set of test cases is the minimal set that covers the equivalence partitions for a discount type?

(A) TC1, TC2, TC3, TC4, TC5, TC6
(B) TC1, TC2, TC4
(C) TC1, TC3, TC4, TC5
(D) TC2, TC3, TC4

Question 13.
Which of the following is *not* an example of a test objective?

(A) Correcting the defect found
(B) Preventing from defect occurrence
(C) Gaining confidence about the system quality
(D) Providing to stakeholders an information about system quality

Question 14.
Choose the factor influencing the test effort and related to the product characteristics.

(A) Time pressure
(B) Requirements for usability
(C) Maturity of the organization
(D) Skills of the people involved

Question 15.
Unreachable code is an example of a defect that:

(A) Will always be detected in testing
(B) Will never be detected in testing
(C) May result in a failure
(D) Will never result in a failure

Question 16.
You are testing a book prolong process in a university library defined as the following procedure (executable statements are numbered):

```
1 INPUT UserType (possible values: Student, Professor)
2 INPUT ActualBorrowTime (possible values: positive integers)
3 IF (ActualBorrowTime > 60) THEN
4    Do not allow to prolong
  ELSE
5    IF (ActualBorrowTime > 30) THEN
6       IF (UserType == Professor) THEN
7          Allow to prolong
       ELSE
8          Do not allow to prolong
       END IF
    ELSE
9       Allow to prolong
    END IF
  END IF
```

You have two test cases:
(UserType = Professor, ActualBorrowTime = 20)
(UserType = Professor, ActualBorrowTime = 45)
What statement coverage is achieved by these two tests?

(A) 3/9
(B) 5/9
(C) 8/9
(D) 7/9

Question 17.

A methodical approach that uses a list of possible mistakes, defects, and failures, and designs tests that will expose those failures, called "fault attack," is:

(A) A form of exploratory testing
(B) A structured approach to the error guessing technique
(C) A form of checklist-based testing technique
(D) A structured approach to the walkthrough

Question 18.

Which of the following is the example of the trigger for the maintenance testing?

(A) Retirement of a system
(B) Testing the correctness of a data migration process
(C) A necessity of performing the risk analysis
(D) Implementing patches to newly discovered defects and vulnerabilities

Question 19.

Consider the following piece of code:

```
INPUT x, y
IF (x > 0) THEN
  y := y + 1
END IF
IF (y > 0) THEN
  x := x - 1
END IF
```

What is the minimal number of test cases for achieving decision coverage?

(A) 1
(B) 4
(C) 2
(D) 3

Question 20.

Which of the following is an example of a model that may be used by the white-box testing on the integration level?

(A) Call graph, which presents the relationships between subroutines in a program.
(B) Control flow graph, which models all possible control flows through a component or system.
(C) Tree-like menu structure, which presents all possible options that a user can choose from the application's main menu.
(D) White-box testing cannot be performed on the integration level, so there is no such a model.

Question 21.
In order to implement effective monitoring and control, it is critical to:

(A) Establish traceability between the test basis and the various test work products.
(B) Understand where we are at any time in the project.
(C) Provide the basis for relating testing work products to stakeholders in terms that they can understand.
(D) Evaluate the test coverage against requirements.

Question 22.
Which of the following review types is *not* an example of an informal review?

(A) Moderated code review
(B) A technical conversation in the office's kitchen during the break
(C) Pair review
(D) Perspective-based buddy check

Question 23.
During the risk analysis, the following product risk items were identified:

   Risk 1: Low testability of the component X because of its high cyclomatic complexity.

   Risk 2: Response time of the component Y may be too long.

   What are the most reasonable actions that you, as a tester, should implement during the testing phase regarding these two risks?

(A) Thorough acceptance testing of X, usability testing of Y.
(B) Component testing of Y, Integration testing of Y.
(C) No action for X, nonfunctional testing of Y.
(D) Inspection of X, performance testing of Y.

Question 24.
You perform a checklist-based review of a requirement specification. The checklist looks as follows:

Checklist for Requirements Specification Reviews

   R1: Do any requirements conflict with or duplicate other requirements?
   R2: Is each requirement uniquely and correctly identified?
   R3: Are all requirements actually requirements, not design or implementation solutions?

The requirement specification under review looks as follows:

Functional Requirement 1
ID: FR1
Title: Download mobile application
Description: A user should be able to download the mobile application through an application store. The application should be free to download.

Functional Requirement 2
ID: FR3
Title: User registration
Description: Given that a user has downloaded the mobile application, the user should be able to register through the mobile application. The user must provide username, password, and e-mail address. The user data should be kept in the MySQL relational database in a table "UserData" with columns "user_id," "username," "password," and "email," where user_id is the primary key.

Functional Requirement 3
ID: FR3
Title: User logging
Description: Given that a user is registered, the user should be able to log in to the application with his/her username and password.

Which statements from the checklist are violated and which are not?

(A) R3 is violated. R1 and R2 are not violated.
(B) R2 and R3 are violated. R1 is not violated.
(C) R1, R2, and R3 are violated.
(D) R1 and R2 are violated. R3 is not violated.

Question 25.
A system state is described by a pair of numbers (First, Second), where First and Second can be 0, 1, or 2. The initial state is (0, 0) and the final state is (2, 2). There are two possible events in this system: FirstUp and SecondUp. An event FirstUp moves us form a state (First, Second) to a state (First+1, Second) and SecondUp moves us from (First, Second) to (First, Second+1). If the number to be increased reached its maximal value, the corresponding event cannot occur.

What is the minimal number of test cases to achieve state coverage and transition (0-switch) coverage in this machine?

(A) 4 tests for state coverage; 4 tests for 0-switch coverage
(B) 3 tests for state coverage; 4 tests for 0-switch coverage
(C) 8 tests for state coverage; 12 tests for 0-switch coverage
(D) 4 tests for state coverage; 8 tests for 0-switch coverage

Question 26.
In white-box techniques the test conditions, test cases and test data are derived from the test basis that typically include:

(A) Specification
(B) Experience of a tester
(C) Software architecture
(D) Software requirements

Question 27.
You test a function isLeapYear, which takes a positive integer X as input and returns TRUE if X is a leap year or FALSE otherwise. The specification defines the leap year in the following manner: "A year is a leap year if it is divisible by 4 with exception of begin divisible by 100 and not divisible by 400." For example:

- 2003 is not a leap year, because it is not divisible by 4.
- 2004 is a leap year, because it is divisible by 4 and not divisible by 100.
- 2100 is not a leap year, because it is divisible by 4 and 100, but not by 400.
- 2400 is a leap year, because it is divisible by 4, 100, and 400.

You want to apply equivalence partitioning for the isLeapYear output to check if the isLeapYear function works correctly. Which set of test cases gives you the 50% coverage?

(A) 2003, 2004
(B) 2003
(C) 2003, 2100
(D) 2004, 2400

Question 28.
What is the difference between static and dynamic techniques, with respect to their objectives?

(A) Static techniques directly detect defects, while dynamic techniques directly detect failures.
(B) Static techniques are usually applied at the early SDLC phases, while dynamic techniques at the later phases.
(C) There is no difference, because they both try to detect defects as early as possible.
(D) Static techniques require programming skills, while dynamic techniques don't.

Question 29.
You executed a test script which has passed. During the later phases, it turned out, however, that the expected result was different, so the test should fail. This is an example of which of the tool-related risks?

(A) Over-reliance on the tool
(B) Unrealistic expectations for the tool
(C) Underestimating the effort required to maintain the test assets generated by the tool
(D) Poor response from vendor for support, upgrades, and defect fixes

Question 30.
Which of the following is an example of a reactive test strategy?

(A) Exploratory testing
(B) Risk identification
(C) Requirements-based testing
(D) Fault attacks

Question 31.
Which of the following skills is the least important one in testing?

(A) Programming skills
(B) Curiosity
(C) Attention to detail
(D) Communication skills

Question 32.
Which test estimation approach is the most recommended one and why?

(A) There is no single best approach. The applicability and effectiveness of the approach depends on many factors.
(B) Metrics-based approach is the best estimation approach, as it operates on data and facts, so it is always able to give us the accurate estimates.
(C) Expert-based approach is the best estimation approach, because it takes advantage on the experts' knowledge, experience, and intuition.
(D) It is not recommended to use any estimation approach, because estimates are never accurate and hence, wrong estimation may lead the team to wrong conclusions, putting the project at risk.

Question 33.
Connect the report types with their appropriate audience.
    Report types:

(a) Burndown chart
(b) Detailed information on defect types and trends in number of defects found and fixed
(c) Status summary of defects by priority

    Audience:

1) Development team
2) Test team
3) Project manager

(A) 1a, 2c, 3b
(B) 1a, 2b, 3c
(C) 1b, 2a, 3c
(D) 1c, 2b, 3a

Question 34.
You are analyzing the following use case to design the test cases.

Use case UC-02-001: printing a ticket
Use case steps:
1. User logs in to the system.
2. System verifies in the database the User's age. If age > 18, the use case continues in Step 4.
3. System informs the User that a reduced ticket has been admitted because of the User's age.
4. System prints the ticket.
5. User logs out.
Exceptions: there are no exceptions in this use case.

Which of the following answers describes best the conclusion you should draw from the analysis of this test case?

(A) It is incorrect, as it has no exceptions.
(B) It is incorrect, as it does not have one main scenario.
(C) It is correct and 1 test is needed to cover this use case.
(D) It is correct and 2 tests are needed to cover this use case.

Question 35.
You want to perform an impact analysis to estimate the effort needed to modify the test suite after some requirements have been changed. Choose the reason why this impact analysis may be difficult.

(A) There is no traceability from test cases back to requirements.
(B) We have no information about risks and their impact related to these requirements.
(C) Testers lack programming skills.
(D) There is no time for modifying test cases.

Question 36.
Black-box testing is mainly performed for two types of testing. Which ones?

(A) Functional and structural testing
(B) Functional and nonfunctional testing
(C) System and nonfunctional testing
(D) System and acceptance testing

Question 37.
You work as a tester in a project that follows V-model. You are currently in the requirement phase and, during the requirement review, you notice that two requirements contradict each other. You were asked to write a defect report about this finding. What would be the reason for doing that?

(A) There is no reason, as it makes no sense to write a defect report in the initial project phase.
(B) To provide architects feedback about the problem to enable its correction.
(C) To provide ideas for test process improvement.
(D) To provide developers feedback about the problem to enable its isolation.

Question 38.
After test execution, it turned out that one test is implemented incorrectly. This test returned to the implementation phase. During the re-implementation, it turned out that it is not only incorrectly implemented, but also incorrectly designed. It turned back to the design phase, where it was corrected, and then implemented and executed once again.

What can we say about this situation from the testing process point of view?

(A) This situation is impossible, because the wrong design should be detected in the implementation phase, not in the execution phase, as the implementation phase precedes the execution phase.
(B) This situation is impossible, because we cannot go back from execution phase to earlier phases, as the phases in the testing process follow the sequential order.
(C) This situation is possible, because prior to designing the test first time, we had to perform the analysis phase so that we were able to derive this test from the test basis.
(D) This situation is possible, because the process phases are not sequential and we can go back from one phase to another.

Question 39.
Pareto rule says that a small number of causes are responsible for the major part of the effects. This rule is a basis of which testing principle?

(A) Defect clustering
(B) Early testing
(C) Pesticide paradox
(D) Exhaustive testing is impossible

Question 40.
Which of the following configuration management activities is most important from a testing point of view?

(A) Ensuring that all test cases are version controlled and related to development items
(B) Ensuring that all testware are collected in a single repository
(C) Ensuring that the repository contains only the newest version of all items of testware
(D) Ensuring that all software configurations were tested

Chapter 9
Sample Exam: Question Set 4

Question 1.
The results of a test planning for a certain project may be documented in:

(A) Test strategy
(B) Test policy
(C) Integration level test plan
(D) Test report

Question 2.
In developing which type of products it is typical to apply separate software development life cycle models for each object and a strong emphasis is placed on the later phases of the software development life cycle after they have been introduced to operational use?

(A) Internet of Things systems
(B) Commercial off-the-shelf systems
(C) Systems of systems
(D) User interfaces

Question 3.
Suppose that the code under test contains only one decision shown below.

```
IF (CustomerAge > 18 AND TotalAmount > $100) THEN
   Assign a discount
```

Your tests achieved 100% decision coverage of this code. What is the consequence of this fact?

© Springer Nature Switzerland AG 2018
A. Roman, *A Study Guide to the ISTQB® Foundation Level 2018 Syllabus*,
https://doi.org/10.1007/978-3-319-98740-8_9

(A) We tested at least one situation in which CustomerAge is greater than 18 and at least one situation in which total amount did not exceed $100.
(B) We tested at least one situation in which customer's age is greater than 18 and at least one situation in which customer's age did not exceed 18.
(C) We tested at least one situation in which a customer was assigned a discount and at least one in which the discount was not assigned.
(D) We tested at least one situation in which customer's age did not exceed 18 and at least one situation in which total amount did not exceed $100.

Question 4.

You consider a variable Year, which can accept only positive integer values. From the specification you know that the complete set of the boundary values for this variable is as follows: 0, 1, 1976, 1977, 2019, 2020. Which of the following is the correct equivalence class for this variable?

(A) {2020, 2021, 2022, ...}
(B) {1, 1976, 1977, 2019, 2020}
(C) {0, 1, 1975, 1976, 1977, 1978, 2018, 2019, 2020, 2021}
(D) {1, 2, ..., 2018, 2019}

Question 5.

Your project follows a sequential SDLC, which defines only three sequential phases of testing, as shown in Fig. 9.1. Testing is done only in these three phases.

In each phase, each test will be executed only once. Which of the following is a set of all possible phases in which we can conduct regression testing?

(A) Test phase 2, Test phase 3
(B) Test phase 1, Test phase 2, Corrections, Test phase 3
(C) Test phase 1, Test phase 2, Test phase 3
(D) Test phase 1, Implementation of changes, Test phase 2, Corrections, Test phase 3

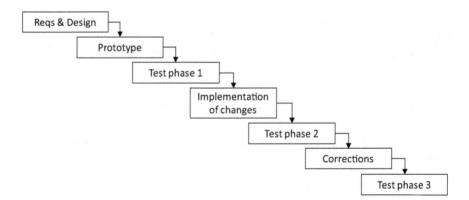

Fig. 9.1 A sequential SDLC model with 3 testing phases

Question 6.
You test the application that calculates the risk of a patient's brain hemorrhage (low or high) based on three conditions: age (young or old), does the patient take the medicines (yes or no), and did he have a stroke (yes or no). The rules are as follows:

- If the patient is young and takes the medicines, the risk is low.
- If the patient is old and did not have a stroke, the risk is low.
- Otherwise, the risk is high.

What is the minimal number of columns in the collapsed decision table for this problem?

(A) 2
(B) 3
(C) 4
(D) 6

Question 7.
You need to execute the following test cases in functional and performance areas:

TC1: functional test with high priority
TC2: performance test with high priority
TC3: functional test with low priority
TC4: functional test with high priority
TC5: performance test with low priority

The test strategy assumes that covering each area with at least one test as quickly as possible is the most important criterion. The less important criterion says that the tests should follow their priorities.
Which of the following is the most reasonable test execution ordering that follows this strategy?

(A) TC2, TC3, TC5, TC1, TC2
(B) TC1, TC4, TC3, TC2, TC5
(C) TC5, TC3, TC2, TC1, TC4
(D) TC1, TC2, TC4, TC3, TC5

Question 8.
Which of the following *best* describes the test basis?

(A) Information used as the basis for achieving specific test objective
(B) Information used as the basis for test monitoring and control
(C) Information used as the basis for the oracle when determining the expected result
(D) Information used as the basis for test analysis and design

Table 9.1 State transition table for a state machine

Next state		State					
		S1	S2	S3	S4	S5	S6
Event	E1	S2	S5	S4			
	E2	S3			S6		
	E3		S4			S4	

Question 9.

You test a state transition machine given by the state transition table shown in Table 9.1. The initial and final states are, respectively, S1 and S6.

What is the minimal number of test cases to achieve transition (0-switch) coverage?

(A) 1
(B) 2
(C) 3
(D) 4

Question 10.

Which of the following, according to the Foundation Level Syllabus, is an example of a tool used by a tester rather than a developer?

(A) A tool that calculates cyclomatic complexity and other code metrics
(B) A tool that calculates statement coverage achieved by the unit tests executed
(C) A tool that compares the content of two files
(D) A dynamic analysis tool

Question 11.

Typically, the person responsible for fixing the defect in the artifact under test is:

(A) Artifact's author
(B) Tester
(C) Debugger
(D) Client

Question 12.

The block diagram shown in Fig. 9.2 presents an algorithm for computing the mean value of the set of N numbers given by the user as an input.

What is the decision coverage for this program achieved by the following suite of two tests?

TC1: User enters N = 299.
TC2: User enters N = 0.

(A) 1/2
(B) 5/6
(C) 7/10
(D) 2/3

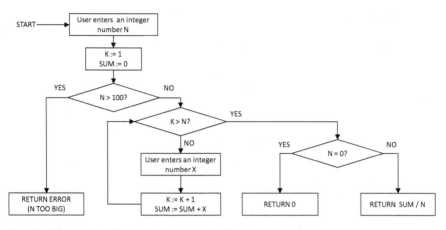

Fig. 9.2 Block diagram for the algorithm computing the mean value

Question 13.
Which of the following work products is the best candidate to perform a static analysis on it?

(A) Architectural design
(B) Test plan
(C) Requirement specification
(D) Source code

Question 14.
In what way do static and dynamic techniques complement each other?

(A) They are applied at different test levels.
(B) Static techniques don't use tools, while dynamic techniques use them.
(C) They are performed by different roles.
(D) They find different types of defects.

Question 15.
Consider the following two test reports:

TEST REPORT 1
Module: browseCatalog
test cases planned vs. implemented: 56/54
test cases executed (pass/fail/blocking/other): 54 (34/10/2/8)
Decision coverage (required): 56% (50%)
Condition coverage (required): 77% (70%)
Blocking test cases id: TC004-34, TC-004-50

TEST REPORT 2

Module	Test status	Requirements coverage (%)
logIn	PASS	100
browseCatalog	PASS	80
pay	FAIL	100
finalize	PASS	100

What is the best audience for these reports?

(A) Test report 1 is better for a client, and test report 2 is better for a test automation engineer.
(B) Test report 1 is better for the IT director, and test report 2 is better for a developer.
(C) Test report 1 is better for a client, and test report 2 is better for a tester.
(D) Test report 1 is better for a tester, and test report 2 is better for a client.

Question 16.
The quality of the specification, size of the product, and complexity of the product domain are the factors that affect:

(A) Skills of the team members
(B) Tools used by the testers
(C) Test effort
(D) Stability of the organization

Question 17.
Which of the following is a test type?

(A) Code review
(B) System testing
(C) Functional testing
(D) Boundary value analysis

Question 18.
Which of the following is *not* a trigger for maintenance testing?

(A) Migration of the software from one platform to another
(B) Retirement of the software, so that data-archiving process needs to be tested
(C) Acquisition of a new test automation framework
(D) A need to test the emergency fix

Question 19.
Select the sentence that correctly explains the issue of using test techniques during the exploratory testing session.

(A) All test techniques are allowed, because exploratory testing does not impose on tester any particular way of acting.
(B) All test techniques are forbidden, because exploratory testing is based on knowledge, intuition, and experience.
(C) All test techniques are forbidden, because exploratory testing is not a scripted testing and test actions cannot be planned in advance.
(D) All test techniques are allowed, because exploratory tester needs to have a test basis from which he derives test ideas.

Question 20.
Which of the following is an example of an error?

(A) One of the source code instruction is 'x := x + 1', but it should be 'x := y + 1'.
(B) A tester makes a mistake and introduces a defect into the test script.
(C) A software crashes because of overheating of the processor
(D) An ATM machine should dispense $10, but it dispended $20.

Question 21.
Which of the following is a part of the "initiate review" activity?

(A) Selecting the people to participate in the review and allocating roles
(B) Gathering metrics
(C) Answering any questions that participants may have about the review
(D) Defining the purpose of the review, what document to review, and the quality characteristics to be evaluated

Question 22.
A test team has decided about which test tool should be selected. The tool was bought. What should be the next step?

(A) The test team should conduct a pilot project in some part of the organization.
(B) The test manager should introduce the tool in the whole organization.
(C) The test team should evaluate the tool vendor in terms of the training, support, and commercial aspects.
(D) The test manager should evaluate the tool against clear requirements and objective criteria.

Question 23.
Which of the following is an example of a benefit from independent testing?

(A) Isolation from the development team.
(B) Unbiasness of the testers.
(C) Independent testers can work from a different location.
(D) It is cheaper than testing in a situation, where there are no independent testers.

Question 24.
Test conditions are exercised by which of the following test artifacts?

(A) Risk items
(B) Test cases
(C) Requirements
(D) Test data

Question 25.
You design a set of test cases to cover a use case having 11 steps in which 3 different exceptions can occur: E1, E2, and E3. Exception E1 occurs in steps 4, 8, and 9, and E2 in steps 3 and 4. Exception E3 occurs in all steps with the occurrence of at least one other exception, and in no other steps.

How many test cases should be designed to achieve the coverage of this use case, according to the use case coverage defined in the Foundation Level Syllabus?

(A) 12
(B) 9
(C) 10
(D) 11

Question 26.
In the last few days, all the test team members were trying to figure out why a strange failure occurs in the software. Unfortunately, no one has any idea about that. It was decided that the test team will "simulate the compiler," which will take form of some dry runs of a software, in order to understand what exactly happens in the code.

Which review type would be the most appropriate for this activity?

(A) Inspection
(B) Informal review
(C) Technical inspection
(D) Walkthrough

Question 27.
Assign examples of defects/failures to the phases, in which these defects/failures are most likely to be discovered.

1—Unreachable code
2—Data sent from one component as parameters of some API call are understood by the receiving component in wrong order
3—Application does not round the result when multiplying two values

(A) 1—system testing. 2—component testing. 3—acceptance testing
(B) 1—component testing. 2—system testing. 3—acceptance testing
(C) 1—system testing. 2—acceptance testing. 3—integration testing
(D) 1—component testing. 2—integration testing. 3—system testing

Question 28.
Which standard describes the testing process as a multilayer model?

(A) IEEE 829
(B) ISO/IEC/IEEE 29119
(C) ISO/IEC/IEEE 25000
(D) ISO 9126

Question 29.
In a checklist-based approach, a checklist used by a tester may include:

(A) An excerpt from the test plan describing test levels and test types defined in the project
(B) A list of typical functional defects that were found in the previous versions of a software
(C) A list of tools that should be bought prior to introducing the automation project
(D) Nielsen heuristics that describe the desired usability characteristics of a software

Question 30.
Which of the following items can be identified when using a test technique?

  i) Test conditions
 ii) Test cases
iii) Test data

(A) i), ii), and iii)
(B) Only i) and ii)
(C) Only i)
(D) Only ii) and iii)

Question 31.
You are responsible for functional testing of the new mobile application for tourists. The application allows a user to plan a route, modify it, read info about the monuments, etc. All these functional requirements are documented in a form of the use cases. Together with your team, you are planning to perform a review of the application regarding its functionality. Which review type will probably be the most beneficial in this case?

(A) Scenarios and dry runs
(B) Checklist based
(C) Perspective based
(D) Role based

Question 32.

Choose the best example of a failure that results from the following root cause: "'a low quality of a functional requirement specification."

(A) Functional requirement specification cannot be a subject to a review process.
(B) A bank system incorrectly calculates interest rate.
(C) System response time is too long when more than 100 users are logged to the system at the same time.
(D) The requirement id number does not follow the numbering rules accepted and used in the organization.

Question 33.

Let D, C, T denote respectively:

- Number of defects found in the software
- Size of the software (in Lines of Code)
- Time used for testing

Which metric measures the defect density?

(A) $\frac{C}{D}$

(B) $\frac{D}{T}$

(C) $\frac{D}{C}$

(D) $\frac{D}{C \cdot T}$

Question 34.

You test a function isLeapYear which takes a positive integer X as input and returns TRUE if X is a leap year or FALSE otherwise. The specification defines the leap year in the following manner: "A year is a leap year if it is divisable by 4 with exception of begin divisible by 100 and not divisible by 400." For example:

- 2003 is not a leap year, because it is not divisible by 4.
- 2004 is a leap year, because it is divisible by 4 and not divisible by 100.
- 2100 is not a leap year, because it is divisible by 4 and 100, but not by 400.
- 2400 is a leap year, because it is divisible by 4, 100 and 400.

You test the domain of the isLeapYear function (the set of all positive integers) and you want to apply a 2-point boundary value analysis to verify if it calculates the leap year correctly. What is the minimal number of test cases to achieve 100% BVA coverage?

(A) 2.
(B) 4.
(C) It is impossible to achieve 100% coverage.
(D) 5.

Question 35.
Select the correct statement about the objectives of testing.

(A) Testing objectives may vary depending upon the context of the system under test.
(B) One of the testing objectives is to correct defects raised during the development process.
(C) During the acceptance testing, the main objective is to cause as many failures as possible.
(D) During the acceptance testing, the main objective is to gain confidence in the system.

Question 36.
You follow the 2-point boundary value analysis for testing the following requirement:

A system receives an input value X from the set {1, 2, ..., 100} of integers. It is not possible to force as an input the values outside this range. If X is greater than 90, the system returns a message "student passed with distinctions." Else, if X is greater than 50, the system returns a message "student passed." In any other case, the system returns "student failed."

You define the equivalence classes for X regarding the system's output. You have already prepared the test suite that covers 2-point boundary value analysis. However, your manager was told that your team has some additional time and he decides that instead of 2-point, you will follow the 3-point boundary value analysis for this problem.
How many additional test cases you have to design?

(A) 3
(B) 4
(C) 6
(D) 8

Question 37.
Building a state machine of the System Under Test and deriving from it the tests that cover all 1-switches is an example of which test strategy?

(A) Analytical
(B) Methodical
(C) Process compliant
(D) Model based

Question 38.
Your organization uses the following structure of the defect reports for the projects following an iterative life cycle model:

- Defect report id, tester's name
- Version of the environment and product used
- Bug description
- Bug type (selected from a drop-down list)
- Iteration in which the defect was discovered
- Severity
- Steps to reproduce

The defect reports are stored in a central repository, which can be used to produce different reports, statistics, and so on. In what way such a repository can help test manager to track the quality of the system?

(A) By creating an aggregated report of the number of defects broken by bug types
(B) By performing a detailed analysis of bug descriptions and steps to reproduce the bugs
(C) By analyzing the number of defects (together with their severity) found in the consecutive iterations
(D) By arranging the bugs in the severity order, filtering out the ones with the low severity, and calculating the number of the high severity bugs raised by each tester

Question 39.
Which of the following is the best example of a quality assurance activity not related to the quality control?

(A) Defining requirement engineering process in a way that ensures the requirements are defined at the proper level of detail
(B) Measuring the product to give information about its quality, so that managers can undertake conscious decisions about the product and project
(C) Conducting the inspection for an architectural design to detect as many architectural defects as possible
(D) Raising a defect report through the defect management system

Question 40.
Which of the following is an example of a quality risk?

(A) The project will be delayed due to short staffing.
(B) The system will work slowly due to an ineffective implementation.
(C) The software will return a wrong result due to inaccuracies in computations.
(D) The application will not provide the full functionality to a user due to lack of time.

Chapter 10
Sample Exam: Question Set 5

Question 1.
What is represented in the following picture? (Fig. 10.1)

(A) Traceability
(B) Test suite
(C) Impact analysis
(D) Test basis

Question 2.
Which of the following is an example of why static techniques are beneficial?

(A) During the requirements review the team realized that one requirement was missing from the document.
(B) A developer writes better code when following Test-Driven Development and executing automated component tests.
(C) A tester helped his manager to estimate the test effort for the forthcoming test level.
(D) Automating manual tests and executing them many times saved a lot of time in the project.

Question 3.
A tester analyzes the user stories as a test basis. From them, he derives the test cases using state machine testing, executes them and measures the transition (0-switch) coverage achieved by his tests. This is an example of using which test technique?

(A) Specification-based technique
(B) Structure-based technique
(C) Experience-based technique
(D) Risk analysis

© Springer Nature Switzerland AG 2018
A. Roman, *A Study Guide to the ISTQB® Foundation Level 2018 Syllabus*,
https://doi.org/10.1007/978-3-319-98740-8_10

Fig. 10.1 A certain
structure

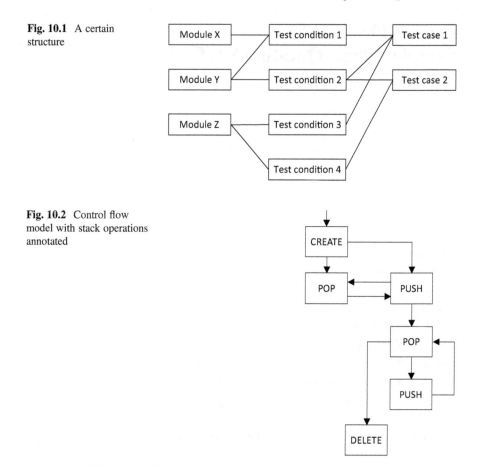

Fig. 10.2 Control flow
model with stack operations
annotated

Question 4.
Entry criteria:

(A) Prevent us from proceeding with the next phase of our test activities when we
are not prepared for performing them well
(B) Define what must be achieved in order to complete a test level
(C) Can be defined only before entering a new test level
(D) Are defined by clients

Question 5.
Figure 10.2 presents the control flow graph with operations on a data structure called
stack. These operations are:

- create—creates an empty stack
- push—insert an element on the top of stack
- pop—return the top element and remove it from the stack
- delete—remove the stack

You perform a checklist-based review of this model against the following checklist:

1. Check that every PUSH and POP operation is done after the stack has been CREATED.
2. Check that it is impossible to POP an element from an empty stack.
3. Check that a stack can be DELETED only if it is empty.
4. Check that the number of elements on the stack will never exceed 10.

Which points from the above checklist are related to the possible problems with the model?

(A) 2 may not be fulfilled. 1, 3, and 4 are always fulfilled.
(B) 2 and 4 may not be fulfilled. 1 and 3 are always fulfilled.
(C) 1, 3 and 4 may not be fulfilled. 2 is always fulfilled.
(D) 3 may not be fulfilled. 1, 2, and 4 are always fulfilled.

Question 6.
You are involved as a tester in the project X, Your manager decided to move you for one week to another project Y in order to support testing in that project, because the project Y is short on testing stuff. The manager also decided that system tests in project X will be done by one of the developers. What can you say about this decision from the Foundation Level Syllabus point of view?

(A) It is not forbidden, because different people may take over the role of tester.
(B) It is a bad decision, because developer cannot take over the responsibilities of another role.
(C) It is a bad decision, because the better idea would be to give the responsibility of system testing in project X to some other tester moved to project X from project Y.
(D) It is not forbidden, because it is manager who is responsible for the project, and thus, he can make any decision he want.

Question 7.
Figure 10.3 presents a state machine for a system under test. The transitions are labeled by strings of the form: Event [Condition]/Action, where [Condition] as well as Action can be omitted. A label Event [Condition]/Action means that the corresponding transition can be executed only if Event occurred AND the Condition is true.

The initial state is S1 and the initial value of the variable x is 0. Choose the correct sequence of events which, if applied to this machine, forms a test case that achieves transition (0-switch) coverage.

(A) Inc, Inc, Inc, Dec, Inc, Fire, Inc, Inc, Fire
(B) Inc, Dec, Inc, Inc, Fire, Inc, Fire
(C) Inc, Inc, Inc, Fire, Inc, Fire
(D) Inc, Inc, Dec, Inc, Inc, Fire, Inc, Fire

Fig. 10.3 State transition
system with events, actions
and conditions

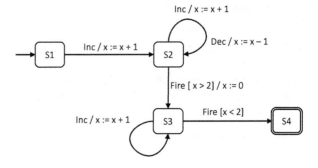

Question 8.
Which of the following sequences orders the criteria for the test execution ordering
from the most important to the least important?

(A) Logical dependencies, priority, test execution time
(B) Priority, logical dependences, test execution time
(C) Test case execution time, priority, logical dependencies
(D) Priority, test case execution time, logical dependencies

Question 9.
Which of the following is a measurable criterion used to validate the test basis?

(A) Test case
(B) Test step
(C) Test condition
(D) Test suite

Question 10.
You want to integrate a recently purchased commercial off-the-shelf system into
your existing system. What would be the most reasonable test activity to perform at
this moment?

(A) System and acceptance testing of the commercial off-the-shelf system
(B) Integration testing at the system and acceptance levels
(C) System and acceptance testing of your existing system
(D) Integration testing of the commercial-off-the-shelf system

Question 11.
Which testing activity is impossible to be supported with the tools?

(A) Usability testing, as usability cannot be measured in a mechanical,
     automatic way.
(B) Test design, because designing is an intellectual activity, impossible to perform
     by a tool.
(C) Test reporting, because reports need to be interpreted by humans, not tools.
(D) All test activities can be supported with the tools.

Question 12.
Which of the following is an example of a nonfunctional test?

(A) Cover a certain combination of conditions and observe what actions are executed to verify the correctness of a certain business rule.
(B) Cover a "true" outcome of a decision "if $(x > 5)$ then ..." in the code.
(C) Check if the system correctly validates the syntax of an e-mail entered by a user in a user registration form.
(D) Check if the system response time is less than 5 ms when there are more than 1000 users logged in.

Question 13.
You are testing the SmartBikeShop system that verifies the correctness of the orders placed by the consumers via the web-based software. Every order needs to follow two restrictions:

• The maximal number of items in the basket is 4.
• The total weight of all the ordered items cannot exceed 10 kg.

The total weight is measured with the precision of 0.1 kg. The list of available items is presented in Table 10.1.

You want to test the correctness of the weight criterion using the 2-point boundary value analysis. Select the minimal set of test cases to achieve this coverage.

(A) TC1: wheel, frame, saddle area, brakes
    TC2: wheel, frame, saddle area, pedals
(B) TC1: wheel, frame, saddle area, brakes
    TC2: wheel, frame, saddle area, pedals
    TC3: five front sets
(C) TC1: wheel, frame
    TC2: saddle area, front set
    TC3: brakes, pedals
(D) TC1: wheel, frame, saddle area, brakes
    TC2: wheel, frame, saddle area, pedals
    TC3: frame, two saddle areas, two brakes

Table 10.1 List of available products, their weights, and prices

Id	Product name	Weight (kg)	Price
1	Wheel	1.5	$50
2	Frame	6.8	$650
3	Front set	1.0	$95
4	Saddle area	1.3	$135
5	Brakes	0.3	$30
6	Pedals	0.4	$45

Question 14.
If it is difficult to predict what the final product should look like, and hence, it is necessary to provide flexibility to make changes up to a certain point in the development life cycle, which SDLC model is it best to choose in such situation?

(A) Sequential
(B) Incremental
(C) Any SDLC model will be equally good
(D) Iterative

Question 15.
Comparing with static testing, which of the following problems can be easier to found through dynamic testing?

(A) Performance requirement saying that "the system should work efficiently" is ambiguous.
(B) High coupling and cyclomatic complexity of a component will cause maintainability problems.
(C) The system allows to obtain the admin rights by an unauthorized user.
(D) Developers do not follow the variables naming standard while writing code.

Question 16.
During the review, which of the following is the typical responsibility of a person being in a role of an author?

(A) Mediating between the various points of view
(B) Identifying potential defects in the work product under review
(C) Collecting potential defects found during the individual review activity
(D) Fixing defects in the work product under review

Question 17.
Figure 10.4 presents the control flow of some source code with 8 statements (denoted by numbered nodes).
    What is the statement coverage achieved by a test that goes through the nodes 1, 3, 4, 3, 5, 6, 8?

(A) 87.5%
(B) 75%
(C) 60%
(D) 100%

Question 18.
Which of the following does *not* justify using the exploratory testing?

(A) We need to test a new functionality, but we have only 1 day for this.
(B) Our test team consists of inexperienced testers who do not know the product well.
(C) The software specification is outdated and inadequate.
(D) We want to augment other, more formal testing techniques used earlier.

Fig. 10.4 Control flow of a
source code

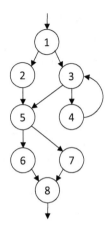

Question 19.
Which test technique is used to anticipate the occurrence of failures, based on the tester's knowledge, including how the application worked in past and what kind of failures have occurred in other, similar applications?

(A) Exploratory testing
(B) Checklist-based testing
(C) Use case testing
(D) Error guessing

Question 20.
Inspection will be better performed if:

(A) Its main goal will be defined as "evaluate alternatives."
(B) Manager will attend the review meeting.
(C) People attending the review meeting will be trained in review techniques.
(D) Metrics will not be collected during the inspection process.

Question 21.
A tester raised a bug in the program that calculates the mean value of a set of variables: when the input set of variables is empty, the software crashes. Developer found that this is caused by the division by 0 in the instruction:

```
meanValue := SumOfVariables / NumberOfVariables
```

He changed this instruction into the following code:

```
IF (NumberOfVariables> 0) THEN
   meanValue := SumOfVariables / NumberOfVariables
ELSE
   meanValue := 0
```

The developer's activity in this scenario is:

(A) Inspection
(B) Debugging
(C) Testing
(D) Code review

Question 22.
In computability theory, the halting problem is the problem of determining, whether the program will finish or continue to run forever for a given input. In 1936 Alan Turing proved that a general algorithm to solve the halting problem for all possible program-input pairs cannot exist. This is a formal proof of which of the Seven Testing Principles?

(A) Absence-of-errors fallacy.
(B) Exhaustive testing is impossible.
(C) Testing shows presence of defects.
(D) Pesticide paradox.

Question 23.
Which of the following is *not* recommended when introducing the tool into the organization?

(A) Adapt the test process to fit with the use of the tool.
(B) After tool acquisition immediately roll it out to all departments in the organization.
(C) Provide support for the test team for a given tool.
(D) Define usage guidelines.

Question 24.
If software specification is out of date and test cases are not documented, which type of test activity can be difficult to perform?

(A) Requirement analysis
(B) Exploratory testing
(C) Impact analysis
(D) Review of the specification

Question 25.
A weight sensor detects the lift overload when the total weight of the persons in the lift exceeds 280 kg. You want to verify if the sensor implements correctly this requirement. Each test simulates a certain load (given in kg). Which of the following is the minimal set of test cases that achieves 100% BVA coverage in the 2-point BVA version?

(A) 0, 1, 280, 281
(B) −1, 0, 1, 279, 280, 281
(C) 279, 280, 281
(D) 280, 281

Question 26.
You will be testing a software that calculates points for football teams. You receive the following requirement that describes the way the points should be calculated:

> If a team wins the match, it receives 3 points. If there is a draw, it receives 1 point. If it losses, it gets no points. In case of championships, the draw results in penalty kicks. If there are penalty kicks, only two options are possible: if a team wins them, it receives two points. If it losses, it gets 1 point.

You want to apply decision table technique to test the software. You identify three conditions: match result (win, draw, loss), is the match played on the championships (yes, no), and penalty kicks result (win, loss). The result will be the number of points assigned to a team. What kind of problem will you observe when trying to evaluate the action results based on the requirement analysis?

(A) There will be no problem, because for each combination of conditions there is a well defined action.
(B) There will be a problem with contradictory requirements, because in case of a draw the action will differ, depending on whether it was the championships match or not.
(C) There will be a problem with missing requirement, because there exists some combination of conditions with undefined action.
(D) There will be a problem, because the action is not a logical value, but a number.

Question 27.
Project risks do *not* arise from:

(A) Organizational factors
(B) Technical issues
(C) Product characteristics
(D) Political issues

Question 28.
Your tests achieved 50% decision coverage. What is a consequence of this fact?

(A) Each decision was evaluated with at least one outcome.
(B) You achieved at most 50% statement coverage.
(C) At least one decision had to be evaluated to FALSE.
(D) At least one executable statement was executed.

Question 29.
When manual tests are run repeatedly and we care about the consistence of their execution, which test technique would be the most helpful?

(A) Checklist-based testing
(B) Exploratory testing
(C) Regression testing
(D) User acceptance testing

Question 30.

The likelihood of some risk was defined as "high." What can we say about its impact?

(A) We know nothing about the impact, as it is independent of the risk likelihood.
(B) The impact will also be high, because the risk will occur frequently.
(C) The impact will be low, because it is inversely proportional to the likelihood.
(D) We know nothing about the impact, because it cannot be assessed before the risk occurs.

Question 31.

Every fifth shopping an order processing system assigns a discount for a customer. You want to use the equivalence partitioning technique to check if this rule holds. Which of the following is a minimal set of values representing the number of the shopping that covers all valid equivalence classes for this problem?

(A) 0, 1, 5
(B) 55, 89
(C) 1, 5, 6
(D) 5, 10, 15, 20, 25, 30, 35, . . .

Question 32.

Which of the following is the example of the highest degree of independence in testing?

(A) Operational Acceptance Testing
(B) Unit testing performed by a developer
(C) Unit testing performed by a tester from the team
(D) System testing performed by a tester from the team

Question 33.

Consider the following sequence of events in the project, in which you work as a tester:

1. Execution of Test Case 001 for component X—test failed
2. Execution of Test Case 002 for component X—test passed
3. Execution of Test Case 003 for component Y—test passed
4. Fix done in component X
5. Execution of Test Case 001 for component X—test passed
6. Execution of Test Case 003 for component Y—test passed
7. Execution of Test Case 004 for component Y—test failed

No other test cases were executed apart from the ones mentioned in the list above. In which steps the confirmation tests and in which regression tests were performed?

(A) Confirmation test only in step 6, regression test only in step 5
(B) Confirmation test only in step 5, regression test only in step 6
(C) No confirmation tests, regression tests only in steps 5, 6 and 7
(D) Confirmation tests only in steps 5, 6, and 7, no regression tests

Question 34.
Consider the following excerpt of a document:

The following metrics should be collected:

- Number of defects found, split by defect type and detection phase
- Time to repair (for each raised bug)
- Number of test cases planned, designed, implemented, executed, automated
- Test results for each test run (passed, failed, blocked, not executed)

This is an example of a part of which document?

(A) Test policy
(B) Test design
(C) Test procedure
(D) Test plan

Question 35.
Choose the correct sentence about the developer's and the tester's mindsets.

(A) They are different, because a tester's primary goal is to raise bugs, and a developer's primary task is to debug and fix them.
(B) They are different, because a developer's primary goal is to design and build a product and a tester's primary task is to verify its quality.
(C) They are the same, because the primary goal for both of them is to care about the highest possible product quality.
(D) They are the same, because tester and developer are just the project roles and any person can fulfill both these roles.

Question 36.
Which of the following activities is related to quality control?

(A) Redefining the testing process in the organization
(B) Performing the code review
(C) Organizing a training for developers about good programming practices
(D) Improving the testing process in the organization

Question 37.
Testing is a constructive activity, but it may be perceived as a destructive one. What is the reason of this phenomenon?

(A) Testing is an expensive process and may be perceived as the one that does not bring any added value.
(B) Identifying failures during testing may be perceived as a criticism against the product or developers.
(C) Independent testers may be perceived as a "bottleneck" in the testing process.
(D) Testers who do not have programming skills may be perceived as the useless team members.

Question 38.
Figure 10.5 presents an example of a defect report created by a tester. The report was sent through a defect management application. This report is going to be sent to a developer, who is supposed to debug the application. The debug process should be prioritized, so that the most important bugs can be fixed first.

From the developer's point of view, what important information is missing from this report?

(A) Status of the defect
(B) Expected and actual results
(C) Tester's name
(D) Severity of the impact on the system

Question 39.
In which phase of the test process are entry and exit criteria defined?

(A) Test planning, monitoring, and control
(B) Test analysis
(C) Test design
(D) Test implementation

Question 40.
Figure 10.6 presents two data tables of the configuration management database. The left table presents consecutive versions of test cases, together with the information about traceability of these test cases to requirements. Right table shows which versions of the test cases were used for testing a system build in a given version.
    Suppose the client has raised a problem: the system crashed unexpectedly. You checked in the client database that the client uses the built-in version 1.1.002. The defect analysis shows that the defect is related to REQ 2 and may be caused because of a specific operation system the user has installed.

Title: [IE 11] *Unable to type in search box of www.example-url.com*
Description: *I navigated to www.example-url.com, and clicked on the search box at the top right corner. I noticed that the cursor didn't change, the caret wasn't visible, and you can't click and type in the search box.*
Area: *Broken Site*
Expected behavior: To be able to type in the search box, and complete the search
Steps to reproduce the problem (include URL if applicable):
     1. Launch IE 11
     2. Navigate to http://www.example-url.com
     3. Move cursor to top right corner of the webpage
     4. Click in the search box
     5. Caret is not visible. Can't type in the search box
     6. Refer to search-OK.jpg and search-BROKEN.jpg
Screenshots and attachments: *search-OK.jpg, search-BROKEN.jpg*

Fig. 10.5 An example of a bug report (based on the example from: connect.microsoft.com)

Test case	Version	Traceability to requirements
TC 001	001.1.0	REQ 1, REQ 2
TC 001	001.2.0	REQ 1, REQ 2, REQ 5
TC 001	001.2.1	REQ 1, REQ 2, REQ 5
TC 002	002.1.0	REQ 1, REQ 3, REQ 4
TC 002	002.1.1	REQ 1, REQ 3, REQ 4

Build	TC 001	TC 002
1.0.000	001.1.0	002.1.0
1.1.001	001.1.0	002.1.1
1.1.002	001.2.0	002.1.1
1.2.000	001.2.0	002.1.1
2.0.000	001.2.0	002.1.1

Fig. 10.6 Configuration management database

The developers want to fix the defect and create the newly built 1.1.003. Which test cases should they use to reproduce the failure?

(A) TC001 in version 001.2.0 and TC002 in version 002.1.1.
(B) TC001 in version 001.2.0.
(C) TC001 in version 001.2.1.
(D) TC001 in version 001.2.0 and TC002 in version 002.1.0.

Part IV
Solutions and Answers

Chapter 11
Solutions to Exercises on Test Techniques

Exercise 1: Partitions

(a) The possible partitionings of the domain $\{1, 2, 3, 4\}$ are as follows:

1. $\{1, 2, 3, 4\}$[1]	2. $\{1, 2, 3\}, \{4\}$	3. $\{1, 2, 4\}, \{3\}$	4. $\{1, 3, 4\}, \{2\}$
5. $\{2, 3, 4\}, \{1\}$	6. $\{1, 2\}, \{3, 4\}$	7. $\{1, 3\}, \{2, 4\}$	8. $\{1, 4\}, \{2, 3\}$
9. $\{1, 2\}, \{3\}, \{4\}$	10. $\{1, 3\}, \{2\}, \{4\}$	11. $\{1, 4\}, \{2\}, \{3\}$	12. $\{2, 3\}, \{1\}, \{4\}$
13. $\{2, 4\}, \{1\}, \{3\}$	14. $\{3, 4\}, \{1\}, \{2\}$	15. $\{1\}, \{2\}, \{3\}, \{4\}$	

An example of incorrect partitioning would be, for example, $\{1, 2, 3\}, \{2, 4\}$ or $\{1\}, \{2, 4\}$. In the first case, one element (2) belongs to more than one class. In the second example, one element (3) is missing and does not belong to any partition.

(b) The most reasonable partitioning is $\{1, 3\}$ and $\{2, 4\}$, because we expect that the system behavior should be similar for odd numbers and similar for even numbers.

Exercise 2: Identifying Variables and Their Domains

(a) We can identify at least four variables:

Input variable a with the domain $\{1, 2, 3, \ldots\}$
Input variable b with the domain $\{1, 2, 3, \ldots\}$

(continued)

---

[1]This equivalence partitioning contains only one equivalence class. It is a degenerated example but, still, it is a valid one, as this partitioning fulflls the definition of the correct partitioning. A similar degenerated example is the last one, where each element forms a separate equivalence class.

© Springer Nature Switzerland AG 2018
A. Roman, *A Study Guide to the ISTQB® Foundation Level 2018 Syllabus*,
https://doi.org/10.1007/978-3-319-98740-8_11

Input variable *c* with the domain {1 2, 3, ...}
Output variable *triangleType* with the domain {equilateral, isosceles but not equilateral, scalene, not a triangle}

(b) The most natural partitioning of the *triangleType* variable is {equilateral}, {isosceles but not equilateral}, {scalene}, {not a triangle}, because it reflects the different behavior of the system (i.e., different output). There are no "obvious" partitionings for variables *a*, *b*, and *c*. We could assume, for example, that for each of them, there is one valid class {1, 2, 3, ...} and one invalid class, containing all integers less than 1: {..., −2, −1, 0}. If the interface allows to enter *any* value, we could also define an incorrect classes for non-integers, for non-numerical characters, *etc.*

(c) We cannot create the "isosceles" class, because, in particular, all equilateral triangles are at the same time isosceles triangles. This would result in a class that is a subset of another class, which is an incorrect partitioning. Remember that every domain element (in our case, every triangle) must belong to exactly one class.

Exercise 3: Identifying Partitions from the Specification
The domain of interest is the domain of the variable "user status," as the system behavior depends on it. The domain has three elements: {child, student, adult}, and each value forms a separate equivalence class. So, the partition looks like this:

{child}, {student}, {adult}

Hence, we should provide three test cases: one for status = child, one for status = student, and one for status = adult.

Exercise 4: One Partition with Many Classes
The variable of our interest is CarAge. It is an integer value, so it accepts values from the set {..., −2, −1, 0, 1, 2, ...}. We may assume that the correct age is 0 or more, so all negative integers will fall into one invalid equivalence class.

The rule "IF CarAge < 6" gives us another class: {0, 1, 2, 3, 4, 5}.

If it is not true, but the next rule "IF CarAge ≤ 12" is true, it means that the variable falls into the partition {6, 7, 8, 9, 10, 11, 12}.

If it is not true, then the car's age must fall into the partition {13, 14, 15, ...}.

Hence, we have 4 partitions. Table 11.1 summarizes the partitions, their meaning, the exemplary representant as a test input, and the expected system's behavior.

Table 11.1 Equivalence classes and sample test cases for Exercise 4

#	Partition	Meaning	Sample test input	Expected output
1	{..., −3, −2, −1}	Invalid equivalence class	−5	Error
2	{0, 1, 2, 3, 4, 5}	Valid class for new cars	4	New
3	{6, 7, 8, 9, 10, 11, 12}	Valid class for used cars	8	Used
4	{13, 14, 15, ...}	Valid class for old cars	13	Old

Exercise 5: Many Equivalence Partitionings

We have two input variables: height and weight. From the specification we know that the only valid class for height is {1.00, 1.01, 1.02, . . ., 2.48, 2.49, 2.50}. We also know that the only valid equivalence class for weight is {20, 21, . . ., 299, 300}. As low values are treated differently than high ones (there is a different warning message), we should represent them for each variable as two separate classes:

- Invalid "too low" class for height: {. . ., 0.98, 0.99} (all values less than 1.00 m)
- Invalid "too high" class for height: {2.51, 2.52, . . .} (all values greater than 2.5 m)
- Invalid "too low" class for weight: {. . ., 18, 19} (all values less than 20 kg)
- Invalid "too high" class for weight: {301, 302, . . .} (all values greater than 300 kg)

A test is a pair of height and weight values. We follow a strategy in which first we want to cover as many valid partitions as possible, and then we design a separate test for each invalid class. In the first test, we can cover both valid classes for height and weight domain. For example, this may be the test (1.75 m, 85 kg). Next, we need to provide four tests to cover four invalid classes described above. For example:

- (0.45 m, 55 kg) covers invalid "too low" class for height.
- (3.80 m, 90 kg) covers invalid "too high" class for height.
- (1.91 m, 6 kg) covers invalid "too low" class for weight.
- (1.34 m, 993 kg) covers invalid "too high" class for weight.

Notice that in all such tests only one input variable is invalid, and all the remaining must be valid. This strategy protects us against so-called defect masking, where two invalid inputs might mask each other.

We had to design five test cases to cover all the equivalence partitions according to the above mentioned strategy.

Exercise 6: Hidden Variables

The function *CalcSquareArea()* takes a number x as input. But noice that its output is not *directly* related to x, but to a *function* of x. In our case, it is x^2, the area of the quare. To force "square too small" output, the area needs to be less than 100, so $x^2 < 100$. This means that square will be too small for *input* values $x < 10$. We know that the input is a nonnegative integer, so we have the additional constraint $x \geq 0$. Analogously, the square will be OK if $100 \leq x^2 \leq 400$, which is equivalent to $10 \leq x \leq 20$. Finally, the square will be too big if $x^2 > 400$, which is equivalent to $x > 20$.

Hence, we have three equivalence classes and corresponding classes of input variable x, as shown in Table 11.2

Table 11.2 Test cases covering equivalence classes for CalcSquareArea (Exercise 6)

#	Equivalence class	Corresponding input values	Sample representant for a test input
1	Square too small	From 0 to 10 excl.	5.67
2	Square OK	From 10 to 20 incl.	11
3	Square too big	Over 20	56.3

Minimal valid number of tiles = 9

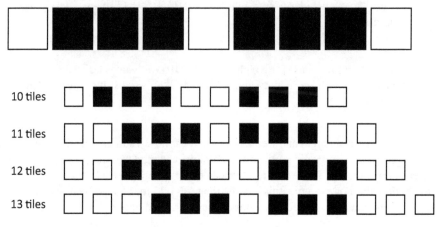

Fig. 11.1 The shortest valid sequence and the examples of some longer ones (Exercise 7)

Exercise 7: Identifying Boundary Values

The shortest sequence for which the requirements are fulfilled is presented in Fig. 11.1 (top part). It must consist of 9 tiles: two black fragments (6 tiles) separated by the shortest possible white fragment (1 tile), starting and ending with the shortest white sequences (1 tile each). Altogether this gives us $1 + 3 + 1 + 3 + 1 = 9$ tiles. Hence, the related equivalence classes are $\{1, 2, \ldots, 8\}$ and $\{9, 10, 11, 12, \ldots\}$. So, the boundary values are 8 and 9. 8 is the largest number of tiles for which the system should return the error message. Notice that for every number of tiles greater than or equal to 9, it is possible to fulfill the requirements (see the bottom part of Fig. 11.1 for some examples).

Exercise 8: Two- and Three-Point Boundary Value Method

The equivalence classes should represent the grades, so we have the following classes:

- $A = \{91, 92, \ldots, 99, 100\}$—representing the values for A
- $B = \{76, 77, \ldots, 89, 90\}$—representing the values for B
- $C = \{61, 62, \ldots, 74, 75\}$—representing the values for C
- $D = \{50, 51, \ldots, 59, 60\}$—representing the values for D
- $F = \{0, 1, \ldots, 48, 49\}$—representing the values for F

Table 11.3 Boundaries and boundary values for 2- and 3-point value method (Exercise 8)

Class	Boundaries	2-point boundary values	3-point boundary values
F	0, 49	0, 49, 50	0, 1, 48, 49, 50
D	50, 60	49, 50, 60, 61	49, 50, 51, 59, 60, 61
C	61, 75	60, 61, 75, 76	60, 61, 62, 74, 75, 76
B	76, 90	75, 76, 90, 91	75, 76, 77, 89, 90, 91
A	91, 100	90, 91, 100	90, 91, 92, 99, 100

Notice that we do not have any other values, since the only valid ones are in range 0–100. This means we do not have the invalid equivalence classes. In Table 11.3, the consecutive columns show: the equivalence class, its boundaries, the boundary values identified with the 2-point boundary value approach, and the boundary values identified with the 3-point boundary value approach.

Hence, we have the following sets of boundary values:

- for the 2-point value method: 0, 49, 50, 60, 61, 75, 76, 90, 91, 100
- for the 3-point value method: 0, 1, 48, 49, 50, 51, 59, 60, 61, 62, 74, 75, 76, 77, 89 90, 91, 92, 99, 100

Notice that we do not have values -1 and 101, because, according to the specification, they are infeasible.

Exercise 9: Boundary Values and Equivalence Partitioning

(a) The equivalence classes are $\{\ldots, 1898, 1899\}$, $\{1900, 1901, \ldots, 2019, 2020\}$, $\{2021, 2022, \ldots\}$. The boundary values are 1899, 1900, 2020, 2021, so we must use them. Notice that a boundary value belonging to a class C is also the value from this class, so it covers the partition C. Hence, four tests are enough and the correct answer is D.

(b) The equivalence classes are $\{\ldots, -2, -1\}$, $\{0\}$, $\{1, 2, \ldots\}$. The boundary values are: -1, 0, 1. Applying the 3-value BVA we obtain the following values to be tested:

- For the boundary value -1: $-2, -1, 0$
- For the boundary value 0: $-1, 0, 1$
- For the boundary value 1: 0, 1, 2

Altogether, we obtain the following set of values to be tested: $-2, -1, 0, 1, 2$. Hence, the correct answer is D. Notice that since 0 forms a separate equivalence class, we cannot put all the other values into a single class, since in the BVA approach, the classes cannot have "holes."

Fig. 11.2 The marks before and after rounding (Exercise 10)

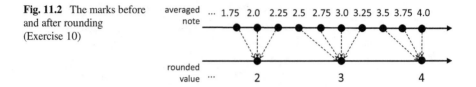

Exercise 10: Rounding

First, notice that the possible averaged value ranges from 1 to 5 by 0.25. We need to find the minimal possible average note, such that its rounding is 3 (a ski jumper is qualified) and the maximal possible average note, such that its rounding is 2 (a ski jumper is not qualified).

It is easy to observe (see Fig. 11.2) that the corresponding values are 2.25 and 2.5. 2.25 is the maximal value that, after rounding, gives the final mark 2. 2.5 is the smallest mean value, which after rounding gives the final mark 3. Hence, the boundary values are 2.25 and 2.5. Now we have to find the two test cases for these values. We need to find four numbers from 1 to 5 with their average value 2.25 (resp. 2.5). The example two test cases are as follows:

- The set 2, 2, 2, 3 of four notes gives $\frac{2+2+2+3}{4} = \frac{9}{4} = 2.25$ after averaging and 2 after rounding
- The set 1, 2, 3, 4 of four notes gives $\frac{1+2+3+4}{4} = \frac{10}{4} = 2.5$ after averaging and 3 after rounding

We found two test cases that verify the boundary values of the averaged result.

Exercise 11: Deriving Classes from Boundary Values

For case A, we have the boundary values 3, 4, 8, and 9. This means that 3 is the right boundary value of a class that does not have the left boundary value. This class must be $\{\ldots, -1, 0, 1, 2, 3\}$. The next class must be bounded by the values 4 and 8: $\{4, 5, 6, 7, 8\}$. Finally, we have the class with 9 as the left boundary value 9 and with no right boundary, so this class must be $\{9, 10, 11, \ldots\}$.

For case B, the corresponding classes are $\{\ldots, 1, 2\}$, $\{3, 4\}$, $\{5, 6, \ldots\}$.

For case C, the corresponding classes are $\{\ldots, -6, -5\}$, $\{-4, -3, \ldots, 0, 1\}$, $\{2\}$, $\{3, 4, 5, 6\}$, $\{7, 8, \ldots\}$. Notice that the value 2 must constitute a separate class, because both its neighbors are also the boundary values.

For case D, the partition is impossible: if 4 is a boundary value, then either 3 or 5 must also be a boundary value.

For case E, the partition is impossible: f 3 is a boundary value, then either 2 or 4 must also be a boundary value.

Exercise 12: Limits of the BVA Method

For A, B, and C, we can apply BVA method, because these domains are ordered. In case of B, there is a question of the number precision in the computer's memory representation: for example, what is the right boundary value for the set (0, 1]? Is it 1.01, 1.00001, 1.0000001, etc.?

For D and E, we cannot apply BVA method, because the elements are incomparable. However, we could introduce the ordering on these sets and then apply the BVA method. For example, in case of strings, we could introduce the classical, lexicographic ordering. Then, each string could be compared with another, for example: aaa < aab, az < ba etc.

Exercise 13: Reading the Full and Collapsed Decision Table

(a) For a 32-year-old man with a monthly salary $11,000 who does not have any other loans, the conditions in the decision table have the following values:

- Age > 21? TRUE (because 32 > 21)
- Gross annual salary ≥ $36,000? FALSE (because $11,000 < $36,000)
- Has other loans? FALSE (stated explicitly in the description)

We look at the column with the combination (TRUE, FALSE, FALSE). This is in column 3. The corresponding actions are: maximal loan value = $1000 and the associated risk = medium. Hence, the maximal loan value in this case is $1000 and the related risk is medium.

(b) Analogously as in case (a) we have the following conditions values:

- Age > 21? FALSE (because it is not true that 21 > 21)
- Gross annual salary ≥ $36,000? FALSE (because 12 * $1,200 < 12 * $36,000)
- Has other loans? TRUE (because he has one other loan)

The combination of conditions (FALSE, FALSE, TRUE) matches the first column (if the age condition is FALSE, the other conditions do not matter). Hence, the maximal loan value in this case is $0, that is, the loan is not granted. This implies that the related risk is not applicable.

(c) We have to give three examples of the test cases that result in three different risk levels (low, medium and high). Notice that risk is defined as low only in column 5, for which the corresponding conditions are: age > 21, gross annual salary ≥ $36,000, and no other loans. Hence, the example of a test case for this situation might be: (33 years old, gross annual salary = $40,000, no other loans). The medium risk is computed in columns 3 and 4. We can choose one of them, say column number 3. The conditions should be (TRUE, FALSE, FALSE), so the example of a test case for this situation might be: (45 years old, gross annual salary = $13,000, 2 other loans). For the high risk, we need to fulfill the conditions from the column 2 (TRUE, FALSE, TRUE), so the example of a test case here might be: (38 years old, gross annual income = $10,000, no other loans).

Exercise 14: Building the Table from Requirements

(a) The exam depends on the results of the three examinations, hence the conditions
are as follows:

- Test 1 result (possible values: 0, 1, 2)
- Test 2 result (possible values: 0, 1, 2)
- Test 3 result (possible values: 0, 1, 2)

The actions:

- Total result. The minimal and maximal values are 0 and 6. If a candidate gets
  0 points for at least one exam, the total result is 0. Hence, the minimal possible
  positive total result is $1 + 1 + 1 = 3$. Thus, the possible total result values are: 0, 3,
  4, 5, 6.
- Entitlements. The possible values are: no entitlements, partial, and full.

(b) As we have three conditions and each of them takes three possible values, the
full decision table would have $3 \times 3 \times 3 = 27$ columns. Notice, however, that
the rule "If a candidate receives 0 for at least one of them, the total result is 0 and
the entitlements are not granted" allows us to collapse the table—see c).

(c) The collapsed table is shown in Table 11.4.

Exercise 15: Unfeasible Combinations

The first three conditions are mutually exclusive, that is, exactly one of them will
always be true. Hence, there are only three combinations of the first three variables:

(YES, NO, NO)
(NO, YES, NO)
(NO, NO, YES)

If condition 4 has value "cash" or "checque," the condition 5 is irrelevant. Hence,
the possible combinations of conditions 4 and 5 are:

Table 11.4 Collapsed table for the system from Exercise 14

Conditions	1	2	3	4	5	6	7	8	9	10	11
Test 1 result	0	–	–	1	1	1	1	2	2	2	2
Test 2 result	–	0	–	1	1	2	2	1	1	2	2
Test 3 result	–	–	0	1	2	1	2	1	2	1	2
Actions											
Total result	0	0	0	3	4	4	5	4	5	5	6
Entitlements	NO	NO	NO	Part.	Part.	Part.	Full	Part.	Full	Full	Full

Part. = partial entitlements

(credit card, YES)
(credit card, NO)
(cash, −)

We have $3 \times 3 = 9$ combinations of the first five conditions. Each of them can be combined in two possible ways with condition 6. Hence, altogether we have $9 \times 2 = 18$ conditions. Considering all the restrictions, all the possible combinations of *all* the conditions are given in Table 11.5, Table 11.6, and Table 11.7.

Exercise 16: Collapsing the Decision Table

First let us find the groups of columns that can potentially be collapsed. We split the columns into four sets, according to the combination of actions, because we can collapse only the columns that have the same combination of actions.

Table 11.5 Conditions of the decision table with all feasible conditions for Exercise 15

Condition	1	2	3	4	5	6
1 Age < 18?	YES	YES	YES	YES	YES	YES
2 18 ≤ age ≤ 35?	NO	NO	NO	NO	NO	NO
3 Age > 35?	NO	NO	NO	NO	NO	NO
4 Payment type	card	card	card	card	cash	cash
5 PIN correct?	YES	YES	NO	NO	−	−
6 Payment value	<$100	≥$100	<$100	≥$100	<$100	≥$100

Table 11.6 Conditions of the decision table with all feasible conditions for Exercise 15 (cont'd)

Condition	7	8	9	10	11	12
1 Age < 18?	NO	NO	NO	NO	NO	NO
2 18 ≤ age ≤ 35?	YES	YES	YES	YES	YES	YES
3 Age > 35?	NO	NO	NO	NO	NO	NO
4 Payment type	card	card	card	card	cash	cash
5 PIN correct?	YES	YES	NO	NO	−	−
6 Payment value	<$100	≥$100	<$100	≥$100	<$100	≥$100

Table 11.7 Conditions of the decision table with all feasible conditions for Exercise 15 (cont'd)

Condition	13	14	15	16	17	18
1 Age < 18?	NO	NO	NO	NO	NO	NO
2 18 ≤ age ≤ 35?	NO	NO	NO	NO	NO	NO
3 Age > 35?	YES	YES	YES	YES	YES	YES
4 Payment type	card	card	card	card	cash	cash
5 PIN correct?	YES	YES	NO	NO	−	−
6 Payment value	<$100	≥$100	<$100	≥$100	<$100	≥$100

The actions (A1 = TRUE, A2 = FALSE) are in columns 3, 4, 9, and 10. Notice that in all these columns, C2 is constant and C1 and C3 form all the possible combinations (C1 = TRUE, C3 = TRUE), (C1 = TRUE, C3 = FALSE), (C1 = FALSE, C3 = TRUE) and (C1 = FALSE, C3 = FALSE). This means that we can collapse these four columns into one, denoting the combination $(\star, B, \star)$ (where $\star$ denotes the arbitrary value).

The actions (A1 = TRUE, A2 = TRUE) are in columns 2 and 8. They can also be collapsed, because the actions depend only on A2 and A3—we have the combination $(\star, A, FALSE)$ here.

The actions (A1 = FALSE, A2 = TRUE) are in columns 1, 7, and 12. In columns 1 and 7, the actions depend only on C2 and C3. Hence, we can collapse them to $(\star, A, TRUE)$. We cannot collapse column 12, as it does not fit to this schema.

The actions (A1 = FALSE, A2 = FALSE) are in columns 5, 6, and 11. In columns 5 and 6, the actions depend only on C1 and C2, so we can collapse them to $(TRUE, C, \star)$. Column 11 cannot be collapsed.

Altogether, we have 6 columns in the collapsed decision table, with the rules:

$(\star, B, \star)$,
$(\star, A, FALSE)$,
$(\star, A, TRUE)$,
$(FALSE, C, FALSE)$,
$(TRUE, C, \star)$,
$(FALSE, C, TRUE)$.

The collapsed table is presented in Table 11.8.

Exercise 17: Using Decision Table to Detect Defects in Requirements

When designing the full decision table for this problem, one of the combinations of conditions will be:

- Has gold card? TRUE
- Economy class full? TRUE
- Business class full? TRUE

Table 11.8 Collapsed table for the problem from Exercise 16

Conditions	1	2	3	4	5	6
C1	–	TRUE	–	–	FALSE	FALSE
C2	B	C	A	A	C	C
C3	–	–	FALSE	TRUE	TRUE	FALSE
Actions						
A1	TRUE	FALSE	TRUE	FALSE	FALSE	FALSE
A2	FALSE	FALSE	TRUE	TRUE	FALSE	TRUE

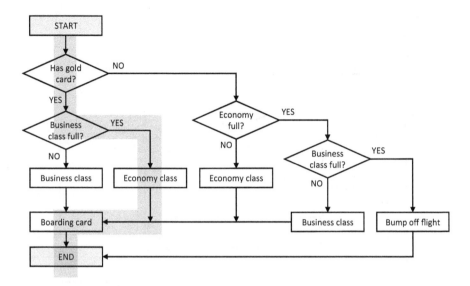

Fig. 11.3 A path in the workflow for a certain test case for Exercise 17

Let us try to derive the expected actions from the specification. In Fig. 11.3 the corresponding path is denoted with gray color.

Notice that when we check if the business class is full (YES) and we go to the next step, we immediately assign a client to the economy class. But one of our conditions says that the economy class is full! We discovered the flaw in the requirements—it is impossible to assign a client to the economy class in this situation.

This is a typical example of using the formal test case design technique as a form of a static testing. There may be no single line of code written, but yet we are able at this stage of the development process, detect a serious problem in the requirements. The cost of fixing this error is very low—we just need to correct the flow diagram. The corrected diagram should always check—in case that one class is full—whether the other one is also full. An example of the fixed diagram is presented in Fig. 11.4.

This fix is of course only one of the possible corrections. We do not really know what should happen with a gold card member in case that both classes are full. He may be bumped off the flight, but we could imagine as well that in such a case, some passenger who does not hold a gold card should be bumped off from the economic class and this place should be reserved for the gold card member. The solution must be definitely discussed with a client/architect/business analyst.

Exercise 18: Identifying the Correct Behavior of a State Machine

(d) We need to check if the state diagram defines the following situation: "when the system shows the client's basket, the client can make payment". This means that we are in the state BASKET and we expect the action Payment to occur. However, the only possible events that can be handled in this situation are

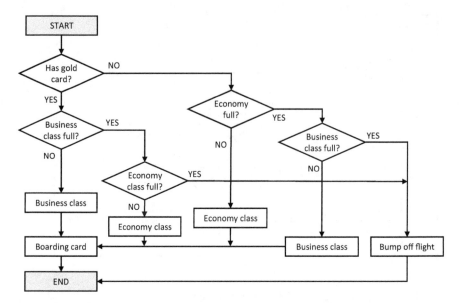

Fig. 11.4 An example of the corrected business flow for the Exercise 17

ToCatalog (we then move to BROWSE) and Finalize (we then move to CHECKOUT). It is impossible to invoke Payment when being in BASKET.

(e) We need to check if the state diagram defines the following situation: "being in the checkout, the client can go back to his basket". It is possible, as there is the transition GoBack, which—when occurs—moves us from CHECKOUT to BASKET.

(f) We need to check if the state diagram defines the following situation: "when paying, if error occurs, the system goes back to the checkout screen". Notice that when we are in the PAY state, it is impossible to go back to CHECKOUT. The only possible transition (TransactionConfirmed) moves us to LOGOUT. Hence, this situation is impossible.

Exercise 19: Identifying Correct Sequences

(A) Possible—realized by the sequence BROWSE → AddItem → BASKET → Finalize → CHECKOUT → GoBack → BASKET → Finalize → CHECKOUT.

(B) Possible—realized by the sequence LOGIN → ToCatalog → BROWSE → AddItem → BASKET → Finalize → CHECKOUT → Payment → PAY. The beginning of the path might be as well BASKET → ToCatalog → BROWSE → . . .

(C) Possible—realized by the sequence CHECKOUT → GoBack → BASKET → ToCatalog → BROWSE.

(D) Impossible—we cannot invoke two consecutive ToCatalog events.

Fig. 11.5 Graphical representation of the machine from the Exercise 20

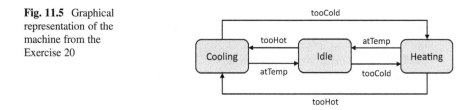

(E) Impossible—after AddItem we are in the BASKET state, from which we cannot invoke Payment.

(F) Possible—realized by the sequence of the following state transitions: LOGIN → ToCatalog → BROWSE → AddItem → BASKET → ToCatalog → BROWSE → AddItem → BASKET → Finalize → CHECKOUT → GoBack → BASKET → Finalize → CHECKOUT → Payment → PAY.

Exercise 20: Working with Different Representations of a State Machine

(a) There are three states (Idle, Cooling, Heating) and three different events (atTemp, tooCold, tooHot).

(b) The example of an invalid transition may be (Cooling, tooHot): in the Cooling state, the event tooHot is not defined. In fact, any combination of state and event for which the cell in the transition table is empty, represents the invalid transition.

(c) The graphical representation of the machine is presented in Fig. 11.5.

(d) The initial state is Idle. The corresponding sequence of states (given in bold) is as follows: **Idle** → tooCold → **Heating** → atTemp → **Idle** → tooCold → **Heating** → tooHot → **Cooling** → tooCold → **Heating**. Hence, the last state after the given sequence of events is Heating.

Exercise 21: Identifying and Counting 0-Switches and 1-Switches

(a) The number of 0-switches equals the number of transitions. In our machine, there are six transitions:

(1) (**Closed**, PushedOpenButton/RaiseTheGate, **Raising**)
(2) (**Closed**, CarAtGate/RaiseTheGate, **Raising**)
(3) (**Raising**, GateOpened/set time = 0s, **Opened**)
(4) (**Opened**, PushedCloseButton/LowerTheGate, **Lowering**)
(5) (**Opened**, NoCarAtGate [time > 10s], **Lowering**)
(6) (**Lowering**, GateClosed, **Closed**)

Notice that there are only four arrows in the figure, but some of them represent more than one transition!

(b) When a car arrives at gate, the gate starts raising and during this process the car drives away, before the system reaches the state Opened, the gate will be raised until the GateOpened occurs. Then, the system moves to the state Opened. Now, either the "Close" button will be pushed, and the gate will start lowering, or—in case no one pushes the button—after ten seconds the event NoCarAtGate holds, as there is no car at gate at this moment. So, either way, the system will move to the state Lowering.

(c) When a user presses the "Close" button when the gate is being raised, nothing should happen, as the model does not define the transition PushedCloseButton when being in state Raising.

(d) We have to count the 1-switches starting from the state Raising. First, let us find all 0-switches that start in Raising and then we will extend them to 1-switches. The only 0-switch starting from Raising is (Raising, GateOpened/set time = 0s, Opened). It can be extended with one more 0-switch in two ways: (Opened, PushedCloseButton/LowerTheGate, Lowering) and (Opened, NoCarAtGate [time > 10s], Lowering). Hence, we have two 1-switches starting from Raising:

- **(Raising**, GateOpened/set time = 0s, **Opened** PushedCloseButton/ LowerTheGate, **Lowering)**
- **(Raising**, GateOpened/set time = 0s, **Opened**, NoCarAtGate [time > 10s], **Lowering)**

Exercise 22: Designing Tests for Achieving Different Types of Coverage

(a) To achieve the 0-switch coverage we need at least two test cases:

- **Closed** → PushedOpenButton → **Raising** → GateOpened → **Opened** → PushedCloseButton → **Lowering** → GateClosed (which covers 4 out of 6 transitions)
- **Closed** → CarAtGate → **Raising** → GateOpened → **Opened** → NoCarAtGate [time > 10s] → **Lowering** → GateClosed → **Closed** (which additionally covers two other transitions)

Notice that we cannot achieve the 0-switch coverage with only one test, as going from the Closed state, we can cover only one out of two outgoing transitions (PushedOpenButton or CarAtGate) and—according to the specification—when we reach the Closed state, we have to end out test case.

(b) First let us define all 1-switches in this machine (the states are bolded):

(continued)

(1) **Closed** → PushedOpenButton → **Raising** → GateOpened → **Opened**
(2) **Closed** → CarAtGate → **Raising** → GateOpened → **Opened**
(3) **Raising** → GateOpened → **Opened** → PushedCloseButton → **Lowering**
(4) **Raising** → GateOpened → **Opened** → NoCarAtGate [time > 10s] → **Lowering**
(5) **Opened** → PushedCloseButton → **Lowering** → GateClosed → **Closed**
(6) **Opened** → NoCarAtGate [time > 10s] → **Lowering** → GateClosed → **Closed**
(7) **Lowering** → GateClosed → **Closed** → PushedOpenButton → **Raising**
(8) **Lowering** → GateClosed → **Closed** → CarAtGate → **Raising**

Notice that (7) and (8) are infeasible, as we must end the test case once we reach the state Closed. Hence, we have only six 1-switches to cover: (1), (2), (3), (4), (5), (6). We can do it with the same two test cases as in a). The first one covers 1-switches (1), (3), (5), the second one covers (2), (4) and (6).

(c) To achieve the state coverage, it is enough to take any of the two test cases defined in a). Each of them covers all four states: Closed, Raising, Opened, and Lowering.

Exercise 23: Automata with Conditions

(a) All 1-switches are presented below:

(1) IDLE → CardEntered → VALIDATE → CardNotOK → END
(2) IDLE → CardEntered → VALIDATE → CardOK → ASK FOR PIN
(3) VALIDATE → CardOK → ASK FOR PIN → PinOK → USER LOGGED
(4) VALIDATE → CardOK → ASK FOR PIN → PinNotOK [attempts < 3] → ASK FOR PIN
(5) VALIDATE → CardOK → ASK FOR PIN → PinNotOK [attempts = 3] → BLOCK CARD
(6) ASK FOR PIN → PinNotOK [attempts < 3] → ASK FOR PIN → PinOK → USER LOGGED
(7) ASK FOR PIN → PinNotOK [attempts < 3] → ASK FOR PIN → PinNotOK [attempts < 3] → ASK FOR PIN
(8) ASK FOR PIN → PinNotOK [attempts < 3] → ASK FOR PIN → PinNotOK [attempts = 3] → BLOCK CARD

(b) After the transition VALIDATE → CardOK → ASK FOR PIN the action "attempts := 1" was invoked, so at this moment, the variable *attempts* equals 1. Now, the event PinNotOK is triggered. Notice that we have two possible target states in this situation: ASK FOR PIN or BLOCK CARD. We chose the

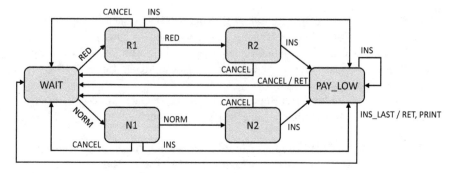

Fig. 11.6 The state diagram for the ticket machine from Exercise 24

state by checking which condition holds: [attempts < 3] or [attempts = 3]. Because attempts = 1, the first condition holds, so we move to ASK FOR PIN and invoke the action "attempts := attempts + 1". After executing this transition, the value of the variable *attempts* increases by one, so now it equals 2. If the next action is PinNotOK the same transition is triggered (as *attempts* is still less than 3), so we move to ASK FOR PIN and the value of *attempts* again increases by one, so now *attempts* equals 3.

(c) It is not possible to cover all 1-switches. In particular, it is impossible to cover the 1-switch (5) from (a), because after the transition VALIDATE → CardOK the variable attempts equals 1. So, it is impossible to immediately go to BLOCK CARD through the PinNotOK [attempts = 3], because *attempts* equals 1, so this condition is false at the moment.

Exercise 24: Building a State Machine and Deriving Test Cases

(a) The state machine is presented in Fig. 11.6. Only the transitions that can be deduced from the specification are defined.

(b) As there are 6 incoming transitions to the final state WAIT, we immediately see that we will need at least six test cases to cover all 0-switches. However, in fact we will need eight test cases (the explanation is given below). We have 15 - 0-switches to cover (states are bolded):

(1) **WAIT** → RED → **R1**	(2) **WAIT** → NORM → **N1**
(3) **R1** → CANCEL → **WAIT**	(4) **R1** → INS → **PAY_LOW**
(5) **R1** → RED → **R2**	(6) **N1** → CANCEL → **WAIT**
(7) **N1** → NORM → **N2**	(8) **N1** → INS → **PAY_LOW**
(9) **R2** → INS → **PAY_LOW**	(10) **R2** → CANCEL → **WAIT**
(11) **N2** → CANCEL → **WAIT**	(12) **N2** → INS → **PAY_LOW**
(13) **PAY_LOW** → CANCEL/RET → **WAIT**	(14) **PAY_LOW** → INS → **PAY_LOW**
(15) **PAY_LOW** → INS_LAST/RET, PRINT → **WAIT**	

Table 11.9 Test cases that achieve the 0-switch coverage for the ticket machine from Exercise 24

TC #	Test case (sequence of events)	0-switches covered
1	RED, CANCEL	**(1)**, **(3)**
2	NORM, CANCEL	**(2)**, **(6)**
3	RED, INS, INS, CANCEL/RET	(1), **(4)**, **(14)**, **(13)**
4	RED, RED, CANCEL	(1), **(5)**, **(10)**
5	RED, RED, INS, INS_LAST/RET, PRINT	(1), (5), **(9)**, **(15)**
6	NORM, NORM, CANCEL	(2), **(7)**, **(11)**
7	NORM, NORM, INS, INS_LAST/RET, PRINT	(2), (7), **(12)**, (15)
8	NORM, INS, CANCEL/RET	(2), **(8)**, (13)

Table 11.9 shows the six test cases and the 0-switches they cover. The bolded 0-switches denote the ones that are covered the first time.

Why do we need eight test cases? Because no two of the 0-switches (3), (4), (6), (8), (9), (10), (11), (12) can be covered in one test case.

(c) If the machine can accept a 50c coin, there is a new situation possible, which couldn't happen in the machine from a). Namely, when a user pushes the RED button and inserts 50c, the total amount inserted exceeds the ticket price (25c), so this triggers the INS_LAST event. Hence, we need to immediately return from N1 to WAIT with action RET, PRINT. So we need one more transition: R1 $\rightarrow$ INS_LAST/RET, PRINT $\rightarrow$ WAIT. To cover the new machine we need one more test that covers this transition, so we need nine test cases in total.

(d) The example of situations that could happen, but are not described explicitly in the requirements are

- Pushing NORM when being in R1 or R2
- Pushing RED when being in N1 or N2
- Pushing NORM or RED when being in PAY_LOW
- Trying to invoke INS when being in WAIT (inserting a coin before ticket selection)

Notice, that all of the above are physically possible, as the machine under test is a physical device. Hence, we should definitely use the invalid transition coverage to exercise these situations.

Exercise 25: Analyzing a Use Case

(a) We need one test case for the main scenario, two another for the two alternative paths and one more for the exception path. Altogether, we need four test cases:

- (Main path): 1, 2, 3, 4
- (Alternative path 3a): 1, 2, 3a
- (Alternative path 3b): 1, 2, 3b
- (Exception 2): 1, 2E

(b) The TC1 does not cover anything in our use case, as in this test case, the user selects the "Soda-2," not the "Soda-1" beverage. TC2, TC3, and TC4 cover respectively: the alternative path 3a, the alternative path 3b, and the exception in step 2. Altogether, these four tests cover 3 out of 4 use case paths, so they achieve $3/4 = 75\%$ coverage.

(c) The alternative path 3b is covered by the TC3.

Exercise 26: Designing the Test Cases from a Use Case

(a) The sample test case that covers the main path of the use case may look like as follows.

Test case TC 001—successful shopping with a 5% discount	
Precondition: The total amount of the previous shoppings for a registered client X is $1000.01.	
Test steps:	
Action	**Expected result**
1. The user X logs into the system.	The system verifies the user, recognizes that X has a 5% discount and shows the message "you are a premium client with a 5% discount"; the basket is empty.
2. The user X inserts the product Y (worth $200) to the basket.	The basket contains Y; the total sum before the discount is shown to the client ($200).
3. The user X clicks the "Pay" button.	The system shows the discounted price ($190).
4. The user accepts the transaction.	The system asks for the credit card credentials.
5. The user enters the credit card credentials.	The system performs the payment transaction; the system verifies that the transaction is OK and informs the client about that; the system generates the shipment ordering and sends user an e-mail with the shipment confirmation and the order details.
Postcondition: Number of products Y in the database decreased by 1; user's X credit card charged for $190.	

(b) There is one main path and 8 exceptions: 1a, 1b, 3a, 5a, 6a, 7a,7b, 7c. Hence, we need nine test cases to cover this use case.

Exercise 27: Exceptions and Alternate Flows

The possible alternate paths

Fig. 11.7 CFG for the code
from Exercise 31

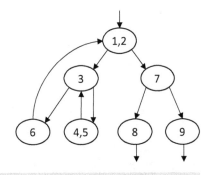

> 1a. The user selects "My courses" and then "Show the available courses."
> 3a. The user selects more than one checkbox.

The possible exceptions:

> 2a. The system has lost connection to the database.
> 2b. There are no courses available for the student.
> 3a. The user cancels the operation.
> 4a. The system cannot enroll the student, because she did not fulfill the prerequisites for this course.

Exercise 28: Transforming the Code into the Control Flow Graph
The CFG for the code is presented in Fig. 11.7.

Exercise 29: Calculating the Coverage

(a) There are four decisions in the code (in nodes A, B, C and E). The outcomes of these decisions are: $A \rightarrow B$, $A \rightarrow C$, $B \rightarrow D$, $B \rightarrow F$, $C \rightarrow E$, $C \rightarrow F$, $E \rightarrow C$, $E \rightarrow G$.

(b) The seven test conditions for the statement coverage are: A, B, C, D, E, F, G. The three given tests altogether cover the nodes: A, B, C, E, F, G, so they cover 6 out of 7 nodes. Hence, the statement coverage is $6/7 \approx 86\%$. The tests cover the following decision outcomes: $A \rightarrow B$, $B \rightarrow F$, $A \rightarrow C$, $E \rightarrow C$, $E \rightarrow G$. So they cover 5 out of 6 decision outcomes, hence the decision coverage is $5/6 \approx 83\%$.

(c) We need two tests to achieve the statement coverage (because we cannot cover B and C in one test). The example test suite that achieves this coverage is

   1. Test 1: $A \rightarrow B \rightarrow D \rightarrow B \rightarrow F \rightarrow G$ (covers A, B, D, F, and G)
   2. Test 2: $A \rightarrow C \rightarrow E \rightarrow G$ (additionally covers C and E)

(d) We need three tests to achieve the decision coverage (because no two out of the decision outcomes $A \rightarrow B$, $C \rightarrow F$ and $C \rightarrow E$ can be covered within one test case. The example test suite that achieves the decision coverage is

1. Test 1: $A \rightarrow B \rightarrow D \rightarrow B \rightarrow F \rightarrow G$ (covers $A \rightarrow B$, $B \rightarrow D$ and $B \rightarrow F$)
2. Test 2: $A \rightarrow C \rightarrow F \rightarrow G$ (covers $A \rightarrow C$ and $C \rightarrow F$),
3. Test 3: $A \rightarrow C \rightarrow E \rightarrow C \rightarrow E \rightarrow G$ (covers additionally $C \rightarrow EE \rightarrow C$ and $E \rightarrow G$)

Exercise 30

```
1. IF NumberOfTransactions > 10 THEN
2.    IF TotalAmountSpent > $500 THEN
3.       discount := 5%
      ELSE
4.       discount := 2%
    ELSE
5.    discount := 0%
```

(a) The 5% discount is admitted in line 3. To reach this line we need to reach the line 2. and the condition TotalAmountSpent>$500 must be true. To reach line 2., in turn, the condition NumberOfTransactions>10 must be true in line 1. So a test case that results in admitting the 5% discount must be the one in which TotalAmountSpent is greater than $500 and NumberOfTransactions is greater than 10. For example, (12, $880).

(b) The test case (9, $600) results in the control flow that goes through nodes: 1 (false), 5. The test case (10, $200) also gives us the control flow 1 (false), 5. Altogether, these two test cases cover 2 out of 5 statements, so the statement coverage in this case is 40%.

(c) There are two decisions (in lines 1 and 2), so we have four test conditions to cover. The test case (15, $50) results in the path 1 (true), 2 (false), 4. The test case (20, $750) in turn results in the path 1 (true), 2 (true), 3. Altogether, these test cases cover the TRUE outcome for decision 1 and both TRUE and FALSE for decision 2. This gives $3/4 = 75\%$ decision coverage.

(d) To achieve the statement coverage we need three tests, because no two out of the statements 3, 4, 5 can be exercised within a single test case. The example test suite is

1. test 1: (5, $50)—exercises the statements 1, 5
2. test 2: (15, $80)—exercises the statements 1, 2, 4
3. test 3: (22, $945)—exercises the statements 1, 2, 3

(e) To achieve the decision coverage we need three tests, because no two out of the decision outcomes: (1, FALSE), (2, TRUE), and (2, FALSE) can be exercised within a single test case. The example test suite may be the same as in the previous point:

1. test 1—exercises decision 1 to FALSE
2. test 2—exercises decision 1 to TRUE and decision 2 to FALSE
3. test 3—exercises decision 1 to TRUE and decision 2 to TRUE

Exercise 31

Notice that in the additional code, there are no additional decisions, so the existing test cases still achieve 100% decision coverage—no additional test cases are needed. The same holds for the statement coverage, because 100% decision coverage guarantees 100% statement coverage. We can also explain it in the other way: each of our tests for the previous version of the code ends after the line 5. So, if we add a single line after line 5, each of the existing test cases will exercise this new line.

Exercise 32: Coverage Criteria Subsumption

(a) The simplest example is an IF statement without the ELSE section and one test case for which the decision in this IF is evaluated to TRUE. Consider, for example, the following code:

```
1. IF (x == 0) THEN
2.    DoSomething
3. END PROGRAM
```

The test case in which x equals 0 goes through all statements: 1, 2, 3, so it achieves 100% statement coverage. However, it achieves only 50% decision coverage, because the decision in line 1 was not evaluated as FALSE.

(b) Suppose we have a test suite that achieves 100% decision coverage for a code with at least one decision. Let us take an arbitrary statement n from this code. We will prove that n is covered by at least one test case. If n is a decision, it must be exercised, as our tests achieve 100% decision coverage. So suppose it is not a decision. Then it must be reached from some other decision node or from the initial node. The first situation comes to the case discussed above. The second one means that our instruction will be reached by all the test cases, because all the paths must go through this node (there are no decision points on the path from the initial node to n).

(c) If there are no decisions in the code, the empty set of tests would achieve decision coverage, but it would not achieve statement coverage (for this we would need one test).

Exercise 33: Provide Test Cases to Achieve a Given Coverage

Correct answer: C

Statement coverage requires that every statement is executed at least once in at least one test case. One test will be enough to execute all the statements within it. Below is the same code with the executable lines numbered. Consider a test case with input values x = 1, y = 1.

```
1 INPUT x, y
2 WHILE (x > 0)
3    WHILE (y > 0)
4       y := y - 1
5       print 'something happened!'
     END WHILE
6    x := x - 1
7    y := y + x
   END WHILE
```

This test will cause the following control flow:

```
Line 1
Line 2 (decision TRUE)
Line 3 (decision TRUE)
Line 4 (y = 0)
Line 5
Line 3 (decision FALSE)
Line 6 (x = 0)
Line 7
Line 2 (decision FALSE)
End.
```

As we can see, every statement was executed at least once. Hence, C is correct and A, B, D are incorrect.

Chapter 12
Answers to Question Set 1

Question 1. (FL-2.4.1)
Correct answer: C

C is correct, because corrective change is one of the modification-related triggers for maintenance. We decided to correct the software by fixing the bug.

A is incorrect, because we do not upgrade software, we have to fix it.

B is incorrect, because we do not perform any migration activities.

D is incorrect. As in fact it is a trigger for maintenance in case of the IoT systems, this is not a case—we need to fix a defect, and we do not introduce any new or modified things into the system.

Question 2. (FL-1.1.1)
Correct answer: D

All these activities are part of the testing process. Implementing a test case is part of the test implementation phase. Performing the review and checking grammar and spelling of a document are the examples of using a static technique for detecting defects. Planning test activities is part of the test planning phase. Designing a test case is part of the test design phase.

Question 3. (FL-4.3.3)
Correct answer: B

100% statement coverage guarantees that every statement in the code will be evaluated at least once. This means that, in particular, if our test suite achieved 100% statement coverage, there must be at least one test in which the instructions within the while loop were executed; hence, in this test, the loop was executed at least once.

A is incorrect, because we may achieve 50% decision coverage with just one test with NumberOfValues = 0. In this case, the decision in the while loop will be false and the loop will not be executed.

C is incorrect, because this test will not execute the loop and we don't know what are the other tests.

© Springer Nature Switzerland AG 2018
A. Roman, *A Study Guide to the ISTQB® Foundation Level 2018 Syllabus*,
https://doi.org/10.1007/978-3-319-98740-8_12

D is incorrect, because both tests may be executed with NumberOfValues less than 1, for example with 0 and −1. Both such tests will not execute the loop.

Question 4. (FL-2.2.1)

Correct answer: B

The type of tests we want to perform is the component integration testing. Architectural design of the components is a typical test basis for this type of tests, as it describes the interfaces, which are used to communicate between different components.

A is incorrect, because integration testing focuses on the integration, not on the components themselves.

C is incorrect, because risk analysis reports are useful more in the system testing rather than in the integration testing.

D is incorrect, because legal regulations are useful for high-level testing, like acceptance testing.

Question 5. (Chapter 1 keyword)

Correct answer: A

According to syllabus: "A person can make an error (mistake), which can lead to the introduction of a defect (fault or bug) in the software code or in some other related work product. (...) If a defect in the code is executed, this may cause a failure, but not necessarily in all circumstances."

Hence, A is correct and B, C, D are incorrect.

Question 6. (FL-4.2.1)

Correct answer: D

The analyzed variable, FinalResult, is the sum of L and E. Its domain is {0, 1, 2, ..., 99, 100}. The final result is "pass" if FinalResult > 50, and "fail" otherwise. Hence, we have two valid equivalence classes for FinalResult:

- class C1 that represents the sum of points for the "fail" result: {1, 2, ..., 49, 50}
- class C2 that represents the sum of points for the "pass" result: {51, 52, ..., 99, 100}

Answer D gives us two values from two different classes: 50 = 35 + 15 and 60 = 40 + 20. Hence, these two tests achieve 100% equivalence partition coverage.

A is incorrect, because both 51 = 1 + 50 and 100 = 50 + 50 belong to C2.

B is incorrect, because both 58 = 39 + 19 and 51 = 28 + 23 belong to C2.

C is incorrect because both 50 = 0 + 50 and 50 = 50 + 0 belong to C1.

Question 7. (FL-1.4.1)

Correct answer: A

The approach to testing is always context dependent and depends on many constraints. It is obvious that the commercial project is way much more important for the company than the internal, on-line room reservation system. Hence, A is correct.

B is incorrect, because critical defects in the room reservation system will not harm our company as much, as the critical defects in the commercial project, discovered by a client after the release.

C is incorrect, because it is commercial project that brings us the money. Hence, it is more important, so it has a higher priority in testing. Sooner or later, we would have to test this system, so we would have to invest in the testing process anyway.

D is incorrect, because the type of an SDLC has nothing to do in this situation: the priorities come from the business rationale.

Question 8. (FL-5.2.4)

Correct answer: D

The test cases need to be ordered according to the decreasing priority, but we need to respect the dependencies between test cases. The only tests that are independent of any others are TC1 and TC4. We should first execute TC1 and then TC4, because TC1 has greater priority. Next, we can execute TC3, which is dependent on both TC1 and TC4. After executing TC3, we can execute TC2 and TC7. We choose TC7, as it has greater priority. After that, notice that apart from TC2, we can also execute TC6 and TC5. Out of these three tests, the one with the greatest priority is TC6, then TC2, and then TC5.

The prioritized sequence of the execution is thus: TC1, TC4, TC3, TC7, TC6, TC2, TC5. The fifth test case is TC6. Hence, D is correct.

A is incorrect, because it follows the opposite direction of the dependence.

B is incorrect, because it follows the dependence, but in the increasing, not decreasing, order of priorities.

C is incorrect, because this sequence takes into account only priorities, not dependencies.

Question 9. (FL-4.2.3)

Correct answer: A

The requirements are contradictory if for one given combination of conditions, we can derive two different actions. In our case, two different actions are "Free ride = TRUE" and "Free ride = FALSE." For "Free ride" to be FALSE, we need to have "Student = TRUE." For "Free ride" to be TRUE, we need to have either "Member of Parliament = TRUE" or "Disabled = TRUE." Test A fulfils these conditions—it fits into both T1 and T3. Notice that these two columns give contradictory actions.

B is incorrect, because this situation fits only into columns T1 and T2, and both of them give the same action.

C is incorrect, because it fits only into T3, so there cannot be any contradiction.

D is incorrect, because it does not fit into T1, T2, or T3. This is an example of a missing requirement, but not an example of contradictory requirements.

The decision table in this question has so-called *nonexclusive rules*. This means that for a certain combination of conditions, more than one rule can be applied. In general, such decision tables should be avoided, as—like in this example—this may lead to some problems.

Question 10. (FL-6.1.1)

Correct answer: B

The tool compares two objects and checks if they are equal—hence, this is a typical example of a comparator.

A is incorrect, because a test oracle gives the expected result, and our tool cannot generate anything—it can only compare.

C is incorrect, because we do not generate any test data with this tool.

D is incorrect, because the tool does not monitor anything.

Question 11. (FL-3.2.1)

Correct answer: B

According to syllabus, the review process comprises the following main activities:

- Planning—including "selecting the people to participate in the review and *allocating roles*"
- Initiate review—including "*distributing the work product* (physically or by electronic means) and other material, e.g., issue log forms, or checklists"
- Individual review—including "*noting* potential defects, *recommendations, and questions*"
- Issue communication and analysis
- Fixing and reporting

Hence, B is correct, and A, C, D are incorrect.

Question 12. (FL-1.1.2)

Correct answer: A

Debugging locates, analyzes, and removes the defects. As the defect was removed by tester, he performed the debugging activity.

B is incorrect, because the developer implemented the code—this has nothing to do with debugging.

C is incorrect, because the architect was only a designer. He made a mistake and inserted a defect into design, but neither located it, nor analyzed or corrected.

D is incorrect, because the test manager has only found the defect—this is a typical testing, not debugging activity.

Question 13. (FL-4.3.2)

Correct answer: A

Decision coverage requires that each decision outcome should be covered by at least one test. Since we have n binary decisions, we have two possible outcomes for each of them (TRUE and FALSE). Hence, the total number of coverage elements is $2n$.

Question 14. (FL-5.3.2)

Correct answer: C

The total repairing time gives the information about the time the software was unavailable. This information is enough for the client to reason about the availability level.

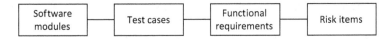

Fig. 12.1 Traceability between different artifacts (Exam set 1, question 15)

A and B are incorrect, because we cannot compute the availability time basing on the information about test cases or defects—these measures may be helpful to measure the test progress in terms of tests or defects, but cannot measure the software availability.

D is incorrect—although availability is related to failures, we have no information about the total time to repair; hence, we cannot calculate the availability metric.

Question 15. (FL-2.4.2)
Correct answer: B

The traceability between different artifacts is presented in Fig. 12.1.

Notice that traceability is transitive: if we know about some change in the risk items, we may trace it back to the functional requirements. Then, using the information about which requirements are impacted by this change, we can trace the changed requirements back to the test cases and finally, the affected test cases to software modules. Hence, the correct answer is B.

Question 16. (FL-5.2.5)
Correct answer: D

The number of defects found is clearly the outcome of the testing activity. It also impacts the testing effort, because the greater the number of defects found, the more the time required for the retests and other testing activities.

A is incorrect—although the size of the product impacts a testing effort, it is not the outcome of the testing activity, but a static property of the system being developed.

B is incorrect, because the number of testers itself does not impact the testing effort.

C is incorrect, because, although client requirements impact the testing effort, they are not the outcome of the testing activity.

Question 17. (FL-3.2.5)
Correct answer: D

According to the syllabus, one of the organizational success factors for reviews is that "review types are applied, which are suitable to achieve the objectives and are appropriate to the type and level of software work products and participants." The moderator was asked to organize a walkthrough, but he organized an inspection, which is not suitable for a code review in this case. Hence, this organizational success factor is missing.

According to the syllabus, one of the people-related success factors for reviews is that "the right people are involved to meet the review objectives." The moderator was asked to organize a code review for the developers, but, apart from the author, he invited only the testers. This will make the code review ineffective. Hence, this people-related success factor is missing.

Therefore, D is correct and A, B, and C are incorrect.

Question 18. (FL-4.4.1)
Correct answer: C

This is a typical example of error guessing—a tester does not use any technique—she just guesses what may go wrong.

A is incorrect, because the scenario does not mention about any specification that might be used.

B is incorrect, because the scenario does not mention that we have access to the internal structure of the problem; also, the tester's idea has nothing to do with analyzing such a structure.

D is incorrect, because the tester got the idea of a test without using any checklist.

Question 19. (Chapter 4 keywords)
Correct answer: A

Decision tables represent complex business rules that a system must implement. The decision table consists of conditions (inputs) and the resulting actions (outputs) of the system. Each column in the decision table represents a business rule in the form "IF (conditions) THEN (actions)." Hence, A is correct.

B is incorrect, because this is the description of the state transition test technique.

C is incorrect, because this is the description of the use-case testing.

D is incorrect, because this is the description of the decision coverage testing. Do not confuse decision tables with decision coverage—they both have "decision" in their names, but they are completely different test techniques (decision table is a black-box technique while decision coverage is a white-box technique).

Question 20. (FL-2.1.1)
Correct answer: A

Answer A is correct, because it rationally justifies the performance of the regression testing due to the nature of the incremental model.

B is incorrect, because it refers to the test level (system testing), not the SDLC model; besides, this explanation is not true–regression can be performed at any test level, not only at the system testing.

C is incorrect, because it does not explain the importance of the regression tests. The fact that in sequential models, we test the whole system does not imply the necessity of performing regression.

D is incorrect, because although it correctly characterizes the iterative models, it does not answer the right question.

Question 21. (FL-2.1.2)
Correct answer: D

Software development model depends on the nature of the project we want to proceed. Hence, it must take into account the context of the project and product characteristics.

A and C are incorrect: it makes no sense to adapt it to test process, as it is exactly the opposite: it is the testing process, which must be aligned with the chosen software development model.

B is incorrect, because user requirements are not about the development processes, but about the product characteristics.

Question 22. (FL-4.2.1)
Correct answer: D

The output variable has four different values: 0%, 10%, 20%, and 25%. Hence, we need four test cases. Test inputs from D cover all of them:

- (0, 300) fulfills R1, so this test covers 0%.
- (200, 50) fulfills R2, so this test covers 10%.
- (300, 50) fulfills R4, so this test covers 20%.
- (300, 300) fulfills R5, so this test covers 25%.

Notice that we do not need an additional test for covering R3, as this rule results in the same bonus as R4. Equivalence partitioning does not distinguish these two cases, as it focuses solely on the bonus value, not on the rules that imply this bonus.

A and B are incorrect, because we need only four tests to achieve the coverage.

C is incorrect, because these four tests fulfill R1, R2, R3 and R4, so they cover 0%, 10% and 20%. None of them covers 25% bonus. Hence, these tests achieve only 75% of the equivalence partitioning coverage, and moreover last two are redundant, as they represent the same equivalence class.

Question 23. (FL-5.1.1)
Correct answer: D

If a developer says that he does not need to care about some quality aspect anymore, this is a clear example of losing the sense of responsibility for quality. Hence, D is correct.

A and B are incorrect—this situation brings no benefits—it is harmful for the product quality.

C is incorrect. Although it is true that the outsourced team is isolated from the developers, it does not answer the right question.

Question 24. (FL-1.2.4)
Correct answer: C

If a developer has a little or no knowledge about algorithms and algorithmic complexity, this may result in an ineffective implementation of the algorithm. Hence, C is correct.

A and D are incorrect, as they may be the effects of the root cause, not the root cause itself—they are the possible consequences, not causes of the developer's mistake.

B is incorrect, because it has nothing to do with the fact that the developer made the mistake.

Question 25. (FL-5.2.2)

Correct answer: B

Analytical strategy is a test approach based on an analysis of some factor which drives the tester's activities. For example, a risk may be such a driver. In this approach, we perform the risk analysis and "follow the risks" by prioritizing the tests according to their risk level. Hence, B is correct.

A is incorrect, because this is an example of a model-based strategy.

C is incorrect, because this is an example of a methodical strategy.

D is incorrect, because this is an example of a regression-averse strategy.

Question 26. (FL-1.2.2)

Correct answer: B

Testing is a form of the quality control (we check if there are defects in the system under test). Quality control is part of the quality assurance, which—in general—tries to prevent defects from being inserted into the product by focusing on processes and improving them. Hence, B is correct and A, C, and D are incorrect.

Question 27. (FL-3.1.1)

Correct answer: A

Static analysis can examine any object. Hence, A is correct.

B is incorrect, because the document says about the analysis of the source code— but the document itself is not a source code; hence, we can apply here some other static techniques, more suitable for documents.

C is incorrect, because the fact that the document is not a source code does not mean that it cannot be examined by a static analysis.

D is incorrect, because static analysis can be used for every kind of software work product.

Question 28. (FL-4.4.3)

Correct answer: D

Checklist-based testing makes testing more consistent, as—when we repeat the tests—it enforces us to perform the actions that check the same things.

A is incorrect, because although checklists may be organized around the nonfunctional testing issues, this is not a general benefit that checklists give us.

B is incorrect, because checklists have nothing to do with formal requirements.

C is incorrect, because using the checklists does not necessarily require the expert knowledge of a tester—this fits more into the exploratory testing.

Question 29. (FL-5.5.1)

Correct answer: B

Risk level is characterized by the probability of its occurrence (likelihood) and the impact, that is—the harm resulting from that event when it occurs). Hence, B is correct and A, C and D are incorrect.

Question 30. (FL-4.2.4)

Correct answer: A

As we have 3 states (Initial, LoginPage, WelcomePage) and 4 transitions, there are 12 possible combinations (state, transition). Since 4 of them are correct (they are shown in the table), we have $12 - 4 = 8$ invalid transitions. Recall that an invalid transition is a transition not defined in the model. These are (represented as a pair (state, transition)):

(Initial, LoginOK)
(Initial, LoginNotOK)
(Initial, LogOut)
(LoginPage, GoToLogin)
(LoginPage, LogOut)
(WelcomePage, GoToLogin)
(WelcomePage, LoginOK)
(WelcomePage, LoginNotOK)

Question 31. (FL-5.2.6)

Correct answer: C

Planning poker and Wideband Delphi estimate the test effort based on the experience of the owners of the testing tasks or by experts. Hence, they are the examples of an expert-based approach. Burning chart and software reliability model estimate the test effort based on metrics of the present or former similar projects, so they are metric-based approaches.

Hence, C is correct and A, B, D are incorrect.

Question 32. (FL-1.5.2)

Correct answer: D

Emotional attitude to their own code results in the fact that developers think positively about their code. If they are asked to test their own code, they will usually design the test cases that confirm their way of thinking about the software—because they wrote this code. Testers do not have such an attitude, so it is easier for them to think about creative ways of testing the software that may reveal a lot of bugs. Hence D is correct.

A and B are incorrect. As these two sentences may be true, they are not the answer for the question (they do not explain why testers may be more efficient in testing than developers).

C is incorrect, because the developer's responsibility is not only to write code, but to write a good quality code. Each team member—including the developers—is personally responsible for the product quality. Besides, developers often perform unit and integration tests of their own code.

Question 33. (FL-1.4.3)

Correct answer: D

High-level test cases are the test cases without concrete values for input data and expected results. Such high-level test cases can be reusable across multiple test cycles with different concrete data, while still adequately documenting the scope of the test case. Hence, D is correct, as this is an example of a test case, containing preconditions, steps to perform, expected results and postconditions.

A is incorrect, because a test suite is a set of (usually ordered) test cases.

B is incorrect, because a low-level test case must have concrete input data and concrete expected results. The artifact operates only with general notions, like "fill up the form with the *valid data*."

C is incorrect, because a test condition is something that can be verified by a test. Usually, this is some function or characteristic of a system under test. Here we have described some test steps to execute, together with the (general) input and expected results. This is definitely not something that can be verified by a test, but an example of a test case.

Question 34. (FL-3.2.4)

Correct answer: B

The business rule says that the file should be rejected if its size exceeds 1 GB, but in the model, the boundary given is not 1 GB, but 1 MB. Hence, there is an inconsistency with the business rule.

A is incorrect. There is a potentially infinite loop in the model, but the business requirement does not restrict the number of tries of sending too large file.

C is incorrect, because the business requirement states that any file can be sent through the form.

D is incorrect, because there is a defect—see B.

Question 35. (FL-4.2.2)

Correct answer: A

From the specification we know that T must be nonnegative, so T belongs to the set {0.01, 0.02, 0.03, …}. $0.01 is the smallest possible value of T that—after rounding (to $0)—results in no discount. $99.49, on the other hand, is the greatest value of T that—after rounding (to $100)—results in no discount. The next value, $99.50, would be rounded to $100, which belongs to another class (5% discount). Hence, A is correct.

B is incorrect, as T cannot accept value of $0.00.

C is incorrect—$100 and $299 are the boundaries of the total rounded price, but not for the domains of the T variable. In the case of "5% discount" class the boundary values would be $99.50 and $299.49.

D is incorrect, because $299.49 and $299.50 are the boundary values for different classes: $299.49 is the upper boundary for the "5% discount" class (because it will be rounded to $299) and $299.50 is the lower boundary for the "10% discount" class (because it will be rounded to $300).

Question 36. (FL-3.1.2)
Correct answer: C

Indeed, it is true that static techniques can be used much earlier in the project life cycle than dynamic techniques. Thanks to that, we can perform testing even when there is no single line of code written, by, for example, reviewing the requirements or software design.

A is incorrect, because the fact that static techniques can find defects other than dynamic techniques is not an advantage (otherwise, we might argue as well, that dynamic techniques are better, because they also find other defects than static techniques).

B is incorrect, because usually static techniques require more effort and therefore are more expensive than dynamic testing. Nevertheless, we cannot say in a definite way that one of these techniques is cheaper than the other.

D is incorrect, because it is exactly the opposite: static techniques can only detect defects, as they do not work on the executable software. Dynamic techniques find failures, because they work only on the executable software.

Question 37. (FL-5.6.1)
Correct answer: B

Notice that your intention is to provide an information for as quick defect reproduction, as possible. Hence, the most useful information will be the information about the environment in which the defect occurred: form name—because there may be many such forms, and system version—because other versions may work correctly. This way we don't force developer to waste time on guessing which environment configuration causes this defect.

A is incorrect, because this information will not help the developer in reproducing the defect.

C is incorrect. As this information may be useful for a developer when he is about to analyze and fix the defect, here we only want to help him in a quick defect reproduction—in this case, this information is useless.

D is incorrect, from the same reasons as A and C.

Question 38. (FL-4.2.5)
Correct answer: C

A standard coverage requires to have one test to cover the main scenario and one test for each exception. We have the following exceptions:

E1 in step 2
E1 in step 4
E2 in step 6
Resignation in step 1
Resignation in step 3
Resignation in step 5

Altogether we have 1 main scenario and 6 exceptions. Hence, we need 7 test cases.

Question 39. (FL-5.4.1)

Correct answer: B

One purpose of configuration management is to established and maintain the integrity of the testware through the project and product life cycle. When a user raises a bug, we need to know which version of the software is used, and which test cases (in which versions) were used for testing this version of the software. When the defect is fixed, a proper set of regression testing can be then done. Hence, B is correct.

A is incorrect, because this activity is connected with defect management, not configuration management.

C is incorrect, because bugs are not version controlled.

D is incorrect, because A is correct.

Question 40. (FL-6.2.1)

Correct answer: A

Answer A describes one of the main principles for tool selection, according to syllabus.

Answers B, C and D are related with the pilot project, so they are done after the tool is acquired.

Chapter 13
Answers to Question Set 2

Question 1. (FL-5.2.1)
Correct answer: B

Test planning is a continuous activity, because a feedback from the different activities impacts our plans, verify planning assumptions, and so on. Hence, B is correct.

A and C are incorrect (see B).

D is incorrect. It is not true that in the iterative models, we should avoid test planning. Every rational approach to testing starts with planning. Otherwise, the project may turn into chaos.

Question 2. (FL-1.3.1)
Correct answer: D

Pesticide paradox says that if the same tests are repeated over and over again, eventually the same set of test cases will no longer find any new defects. To overcome this "pesticide paradox," test cases need to be regularly reviewed and revised, and new and different tests need to be written to exercise different parts of the software or system to find potentially more defects. Hence, D is correct. Notice that the name of this principle is unfortunate, because in fact, there is absolutely no paradox in the above-mentioned fact.

A is incorrect, because the test techniques are a way to somehow "overcome" the other principle, "Exhaustive testing is impossible."

B is incorrect, because this is another testing principle, "Early testing."

C is incorrect, because aligning strategy to context is an example of realization of other testing principle "Testing is context dependent" and has nothing to do with pesticide paradox.

Question 3. (FL-1.2.3)
Correct answer: C

C is correct. Executing the defect in code during testing may result in completely normal and correct situation. Consider the following piece of Java code presenting a

© Springer Nature Switzerland AG 2018
A. Roman, *A Study Guide to the ISTQB® Foundation Level 2018 Syllabus*,
https://doi.org/10.1007/978-3-319-98740-8_13

function numZero() that counts the number of zero elements in a table *x* of integers, given as input to this function.

```
 1 public static int numZero(int [] x) {
 2  // Effects: if x==null throw NullPointerException,
 3  // else return the number of occurences of 0 in x
 4 int count = 0;
 5 for (int i=1; i<x.length; i++)
 6 {
 7   if (x[i]==0)
 8   {
 9    count++;
10   }
11 }
12 return count;
13 }
```

This code has defect in line 5, because in Java table, elements are indexed from 0, not from 1 (so the first element in the table is x[0], not x[1]). Now, suppose we execute this incorrect function giving as the input the array (1, 0, 2, 0, 4, 6). numZero will search zeros from the second element, but fortunately, the first element is a non-zero element. Hence, numZero will correctly return 2. However, if we invoke the same function with the array (0, 1, 2, 3, 4), it will return 0, because it will not analyze the first element.

A is incorrect, because failures are caused by defects, which in turn are caused by errors.

B is incorrect, because code review is a static technique, so we do not execute any software. Failures can be observed only with a software that is running. Static techniques can reveal defects, not failures.

D is incorrect, because some failures can be caused by environmental factors, like radiation, which are independent of human activity. For example, a radiation or a high temperature can damage the electronic circuit with the perfect, defect-free software written on it.

Question 4. (FL-5.2.3)
Correct answer: C

This criterion is a typical thoroughness criterion; hence, it is rather an exit criterion. As it refers to failures, it has to be verified after test execution Hence, it fits as an exit criterion for the test execution phase, so C is correct.

A and B are incorrect. Even if we treat this as an entry criterion, design and implementation phases are too early for this criterion to be applied, since it requires test execution.

D is incorrect, as this is too late—in the completion phase, we don't fix defects, so it makes no sense to condition the end of this phase on number of failures of a given type.

Question 5. (FL-1.4.4)

Correct answer: D

Establishing and maintaining traceability across the artifacts produced within the testing process allows us to implement effective test monitoring and control. In our case, by having the traceability between test cases and risk items, we can calculate the residual risk by analyzing the risks traced back to the tests that were not executed or that were executed and failed. Hence, D is correct.

A is incorrect, because we do not have the traceability between test cases and functional requirements.

B is incorrect, because statement and decision coverage can be calculated during the test cases execution. Traceability between test cases and risk items has nothing to do with these calculations.

C is incorrect, because risk level is specified during the risk analysis. It cannot be derived from the test results. We can, however, calculate the total risk level for the tests that did not pass, but this is the reason why D is correct.

Question 6. (FL-4.1.1)

Correct answer: A

In white-box techniques, a tester derives test cases from the knowledge about the internal software structure. An example of such internal structure is an architectural design, which may be the test basis for integration or system white-box testing. Hence, A is correct.

B is incorrect, because when we derive tests from the specification, we treat the software as a black-box—hence, B refers to the black-box techniques.

C is incorrect, because for generating random inputs, we don't need to know anything about the internal software structure.

D is incorrect, because this is a typical example of an experience-based technique.

Question 7. (FL-2.3.3)

Correct answer: D

Confirmation testing is conducted after a defect is detected and fixed. It confirms that the original defect was indeed removed. As we do not know when a failure related to a given defect will occur, the confirmation testing cannot be planned in advanced. Hence, D is correct.

All other types of testing can be perfectly planned and put in a test plan or test schedule. In case of regression, sometimes it *may* not be able to plan it in advance, when we perform the regression testing after a fix has been done. However, in most cases, regression is performed due to a change. Usually, it can be planned.

Question 8. (FL-5.1.2)

Correct answer: C

According to syllabus, supporting the selection and implementation of tools to support testing is the responsibility of a test manager, not tester.

A and B are incorrect, because preparing test data and test automation are the typical engineering tasks performed by a tester.

D is incorrect. Although tests are planned by a test manager, it is the tester's task to help him in this activity by providing his expert opinion.

Question 9. (Chapter 1 Keywords)
Correct answer: B

A is incorrect, since a comparator is a type of test tool that performs automated test comparison of actual result with expected result. The comparator can only *compare*, it cannot tell us the expected result.

C is incorrect, since test specification is a documentation of the test design, test cases and test procedures for a specific test item. It *may* contain the information about the expected results, but its definition is different from the one in the stem, which refers to the test oracle.

D is incorrect, since test basis is the body of knowledge used as the basis for test analysis and design—this is not the definition of the test oracle.

Question 10. (FL-5.2.4)
Correct answer: B

As test cases have some preconditions on the database content and test cases manipulate with this content, there are some relationships between test cases that should be considered when defining the test execution order.

At the beginning the CRM database is empty. First we should run TC2, because preconditions for TC1 and TC3 are not fulfilled. If T2 passes, the CRM database has 1 record. As TC3 does not change the database state and TC1 requires at least two tests in the database, we can run TC2 again, then TC3, and, as the last one, TC1. Notice that the sequence TC2, TC3, TC2, TC1 would also be correct. Hence, B is correct.

A and D are incorrect, because after executing T2 only once, we are not able to run TC1, as it requires at least two records in the database.

C is incorrect. Despite the test case execution sequence is correct, it is longer than in case of B, so it takes more time.

Question 11. (FL-2.1.1)
Correct answer: B

V-model integrates development with test activities so that each development phase has a corresponding test activity which can begin in the same phase. Requirements are related with the final user needs; hence, they will be tested (using, e.g., validation techniques) at the final, acceptance testing phase. However, V-model allows us to design these tests basing on the requirements in the "Requirements" phase. Therefore, B is correct.

A is incorrect, because V-model gives us the opportunity to perform test tasks within the corresponding development phases.

C is incorrect, because it is too early—we are not ready to perform any activities for iteration testing. We need to have at least the detailed architectural design, but the phase in which it is created has not yet begun.

D is incorrect, because performing a code review requires a code that can be reviewed. We are currently in the "Requirements" phase of the *sequential* process, so the code does not yet exist.

Question 12. (FL-4.2.4)
Correct answer: A

A 0-switch is a single transition that can be described by a triple (state, event, next state). We have 7 such transitions:

1. (S1, LoginOK, S2)
2. (S2, Logout, S5)
3. (S2, PrintReport, S4)
4. (S2, Modify, S3)
5. (S2, NewClient, S3)
6. (S3, SaveData, S2)
7. (S4, ReportFinished, S2)

Notice that although there is only one arrow from S2 to S3, in fact, it represents two parallel transitions: one for the event "Modify" and the other for the event "NewClient." In order to calculate the number of 0-switches, it is better to calculate the number of arrow labels, than the number of arrows themselves, as one arrow may represent more than one transition.

To cover all 0-switches we have to provide a set of test cases such that each transition is present in at least one test. Notice, that we can achieve 0-switch coverage with just one test:

S1 → LoginOK → S2 → Modify → S3 → SaveData → S2 → NewClient → S3 → SaveData → S2 → PrintReport → S4 → ReportFinished → S2 → Logout → S5.

This test covers all seven 0-switches identified above. Hence, A is correct and B, C, D are incorrect.

Question 13. (FL-3.1.1)
Correct answer: D

According to the syllabus, "reviews can be applied to any work product that the participants know how to read and understand." Hence, D is correct.

A is incorrect—although in practice, it indeed may be impractical to perform a review for 50 test scripts, theoretically, it is possible. In case of a critical system, it is likely that such a review would happen.

B is incorrect—although the test plan is a high level document that should be followed, there may be a need to review it, for example in order to weaken some of the exit criteria.

C is incorrect—requirements specification may contain serious architectural defects and definitely should be subject to review.

Question 14. (FL-6.1.1)

Correct answer: A

Every tool a tester uses is a test tool. Since tests can be specified and written using a word processor, it can be classified as a tool supporting test specification. Hence, A is correct and B, C, D are incorrect.

Question 15. (FL-4.2.5)

Correct answer: A

The standard use-case coverage requires one to provide:

- One test for realizing the main scenario (with no exceptions; sometimes this scenario is called a "happy path")
- One test for realizing each exception

Hence, we shouldn't test the occurrence of more than one exception within one test case. In test case A, two exceptions occurred in one test case: E1 and E2. Therefore, A is correct.

B, C, and D are incorrect. In fact, to cover this use-case, we should provide the three test cases described in these three answers.

Question 16. (FL-4.2.1)

Correct answer: C

For a partition of a domain into equivalence classes to be valid, the following two conditions must hold:

- Every domain element must belong to exactly one equivalence class.
- Each equivalence class must be non-empty.

These conditions are fulfilled by partitions described in answers A, B, and D; hence, these answers are incorrect.

C is correct. This is an example of an incorrect partitioning, because elements Mon and Tue belong to two different classes.

Question 17. (FL-1.5.1)

Correct answer: B

Unconstructive communication leads to potential conflicts in the team. Hence, B is correct.

A is incorrect. Decreasing the team effectiveness may be caused by the unconstructive communication, but this would be an indirect cause.

C is incorrect, because causing problems usually don't solve another ones.

D is incorrect. The explanation is similar as in case of A.

Question 18. (FL-4.4.2)

Correct answer: D

Test charters are used by exploratory testers. Test charters contain test objectives to guide the testing during the exploratory testing session. Hence, D is correct and A, B, C are incorrect.

Question 19. (FL-3.2.4)
Correct answer: A

In the role-based reviewing the reviewers evaluate the work product from the perspective of individual stakeholder roles. Typical roles include specific end user types (e.g., experienced, inexperienced, elderly, etc.). This approach is well aligned with the concept of personas—this way the testers will review the interface from the different user types' points of view.

B is incorrect, because the perspective-based approach focuses on different stakeholder viewpoints, like end user, marketing, designer, tester, operations, etc. In our scenario, there is only one stakeholder's viewpoint: an end user who is a bank client.

C is incorrect, because in a checklist-based review, the reviewers detect issues based on checklists that are distributed at review invitation. In our scenario, there are no checklists mentioned.

D is incorrect, because with scenario-based reviewing, reviewers are provided with structured guidelines on how to read through the work product. The concept of personas describes the general types of the clients, but is not a structured guideline on how to review the user interface.

Question 20. (FL-3.2.5)
Correct answer: B

B is correct per syllabus. A, C, and D are incorrect, because they are people-oriented success factors, not organizational factors.

Question 21. (FL-2.4.2)
Correct answer: D

By definition, impact analysis tells us what will be the possible impact of a given change in the different process and product areas. In particular, impact analysis:

- Evaluates the changes that were made for a maintenance release
- Identifies the intended consequences and side effects of a change
- Identifies the areas in the system that will be affected by the change
- Helps to identify the impact of a change on existing tests

Hence, D is correct and A, B, C are incorrect.

Question 22. (FL-2.3.2)
Correct answer: D

Structural testing is not only a development task, since white-box software models can be used on all test levels, even the ones at which developers usually do not test. For example:

- Control flow graph is a model of a code and can be used at the component testing level.
- Call graph is a model of communication between components and can be used at the integration testing level.

- Business process flow modeled in a Business Process Modeling Notation (BPMN) is a model of an end-to-end process realized on a high level and can be used at the system testing.
- Data, operating, or menu structure models can be used as the acceptance system testing.

Hence, D is correct and A, B, C are incorrect.

Question 23. (Chapter 4 Keywords)
Correct answer: B

Boundary value analysis (BVA) is based on the equivalence partitioning, because when we want to apply the BVA, the first thing we have to do is to perform the equivalence partitioning of an ordered domain. Then, we identify the boundary values for each identified class. Hence, B is correct.

A is incorrect, since exploratory testing is an experience-based test technique and has nothing to do with any formal test technique like equivalence partitioning.

C is incorrect, because decision table testing refers to the business logic, while equivalence partitioning refers to the domain analysis. Of course we can apply equivalence partitioning which can be used in the decision tables (e.g., the set of all possible values of a given condition may be represented by the equivalence classes of some domain), but in general, these are two completely different techniques. Decision table testing may use equivalence partitioning, but is not an extension of this technique.

D is incorrect, because "equivalence classes" is a synonym for "equivalence partitioning."

Question 24. (FL-4.2.1)
Correct answer: A

We need to cover the equivalence classes that come from the three different partitions of the set of all possible strings, according to (1) the string length, (2) the presence of at least one digit, and (3) the presence of at least one capital letter. Notice that each of these partitions is the partition of the same set of all strings, but with different partition criterion applied. We have the following classes to cover:

(1 V) – valid class for (1); that is—all strings with six or more characters
(1 INV) – invalid class for (1); that is—all strings with less than six characters
(2 V) – valid class for (2); that is—all strings with at least one digit
(2 INV) – invalid class for (2); that is—all strings without digits
(3 V) – valid class for (3); that is—all strings with at least one capital letter
(3 INV) – invalid class for (3); that is—all strings without capital letters

As partitionings (1), (2), and (3) are independent of each other, each test will cover three equivalence classes—one for each partitioning. From the scenario, we know that each test can cover at most one invalid class for one partitioning. In such a case, the partitions covered for two other partitionings must be valid. Hence, the minimal number of tests is 4: one that covers all valid partitions, and one for covering each invalid one.

Answer A is correct, because

ABC123 covers (1 V), (2 V), and (3 V)—the correct password.

AB1 covers (1 INV), (2 V), and (3 V)—the password with digits and capital letters, but too short.

ABCDEF covers (1 V), (2 INV), (3 V)—the password with valid length and capital letters, but without digits.

123456 covers (1 V), (2 V), and (3 INV)—the password with valid length and with digits, but without capital letters.

B is incorrect. Although there are four tests, the string "ABC" covers two invalid partitions: (1 INV) and (2 INV)—too short and without digits—which violates the imposed rules.

C is incorrect. Although there are four tests, the string "ab1" covers two invalid partitions: (1 INV) and (3 INV)—too short and without capital letters—which violates the imposed rules.

D is incorrect. The strings "Abc12" and "Ab1" cover the same equivalence classes, (1 INV), (2 V), and (3 V), so they are redundant.

Question 25. (FL-4.2.3)

Correct answer: D

If there were no constraints between the variables "age" and "education," there would be $4 \times 3 \times 2 = 24$ combinations of age, education and place ov living. However, we must exclude all combinations with age = "under 18" and education = "undergraduate" or "graduate." These excluded combinations are

1. age = under 18, education = undergraduate, place of living = city
2. age = under 18, education = undergraduate, place of living = village
3. age = under 18, education = graduate, place of living = city
4. age = under 18, education = graduate, place of living = village

As we need to exclude these four infeasible combinations, the corresponding decision table will have $24 - 4 = 20$ columns. Hence, D is correct and A, B, C are incorrect.

Question 26. (FL-5.5.2)

Correct answer: B

Per syllabus. B is an example of a product risk, hence B is correct.

A is incorrect, as this is not a risk.

C and D are incorrect, because these are the examples of the project, not product risks.

Question 27. (FL-5.2.6)
Correct answer: C

This is a classical example of a mathematical modeling which involves different metrics (like the number of defects found in a given phase). The test effort is thus estimated based on metrics and the knowledge about the former similar projects. Hence, C is correct.

A is incorrect, because in an expert-based approach we use the experience of the owners of the testing tasks or experts. Our model does not use any expert knowledge.

B and D are incorrect, because both risk-based approach and methodical approach are the types of the test approach, not a test estimation technique.

Question 28. (FL-5.5.3)
Correct answer: D

The question asks about how product risk analysis may influence the *thoroughness* and *scope* of testing. If the analysis indicates that 70% of the high level risks are related to security issues, and the team concludes that the security testing is therefore very important, this is a classical example of defining the thoroughness and scope of testing. Hence, D is correct.

A is incorrect, because this is an example of a project, not product risk.

B is incorrect, because preparing the contingency plans is not an example of influencing the thoroughness and scope of testing, but rather how to prepare in case that a given risk occurs.

C is incorrect, because *performing* some actions according to the results of the risk analysis is the risk mitigation activity, not a risk analysis activity.

Question 29. (FL-1.2.4)
Correct answer: A

Answer A is a definition of a root cause analysis—the activity of analyzing the defect to identify the cause as well as its containment, corrective and preventive actions so that the defect's reoccurrence can be avoided. Root cause analysis is a part of process improvement.

B is incorrect, as debugging only fixes the defect and does not look deeper, to the root cause of this defect.

C is incorrect, because reviews find defect, but do not analyze the root causes of them.

D is incorrect, because dynamic testing tries to cause failures, not analyze the root causes of defects.

Question 30. (FL-6.1.3)
Correct answer: C

In a keyword-driven approach, each keyword needs to be programmed in the form of a script. Hence, we need some technical expertise in scripting, so C is correct.

A, B, and D are incorrect, because they are irrelevant to the keyword-driven approach.

Question 31. (FL-2.2.1)
Correct answer: C

The objective of the acceptance testing is to check the behavior and capabilities of the whole system or product, usually from the user's perspective. The scenario suggests that we should perform contractual and regulatory acceptance testing, as there are some law regulations regarding invoice processing. Hence, the best test basis will be the legal regulations describing requirements for invoice processing.

A is incorrect, because architectural design may be helpful in system integration testing, when testers try to perform the verification of the correct implementation of interfaces between systems. Architectural design will not be helpful in validating if the whole product fulfils the user's needs.

B is incorrect from the same reason as A.

D is incorrect, because source code may serve as a test basis in low-level, white-box testing, like component testing. It will not be helpful in performing end-to-end scenarios on a fully integrated system.

Question 32. (FL-5.3.1)
Correct answer: B

Per syllabus, metrics are used, among others, to assess the progress against the planned schedule and budget, so they are needed in monitoring and reporting activities. Thanks to them we are able to detect that there is something wrong in the process and undertake conscious and rational actions to overcome these problems. Hence, B is correct and A, C, D are incorrect.

Question 33. (FL-1.4.2)
Correct answer: C

Testability evaluation takes place in the test analysis phase, as this is the analytical activity. Hence, C is correct.

A is incorrect—if we want to check the testability of the test items, we need to have these objects in place, which takes place in the test design phase. So this phase is too early for testability evaluation.

B is incorrect from the same reason that A.

D is incorrect, because during the implementation phase we implement tests, so we need to know that test objects are testable—hence, this phase is too late for evaluating the testability.

Question 34. (FL-3.2.3)
Correct answer: C

Technical review is a type of review during which—among others—a group of technical experts gains consensus by evaluating alternatives, solving technical problems and making decisions. Hence, C is the most appropriate type of review in this situation.

A is incorrect, as the main purpose of an informal review is to detect potential defects. Usually, during the informal review the participants get some small benefit in an inexpensive way. However, in our scenario we need to decide about a very important thing.

B is incorrect, because the main purposes of a walkthrough are to find defects, improve the product, consider alternative implementations, evaluate conformance to standards and specifications.

D is incorrect, as the main purpose of inspection is to find defects.

Question 35. (FL-4.2.2)

Correct answer: B

There are two variables for which we can perform the boundary value analysis:

- Number of PIN digits
- Number of different characters used in PIN

For the first variable, the correct equivalence class is {4, 5, 6}, so the boundary values to be tested are 3, 4, 6, 7. For the second variable, the correct equivalence class is {2, 3, . . .}, so the boundary values to be tested are 1 and 2. Hence, we need to test PIN numbers of lengths 3, 4, 6, 7 and PIN numbers composed of only 1 digit type and of only 2 types of digits. Table 13.1 shows which test cases cover which boundary values.

As we can see, only test suite B covers all the identified boundary values. Hence, B is correct and A, C, D are incorrect.

Question 36. (FL-3.2.1)

Correct answer: A

Formal phases of the review are the following:

- Planning (defining the scope, effort, and timeframe, identifying review charac-teristics, selecting the people to participate, allocating roles, defining the entry and exit criteria for more formal review types, checking that entry criteria are met in case of more formal review types)
- Initiate review (distributing the work product, explaining the scope, objectives, process, roles and work products to the participants)
- Individual review (reviewing the documents, noting potential issues, questions and comments)
- Issue communication and analysis (communicating identified potential defects, analyzing potential defects, assessing ownership and status to them, evaluating and documenting quality characteristics, evaluating the review findings against the exit criteria to make a review decision)

Table 13.1 Test cases covering boundary values for PIN length and number of digits (Exam set 2, question 35)

Test case	PIN length				# of different digits used	
	3	4	6	7	1	2
A	123	1234	123456	1234567	–	–
B	949	0011	123123	6667778	33333	0011
C	123	1111	123456	1234567	1111	–
D	777	8888	999999	4444444	777	–

- Fixing and reporting (creating defect reports, fixing defects found, communicating defects to the appropriate person or team, recording updated status of defects, gathering metrics, accepting the work product when the exit criteria are reached)

Hence, A is correct.

B is incorrect, as defining roles is done at the planning stage.

C is incorrect, as allocating roles is done at the planning stage.

D is incorrect, as preparing for the review is done at the individual preparation; moreover, this activity is done by the reviewers, not moderators.

Question 37. (FL-5.6.1)

Correct answer: A

The system grants loans of no more than $10,000. The tester verifies the algorithm by entering an amount that exceeds this value and system allows for that. This defect shows that the system allows to do something that should not be allowed. The tester did not notice that this is the real problem here and he makes a mistake in step 4 when describing the expected result. The interest rate is not 12%, but is undefined in this situation. Hence, A is correct and B, C, D are incorrect.

Question 38. (FL-4.3.1)

Correct answer: B

The smallest possible decision coverage achieved by the test suite {Test 1, Test 2, Test 3} is 30%. This would hold if Test 1 and Test 2 cover exactly the same decision outcomes, and Test 3—the subset of these outcomes. The largest possible decision coverage is 80%. This would hold if all three tests would cover disjoint set of decision outcomes. So, the possible decision coverage achieved by these three tests is between 30% and 80%.

To illustrate this more figuratively, suppose there are 5 decisions in the code, each with two possible outcomes: TRUE and FALSE, as shown in Fig. 13.1. All the 10 possible decision outcomes are labeled with numbers 1, 2, 3, . . ., 10.

Let us analyze two different examples of a suite of three tests that cover resp. 20%, 30%, and 30% of the possible decision outcomes.

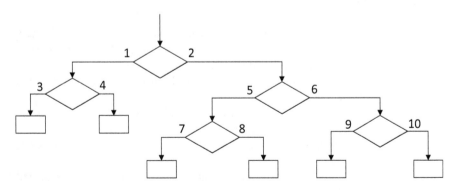

Fig. 13.1 An example control flow graph for a code with 5 decisions (Exam set 2, question 38)

If Test 1 covers the decision outcomes 1 and 3 (20%), Test 2—2, 5 and 7 (30%), and Test 3—2, 6, 10 (30%), altogether these three tests cover 1, 2, 3, 5, 6, 7 and 10, which gives us 70% decision coverage.

If Test 1 covers only the decision outcomes 1 and 3 (20%), and Tests 2 and 3 are identical and cover the decision outcomes 2, 5, 7 (30%), altogether these three tests cover 5 out of 10 decision outcomes (1, 2, 3, 5, 7), which gives 50% decision coverage.

Hence, B is correct. A, C and D are incorrect, because they are either less than 30% or more than 80%.

Question 39. (FL-4.3.3)
Correct answer: A

Achieving 100% statement coverage means to execute every executable statement at least once by our tests. Hence, A is correct.

B is incorrect, because 100% statement coverage doesn't guarantee 100% decision coverage, so we may not be able to test all possible program behaviors. Consider for example the following piece of code:

```
1 IF (x > 0) THEN
2    x := 0
  ENDIF
```

A test with (x=2) goes through executable statements 1 and 2, so it achieves 100% statement coverage, but it does not test the situation in which decision in line 1 is FALSE.

C is incorrect, because 100% statement coverage does not imply 100% decision coverage in general. See the code above.

D is incorrect, because it is possible to achieve 100% statement coverage for a code with decision points. For example, the code above has a decision point in line 1, but the test (x = 2) achieves 100% coverage.

Question 40. (FL-1.2.1)
Correct answer: C

C is correct, because finding contradictions in the requirements allows to fix them and not introduce other defects in the later phases of the SDLC. Usually the defects in the requirements are the design defects and—if not detected early—they can reveal in the later phases and the cost of their removal is usually much bigger than in case of removing them during the requirements inspection.

A is incorrect, because the testing process must be aligned with the SDLC, not the opposite. Besides, this does not explain why testing is necessary.

B is incorrect, because fixing defects is the responsibility of a debugging process, not testing.

D is incorrect, because testing itself has nothing to do with the way it is managed (*non sequitur* logical fallacy).

Chapter 14
Answers to Question Set 3

Question 1. (FL-4.1.1)
Correct answer: B
Foundation Level Syllabus describes five categories of black-box techniques. These are:

- Equivalence partitioning
- Boundary value analysis
- Decision tables
- State transition testing
- Use-case based testing

Answer B contains only black-box techniques, hence is correct.

A is incorrect, because statement coverage is an example of a white-box testing technique and error guessing is an example of an experience-based technique.

C is incorrect, because exploratory testing is an example of an experience-based technique, and system testing is a test level, not a type of test technique.

D is incorrect, because both integration and acceptance testing are test levels, not types of the test techniques. Defect-based testing is an example of an experience-based technique.

Question 2. FL-4.2.2
Correct answer: A
We need to test the following six boundary values:

- For the width: 4, 5
- For the height: 4, 5
- For the area: 35, 36

© Springer Nature Switzerland AG 2018
A. Roman, *A Study Guide to the ISTQB® Foundation Level 2018 Syllabus*,
https://doi.org/10.1007/978-3-319-98740-8_14

A is correct, because:

- The test (4, 9, reject) covers the boundary value 4 for height.
- The test (5, 4, reject) covers the boundary values: 5 for height and 4 for width.
- The test (7, 5, accept) covers the boundary values: 5 for width and 35 for area.
- The test (6, 6, reject) covers the boundary value 36 for area.

Answer B is incorrect, because, as we saw in A, 4 tests are enough. Test (5, 5, accept) is redundant.

Answer C is incorrect, because a test that covers boundary value 35 for area is missing.

Answer D seems to be correct, because we have all boundary values in these three tests: (4, 9, accept) covers boundary value 4 for height and 36 for area, (7, 5, accept) covers boundary value 5 for width and 35 for area and (5, 4, reject) covers boundary values 5 for height and 4 for width. However, there is a problem with test (4, 9, accept)—when height $= 4$, the expected result, according to the model, should be "reject." So we finish the process immediately and we are not able to achieve the decision point "decision < 35."   .

Question 3. (FL-1.2.1)
Correct answer: D

All four answers are good examples of why testing contributes to quality, but only answer D is related directly with validation.

A is incorrect, because validation is usually performed in the later phases and also cares more about the business quality (user's needs) than technical quality (lack of defects).

B is incorrect, because validation is usually performed in the later phases, while requirement analysis is usually done very early in the project, even when no single line of code is written. Validation activities are usually done for the working software.

C is incorrect, because it refers more to verification than validation activities.

Question 4. (FL-2.1.1)
Correct answer: C

Scrum, Kanban, Lean, and Extreme Programming are the examples of the iterative SDLC models (although, to be precise, Extreme Programming is more like a set of good practices rather than a well defined SDLC model). Hence, C is correct and A, B, D are incorrect.

Rational Unified Process, Rapid Application Development, and Boehm Spiral Model are the examples of incremental SDLC models, in which requirements are implemented in a series of short development cycles, called increments. These models often use prototypes, which are then evaluated and guide the following development works.

Waterfall and V-model are the examples of sequential SDLC models, where the development process follows a linear, sequential flow.

Test Maturity Model and Capability Maturity Model are models for assessing and improving the organization maturity. These are not the SDLC models.

Fundamental Test Process is an abstract framework describing the main, typical phases of any test process, so this is not a kind of a particular SDLC model.

Question 5. (FL-5.1.2)

Correct answer: D

According to syllabus, a support in setting up the defect management system and adequate configuration management of testware is the responsibility of a test manager. Hence, D is correct and A, B, C are incorrect.

Question 6. (Chapter 1 Keywords)

Correct answer: C

C is the glossary definition for "verification."

A is incorrect, because validation, although similar to verification, confirms that the requirements for a specific intended use or application have been fulfilled. Hence, validation is performed more from the business or client point of view. Verification, on the other hand, usually focuses on the technical aspects of the so-called internal quality.

B is incorrect, because debugging is a process of finding, analyzing, and removing the causes of failures in software. Hence, the trigger for the debugging process is a problem, not the intention of *verifying* that everything is OK.

D is incorrect, because root cause analysis identifies the root causes of defects. Hence, similar to B, it is triggered by *problems*, not the intention of *verifying* something.

Question 7. (FL-5.2.4)

Correct answer: C

We need to run only the performance tests—these are TC2, TC3, and TC6. TC2 and TC3 have high priority, but they depend on TC1, TC7, and TC6. But TC1 depends on TC7 and TC6—on TC5, which in turn depends on TC1. See Fig. 14.1— the performance test cases are denoted by gray rectangles and the arrows show the dependencies between the test cases. Notice that we do not need to run TC4, as it is not performance related.

So the final order of the test cases is as follows: TC7, TC1, TC2, TC5, TC6, and TC3. The final test case is TC3. Hence, C is correct, and A, B, D are incorrect.

Question 8. (FL-3.2.2)

Correct answer: B

A facilitator (also called moderator) is responsible for ensuring the effective running of review meetings. Hence, B is correct.

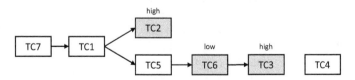

Fig. 14.1 Dependencies between test cases (Exam set 3, question 7)

A is incorrect, as the management is responsible for review planning; decides on the execution of reviews; assigns staff, budget, and time; monitors ongoing cost-effectiveness; and executes control decisions in the event of inadequate outcomes.

C is incorrect, as the author's responsibility may be to present/comment her work during the review meeting (if such a meeting is planned), but author does not have any moderating role.

D is incorrect, as the reviewer reviews the work product, but does not moderate the process.

Question 9. (FL-4.2.3)
Correct answer: A

If Registered user = F, then Action 1 holds and Action 2 and 3 do not hold, no matter what are the logical values of Conditions 2 and 3. Hence, first four columns can be collapsed into one. Also, columns 5 and 7 can be collapsed, because if only Condition 1 holds and Condition 3 does not hold, no matter what is the logical value of Condition 2, no action holds. We are left with columns 6 and 8, which cannot be collapsed, as they have different combinations of actions.

The collapsed table is presented in Table 14.1.

Recall that in some cases, there is more than one possibility to collapse a table. How can we know that 4 columns in our table is really the minimal possible number? Notice that we cannot collapse this table to less than 4 columns, because we have 4 different combinations of actions. Hence, 4 is the minimal number of columns in the collapsed table and A is the correct answer.

Question 10. (FL-6.1.1)
Correct answer: B

One of the important things done during the test execution is measuring the coverage achieved by the tests. This is a typical approach especially in case of white-box unit (component) testing. Hence, B is correct.

A is incorrect, because test data preparation tools are used for test specification, before the test execution phase.

C is incorrect, because configuration management area is not part of the test execution phase.

D is incorrect, because modeling tools support static testing and we perform dynamic testing.

Table 14.1 The collapsed decision table (Exam set 3, question 9)

	1–4	5, 7	6	8
Condition 1: Registered user?	F	T	T	T
Condition 2: Premium user?	–	–	F	T
Condition 3: Account active?	–	F	T	T
Action 1: Show error message "You are not registered"?	T	F	F	F
Action 2: Allow user to log in to the system?	F	F	T	T
Action 3: Assign a discount?	F	F	F	T

Question 11. (FL-3.1.2)

Correct answer: B

This is a classic example of a benefit from static technique (in this case, static analysis). Hence, B is correct.

A is incorrect, because we did not test the running software, we have just analyzed its properties.

C is incorrect, because measuring cyclomatic complexity is not a managerial activity.

D is incorrect, because static analysis is not an example of a formal test technique. Such technique can be equivalence partitioning, boundary value analysis, state transition testing, decision tables, use-case-based testing, etc.

Question 12. (FL-4.2.1)

Correct answer: D

The considered variable—discount—has only three possible values: 5%, 10%, and 20%. Each of them is a separate equivalence class. Hence, we need three tests, one for receiving each discount type. Hence, D is correct, as TC2 refers to 20% discount, TC3—to 5% discount, and TC4—to 10% discount. Notice that in TC4, before the last shopping, the client was typical, but the total amount spent after the last shopping exceeds 5000, so a client receives 10% discount and his status is updated to "regular."

A is incorrect, because three tests are enough.

B is incorrect, because TC1 ad TC2 cover 20% discount and TC4 covers 10% discount. Two tests cover the same equivalence class, and a test that would cover 5% discount is missing.

C is incorrect, because three tests are enough.

Question 13. (FL-1.1.1)

Correct answer: A

Defect correction is the objective of debugging, not testing. All other objectives (B, C, D) are the typical testing objectives.

Question 14. (FL-5.2.5)

Correct answer: B

Per syllabus. The requirements for quality characteristics (like usability, performance, security, reliability, etc.) are the product characteristics that influence the test effort. A, C, and D are the examples of development process or people characteristics.

Question 15. (FL-1.2.3)

Correct answer: D

An unreachable code is definitely a defect. However, as it will never be reached, it will never result in a failure. Hence, D is correct.

A is incorrect, because one of the universal testing rules says that it is impossible to detect all the defects—this may be an example of such defect.

B is incorrect, because unreachable code can be detected in a review.

C is incorrect from the logical consequences of the correctness of D.

Question 16. (FL-4.3.1)
Correct answer: D
Test 1 executes lines 1, 2, 3 (False), 5 (False), 9.
Test 2 executes lines 1, 2, 3 (False), 5 (True), 6 (True), 7.
Altogether these two tests execute lines 1, 2, 3, 5, 6, 7, 9. This is 7 out of 9 lines, so the achieved statement coverage is 7/9. Hence, D is correct and A, B, C are incorrect.

Question 17. (FL-4.4.1)
Correct answer: B
Fault attack is a structured approach to error guessing technique (per syllabus). In a fault attack, a tester generates a list of possible defects and designs tests to "attack" these defects, that is, to enforce a failure caused by them. Hence, B is correct and A, C, D are incorrect.

Question 18. (FL-2.4.1)
Correct answer: A
Retirement of a system is a trigger for maintenance testing: it may result, for example, in performing the testing of data migration or testing the restore/retrieve procedures. B is incorrect, because this is the effect of the trigger, not the trigger itself. C is incorrect, because the necessity of performing the risk analysis has nothing to do with maintenance testing. D is incorrect, because implementing the patches is the effect of a modification, which is one of the triggers for maintenance testing.

Question 19. (FL-4.3.2)
Correct answer: C
To achieve decision coverage, we have to evaluate each decision outcome to FALSE and to TRUE. For input $(x = 1, y = 1)$, both decisions in the code will be executed with TRUE outcome. For input $(x = 0, y = 0)$, both decisions will be executed with FALSE outcome. So, two tests are enough. Hence, C is correct and A, B, D are incorrect.

Question 20. (FL-2.3.2)
Correct answer: A
White-box testing can be performed at all levels, and for each, it can use different models representing the software internal structure, for example,

- Control flow graph or source code—on the component level testing
- Call graphs—on the integration level testing
- Business process models—on the system level testing
- Menu structures—on the acceptance level testing

Call graphs show the relationship between different functions, procedures, and subroutines and visualize how they invoke each other. Hence, A is correct.
B is incorrect, because a control flow graph may be used on the component level testing, as it models only a single component, not an integration between two or more entities.

C is incorrect, because a menu structure is suitable at the system testing level. It is far too general model to perform a white-box integration testing.

D is incorrect, because white-box testing can be performed at all levels.

Question 21. (FL-1.4.4)

Correct answer: A

A is correct per syllabus. B, C, and D are incorrect, as they are the results of having the effective monitoring and control, not the critical things that we have to do in order to achieve this effective monitoring and control.

Question 22. (FL-3.2.3)

Correct answer: A

Moderated review is an example of a walkthrough, technical review or inspection—not an informal review.

B is incorrect, because the casual conversation is an example of an informal review.

C and D are incorrect, because both pair review and buddy check are the examples of an informal review. The fact that the buddy check is perspective-based does not change its informal nature.

Question 23. (FL-5.5.3)

Correct answer: D

The actions we undertake should mitigate the risks. Hence, it is a good idea to perform an inspection of X to ensure that its structure will not be difficult to understand. Also, it is a good idea to conduct the performance testing of Y, as there is a risk of a slow response time.

A is incorrect, because usability has nothing to do with performance. Also, acceptance testing is not a good idea for verifying the complexity of a component.

B is incorrect, because integration testing will not verify the performance issues. Also, component testing will not calculate the cyclomatic complexity—some static analysis methods would be much better here.

C is incorrect, because we should mitigate the risk related to X.

Question 24. (FL-3.2.4)

Correct answer: B

The second requirement has the same ID as the third one (ID FR3), so this violates the statement R2. Also, this requirement imposes a technical (implementation) solution on the way the user data is stored. This violates the statement R3. No requirement conflicts with or duplicates other requirements—hence, the statement R1 is not violated.

Therefore, B is correct, and A, C, and D are incorrect.

Question 25. (FL-4.2.4)

Correct answer: B

The state machine that follows the rules described in the question is presented in Fig. 14.2. As states are pairs of numbers and each of these numbers can have one out of three values, the total number of states is equal to the number of combinations of these numbers, $3 \times 3 = 9$. There are two types of transitions: the ones labeled with

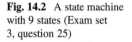

Fig. 14.2 A state machine
with 9 states (Exam set
3, question 25)

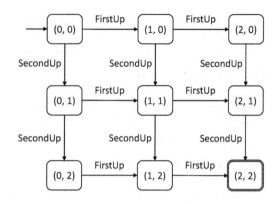

event FirstUp moves us right, and the ones labeled with SecondUp moves us down. Hence, we cannot return to any previously visited state.

To achieve the state coverage, notice that no two of states (2, 0), (0, 2) and (1, 1) can be present in one test case, as we cannot go from one of them to any other. Hence, we need at least 3 test cases to cover state coverage and this is indeed enough, for example,

TC1: (0, 0) → (0, 1) → (0, 2) → (1, 2) → (2, 2)
TC2: (0, 0) → (0, 1) → (1, 1) → (2, 1) → (2, 2)
TC3: (0, 0) → (1, 0) → (2, 0) → (2, 1) → (2, 2)

To achieve 0-switch coverage notice, that none two of the four transitions: (1, 0) → (2, 0), (1, 0) → (1, 1), (0, 1) → (1, 1) and (0, 1) → (0, 2) cannot be together in one test case. Therefore, we need at least 4 test cases and it is easy to see that the four test cases from Fig. 14.3 (denoted with bolded arrows) cover all transitions.

Hence, B is correct and A, C and D are incorrect.

Question 26. (Chapter 4 Keywords)
Correct answer: C

In white-box techniques the test conditions, test cases and test data are derived from the test basis that typically include:

- Code
- Software architecture
- Detailed design
- Any other source of information regarding the *structure* of the software

Hence, C is correct.

A and D are incorrect—these are the typical test basis items from which the test conditions, test cases, and test data are derived in the black-box techniques.

B is incorrect—this is true for the experience-based test techniques.

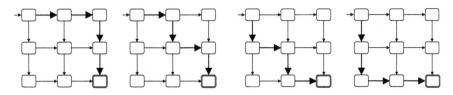

Fig. 14.3   Four test cases covering all 0-switches in the 9-state machine (Exam set 3, question 25)

Question 27. (FL-4.2.1)
Correct answer: B

The set of years is divided into two groups: leap years and non-leap years. Hence, to achieve 50% coverage we need only one test case. In fact, any valid input will be OK, so B is correct. Notice that we are not interested here in different "types" of leap or non-leap years. Each leap year falls into the same equivalence class, as well as each non-leap year falls into the same equivalence class.

A is not correct, because it achieves 100% coverage.

C and D are incorrect, because in each of these cases we obtain 50% coverage but these are not the smallest possible sets.

Question 28. (FL-3.1.3)
Correct answer: C

Static and dynamic techniques have the same objective (see also Sect. 1.1.1): identifying defects as early as possible. Hence, regarding the objective, there is no difference between them.

A is incorrect, because—although the sentence is true—it does not differentiate these approach regarding their goal. Notice that dynamic techniques directly detect failures, but indirectly—by analyzing these failures—they find defects.

B is incorrect, because it is not true—for example, reviews can be done in late phases, while dynamic testing can start during the implementation phase.

D is incorrect, because first it doesn't seem to be true, and second—this is not the answer to the question, in which we are asked about the differences regarding the *objectives*, not *skills required*.

Question 29. (FL-6.1.2)
Correct answer: A

This is a typical example of the overconfidence in a tool: we assumed that the test result must be correct, but probably there is some defect in the test script. Hence, A is correct and B, C, D are incorrect.

Question 30. (FL-5.2.2)
Correct answer: A

In the reactive test strategy, testing is more reactive to events than preplanned, and tests are designed and may immediately be executed in response to knowledge gained from prior test results. An example of this strategy type is the exploratory testing. Hence, A is correct.

B is incorrect, because risk identification is not a test strategy, but a part of the risk management process.

C is incorrect, because requirements-based strategy is an example of the analytical approach, not the reactive one.

D is incorrect, because fault attacks are an example of the methodical approach, not the reactive one.

Question 31. (FL-1.5.2)
Correct answer: A

Programming skills are not necessary to perform good tests. Manual testing is done without any code writing. Curiosity, attention to detail, and communication skills, on the other hand, are crucial for a tester. First two allow her to provide good, effective, and strong tests, which may find defects with high probability. Communication skills are crucial, because the tester is the "messenger of the bad news," so she must be able to communicate the negative things in a neutral, professional way. Hence, A is correct and B, C, D are incorrect.

Question 32. (FL-5.2.6)
Correct answer: A

There is no single best approach to estimation. Besides, a given estimation method may not be applicable under certain conditions. For example, if we do not have subject matter experts, the expert-based approach would not be a very good idea. On the other hand, if we do not have historical data and do not collect any metrics, metrics-based approach will be useless. Hence, A is correct.

B and C are incorrect (see A).

D is incorrect. It is always better to have some estimation—even not very accurate—than don't have any. Estimations are useful in the rational and reasonable planning.

Question 33. (FL-5.3.2)
Correct answer: B

The test reports should be tailored based on the report's audience. Burndown chart is used in the agile development techniques by the whole development team. Detailed information on defect types and trends in number of defects found and fixed is a technical information needed by a test team to drive the testing activities. A general summary of the defect status is an information appropriate for the higher management. Hence, the most typical relation is 1a, 2b, 3c; so, B is correct and A, C, D are incorrect.

Question 34. (FL-4.2.5)
Correct answer: B

A use case has only one main scenario. In this case, we have two main flows:

- Step 1, Step 2, Step 3, Step 4, Step 5
- Step 1, Step 2, Step 4, Step 5

We also know that in this use case, there are no exceptions. Hence, the use case is incorrectly designed. It should be split into two use cases: printing a reduced ticket (for users with age < 18) and printing a normal ticket (for users with age ≥ 18). Hence, B is correct.

A is incorrect, because a use case doesn't necessarily need to have exceptions.

C and D are incorrect, because B is correct.

Question 35. (FL-2.4.2)
Correct answer: A

In order to perform an impact analysis about the effort required to modify the test cases, we need to know which test cases are related to the requirements that have changed. So, we need a traceability between these two types of artifacts. Hence, A is correct.

B is incorrect, because risk does not influence the test case modification effort. Besides, from the scenario, we know nothing about the risk and its role in this process.

C is incorrect. It is true that to modify the automated tests we need to have programming skills and this factor impacts the effort, but we don't know if tests are automated. They may be manual, and hence programming skills are irrelevant.

D is incorrect. The fact that there are some project constraints, which may not allow us to perform some actions, has nothing in common with the possibility to estimate the effort to perform them.

Question 36. (FL-2.3.1)
Correct answer: B

Black-box testing is based on the specification external to the system. Hence (and according to syllabus, cf. Sect. 2.3.1) the typical black-box test types are functional and nonfunctional testing. Structural testing is based on the knowledge about the internal structure of the system, so this is a white-box testing. System and acceptance testing are the test levels, not test types. Hence, B is correct and A, C, D are incorrect.

Question 37. (FL-5.6.1)
Correct answer: B

There are different objectives of writing defect reports. According to syllabus these are:

- Provide developers and other parties with information about any adverse event that occurred, to enable them to identify specific effects, to isolate the problem with a minimal reproducing test, and to correct the potential defects, as needed or to otherwise resolve the problem.
- Provide test managers a means of tracking the quality of the system under test and the impact on the testing.
- Provide ideas for development and test process improvement.

As we raise a bug in the requirements, the reason is to inform about the problem people responsible for this area, who will be fixing it. We are in the requirement phase and the bug is related to the requirements. Hence, the natural recipient of your report should be an architect, who will fix the problem. Therefore, B is correct.

A is incorrect, because, according to syllabus, defects may be reported during coding, static analysis, reviews, dynamic testing, or use of a software product. This makes sense, because raising defects is one of the fundamental means through which the tester has to communicate problems to other stakeholders. Since testing should cover every single aspect of the product development, defect reports should be used throughout the whole life cycle.

C is incorrect, because the issue is related to a concrete bug in the requirements, not to some high-level issues which—when solved—could improve the process.

D is incorrect, because developers will not be fixing this bug. It is not a bug in the code, but a bug in the requirements. The person responsible for that is an architect, not a developer.

Question 38. (FL-1.4.2)
Correct answer: D

The phases of the test process are not sequential and we can go back and forth from one phase to another, skip some phases, return to another one many times, and so on. D is correct, because it directly refers to the situation described in the question (the order of test phases).

A is incorrect, because the fact that a defect was introduced in some phase does not necessarily mean that this defect will be detected in the following phase. It may be detected later, or even never be detected.

B is incorrect, because the test process is not sequential and we can move practically from any phase to any other.

C is incorrect, because—although the sentence may be true itself—it does not answer the question. It does not refer to the situation in which we "move back" in the testing phases.

Question 39. (FL-1.3.1)
Correct answer: A

Applying the Pareto rule[1] to defect distribution we can deduce that a small number of components contain a major part of defects. Hence, A is correct and B, C, D are incorrect.

Question 40. (FL-5.4.1)
Correct answer: A

Configuration management helps to uniquely identify and to reproduce the tested item, test documents, the tests and the test harnesses. It allows us to reconstruct the test object and the tests run against this object. According to the syllabus, "The purpose of configuration management is to establish and maintain the integrity of the

---

[1]The Pareto rule (called also Pareto principle, the 80-20 rule, the law of the vital few or the principle of factor sparsity) states that in many practical situations roughly 80% of effects come from 20% of the causes. If we are able to identify these causes, we can deal with them at first place, thus saving time and effort in eliminating negative effects.

component or system, the testware, and their relationships to one another through the project and product life cycle." Hence, A is correct.

B is incorrect, because it is not necessary that all configuration management data is gathered in one place. The repository may be distributed.

C is incorrect, because configuration management ensures that all items of testware are version controlled. There may be a need to reconstruct some old software, because a client that uses this old version raised a bug and we need to analyze it on this old version of software.

D is incorrect, because it is not the role of configuration management to ensure that something was tested. Besides, testing all software configurations may be impossible.

Chapter 15
Answers to Question Set 4

Question 1. (FL-5.2.1)

Correct answer: C

Test planning activities are recorded in a master test plan or in separate test plans for test levels. Hence, C is correct.

A and B are incorrect, because test strategy and test policy are documents more general than test plans. They describe how and why should testing be conducted within the whole organization. Any test planning must be aligned with these documents.

D is incorrect, because test report is a report, not a plan. It summarizes test activities after they are finished.

Question 2. (FL-2.1.2)

Correct answer: A

According to syllabus, Internet of Things (IoT) systems, which consist of many different objects, such as devices, products, and services, typically apply separate software development life cycle models for each object. This presents a particular challenge for the development of IoT system versions. Additionally, the software development life cycle of such objects places stronger emphasis on the later phases of the software development life cycle after they have been introduced to operational use (e.g., operate, update, and decommission phases). Hence, A is correct.

B is incorrect, because COTS do not necessarily need to consist of many different objects.

C is incorrect, because for the systems of systems, it is not necessarily important to place stronger emphasis on the later phases of the SDLC.

D is incorrect, because user interfaces do not necessarily need to consist of many different objects so that it would justify to apply separate SDLC models.

© Springer Nature Switzerland AG 2018
A. Roman, *A Study Guide to the ISTQB® Foundation Level 2018 Syllabus*,
https://doi.org/10.1007/978-3-319-98740-8_15

Question 3. (FL-4.3.3)

Correct answer: C

100% decision coverage means that we evaluated the *whole* decision at least once to FALSE and at least once to TRUE. The decision has logical form of a conjunction of two conditions: X AND Y, where X = "customer age < 18" and Y = "total amount > $100."

Evaluating this decision to TRUE means that the discount was assigned and evaluating it to FALSE means that the discount was not assigned. Hence, C is correct.

A is incorrect, because we can achieve 100% decision coverage with tests (X = TRUE, Y = TRUE, decision outcome = TRUE) and (X = FALSE, Y = TRUE, decision outcome = FALSE), but none of them has Y = FALSE.

B is incorrect, because we can achieve 100% decision coverage with tests (X = TRUE, Y = TRUE, decision outcome = TRUE) and (X = TRUE, Y = FALSE, decision outcome = FALSE), but none of them has X = FALSE.

D is incorrect (see A).

Question 4. (FL-4.2.1)

Correct answer: A

Since the set of boundary values is 1, 1976, 1977, 2019, 2020, and the boundary values represent minimal and maximal values of equivalence classes, the partitioning of the domain of Year must be as follows:

$$\{1, 2, ..., 1975, 1976\}, \{1977, 1978, ..., 2018, 2019\}, \{2020, 2021, 2022, ...\}.$$

Hence, A is correct.

B and C and incorrect, because boundary value analysis can be applied only to partitions "without the holes." This means that if x and y belong to the same equivalence partition, it follows that all values z such that $x \le z \le y$ must also belong to the same class. For example, 1 and 1976 belong to the class from B, but 2, 3, ..., 1975 do not. This class contains only the boundary values and has "holes."

D is incorrect, because if $\{1, ..., 2019\}$ would be an equivalence class, then 1976 and 1977 would not be the boundary values, as they are neither minimal nor maximal values for this class.

Question 5. (FL-2.3.3)

Correct answer: A

Regression test is any test that is executed to detect the unintended side-effects in case of a fix or a change that has been implemented. This means that the first execution of a test is not a regression. Since tests can be performed only in the test phases, and each test is executed only once in each phase, the only possible phases for regression are Test phase 2 and Test phase 3. Hence, A is correct and B, C, D are incorrect.

Question 6. (FL-4.2.3)

Correct answer: C

The full decision table is shown below (Table 15.1).

Table 15.1 The full decision table (Exam set 4, question 6)

	1	2	3	4	5	6	7	8
Condition 1: is he young?	T	T	T	T	F	F	F	F
Condition 2: does he take drugs?	T	T	F	F	T	T	F	F
Condition 3: did he have stroke?	T	F	T	F	T	F	T	F
Action: risk level	LOW	LOW	HIGH	HIGH	HIGH	LOW	HIGH	LOW

Table 15.2 The collapsed decision table (Exam set 4, question 9)

	1, 2	3, 4	6, 8	5, 7
Condition 1: is he young?	T	T	F	F
Condition 2: does he take drugs?	T	F	–	–
Condition 3: did he have stroke?	–	–	F	T
Action: risk level	LOW	HIGH	LOW	HIGH

We can collapse columns 1 and 2 (Condition 3 is irrelevant), 6 and 8 (Condition 2 is irrelevant), 3 and 4 (Condition 3 is irrelevant), and finally, 5 and 7 (Condition 2 is irrelevant). Hence, we obtain the collapsed table with only 4 columns (Table 15.2).

It is easy to observe that we cannot minimize the table with less than 4 columns. Hence, the correct answer is C.

Question 7. (FL-5.2.4)
Correct answer: D
The strategy implies that within the first two tests, we should cover functional and performance area. As we also have the priority criterion, these two tests should have the highest priority. For the next three tests, we should care only about the priority, as the first criterion will be fulfilled with the first two tests. Hence, D is correct: TC1 and TC2 cover both area and have high priority. TC4 has high priority. The last two tests, TC3 and TC5, have low priority.

A is incorrect, because TC3 should be replaced with functional test with high priority—otherwise, the first criterion is not fulfilled.

B is incorrect, because the ordering is done in a way such that the second criterion is more important than the first one: first we execute high priority tests and then low priority tests.

C is incorrect, because the second criterion is not fulfilled: first we execute low priority tests and then high priority tests. We should do the opposite.

Question 8. (Chapter 1 Keywords)
Correct answer: D
A is incorrect, because this is the definition of the test condition, not the test basis.

B is incorrect, because monitoring and control uses information from the test plans rather than information from the test basis.

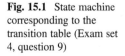
Fig. 15.1 State machine corresponding to the transition table (Exam set 4, question 9)

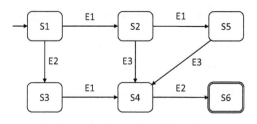

C is incorrect—although a test oracle may analyze test basis in order to derive the expected results, this would narrow the concept of the test basis, which is used primarily by a tester in order to achieve practically any kind of a test objective.

Question 9. (FL-4.2.4)
Correct answer: C

The graphical model of a state machine corresponding to the given transition table is presented in Fig. 15.1. To cover 0-switches (i.e., to cover all the transitions), we need three test cases. Notice that if a test case covers the transition (S1, E1, S2), we cannot return to S1 and cover (S1, E2, S3) within the same test, as there is no possibility of returning to the initial state. Hence, we need at least two test cases:

> TC1—that goes from S1 to S2
> TC2—that goes from S1 to S3

TC2 can continue only through S4 to S6. TC1 can go from S2 to S5 or to S4, but notice that it cannot cover both transitions (S2, E1, S5) and (S2, E3, S4). Therefore, we need one more test TC3. The final set of all three test cases is as follows:

> TC1—S1 → E1 → S2 → E1 → S5 → E3 → S4 → E2 → S6
> TC2—S1 → E2 → S3 → E1 → S4 → E2 → S6
> TC3—S1 → E1 → S2 → E3 → S4 → E2 → S6

As three tests are needed, C is correct and A, B and D are incorrect.

Question 10. (FL-6.1.1)
Correct answer: C

A tool that compares two files is an example of a comparator. Comparators are used by testers rather than developers, hence C is correct.

A and B are incorrect, because these are the examples of code-level tools related to component testing. They are beneficial to developers rather than to testers.

D is incorrect, because, as per syllabus, the dynamic analysis tools are used more often by the developers than the testers.

Question 11. (FL-1.1.2)

Correct answer: A

Debugging searches, analyzes, and removes the defects from the artifact being debugged. So, typically, it is the author who performs these activities, as he knows this artifact best. If this is a code, then debugging is usually done by the developer. Hence, A is correct.

B is incorrect, because testers test, and testing has nothing to do with debugging.

C is incorrect, because a debugger is a tool, not a person.

D is incorrect, because debugging is a technical activity done within the technical phases of SDLC—client do not take part in these activities.

Question 12. (FL-4.3.2)

Correct answer: D

We have three decisions in the code:

$$D1: N > 100$$
$$D2: K > N$$
$$D3: N = 0$$

Hence, we have 6 different decision outcomes to cover: TRUE and FALSE for each of D1, D2, D3.

TC1 (input $N = 299$) goes through D1 and immediately terminates returning error, because D1 is evaluated as TRUE, as $299 > 100$.

TC2 (input $N = 0$) goes through D1, which is evaluated as FALSE (because 0 is not greater than 100), then moves to D2, which is evaluated as TRUE (because $1 > 0$), and finally moves to D3, which is also evaluated as TRUE (because $0 = 0$).

The following table summarizes the decision outcomes coverage by these two tests (Table 15.3).

As we can see, our test suite covers 4 different outcomes out of 6 possible decision outcomes in the code. Hence, the coverage is $4/6 = 2/3$, so D is correct and A, B, C are incorrect.

Question 13. (FL-3.1.1)

Correct answer: D

Static analysis is a synonym of automated static testing. This method is done using a tool and is more applicable at code level rather than other work products such as requirements or other documents. Hence, D is correct. An example of a static analysis may be automated computation of software code metrics, like cyclomatic complexity.

Table 15.3 Decision outcomes coverage (Exam set 4, question 12)

Test case	D1 outcomes covered	D2 outcomes covered	D3 outcomes covered
1	TRUE		
2	FALSE	TRUE	TRUE

A, B, and C are incorrect, because these are the examples of documents, not the code.

Question 14. (FL-3.1.3)

Correct answer: D

Foundation syllabus notices that static and dynamic techniques have the same objectives, such as providing an assessment of the quality of the work products and identifying defects as early as possible. But they complement each other by finding different types of defects. Static techniques are able to find design defects, which are hard to find when performing dynamic testing. Dynamic testing, on the other hand, is able to find failures, which is not possible with static techniques, as static techniques do not work on a running software. Hence, D is correct.

A is incorrect, because both static and dynamic techniques can be applied on the same test levels. For example, both component review and unit testing can be conducted on a component testing level.

B is incorrect, because part of static techniques—static analysis—uses tools. On the other hand, we can perform manual dynamic testing, so we do not need to use tools in this approach.

C is incorrect, because both static and dynamic testing can be performed by tester (reviews, system testing) or by developer (static analysis, unit testing).

Question 15. (FL-5.3.2)

Correct answer: D

The report's abstraction level should be adjusted to the audience and the report's objective. Test report 1 is clearly a technical report, including many detailed metrics and information about particular test cases. It is more suited for a test team. Test report 2 presents the summative, aggregated, high-level information about test project status. Hence, it is more suited for high level management or client. Therefore, D is correct.

A and C are incorrect, because client will usually be completely not interested in technical details about the testing activities.

B is incorrect, because IT director will usually not be interested in a low-level information about some sub-process within a development process of one of the projects conducted in the company.

Question 16. (FL-5.2.5)

Correct answer: C

These are the typical factors influencing the test effort. Hence, C is correct.

A, B, and D are incorrect, because these are the examples of another factors influencing the test effort.

Question 17. (FL-2.3.1)

Correct answer: C

There are three main test types mentioned by a Foundation Level Syllabus. These are:

- functional tests—checking "what" a system does
- nonfunctional tests—checking "how" a system does something

- white-box tests—checking different properties basing on the knowledge of the internal software structure

Hence, C is correct. A and D are the examples of test techniques. B is a test level.

Question 18. (FL-2.4.1)

Correct answer: C

C is correct, because acquisition of a tool for supporting some process activities is not related to the software maintenance process, so it is not a trigger for performing the maintenance testing.

A, B, and D are enumerated in the syllabus as triggers for maintenance testing, so they are incorrect.

Question 19. (FL-4.4.2)

Correct answer: A

Exploratory testing utilizes tester's knowledge, intuition and experience, but gives him a whole room of maneuver for performing his actions. It does not matter if and which techniques he will use—the most important thing is to be effective in finding defects. So, although usually exploratory testing do not use any formal test techniques, it is possible for exploratory tester to use very formal, scripted testing during exploratory testing session. Hence, A is correct.

B and C are incorrect, because using test techniques in exploratory testing is not forbidden (see A).

D is incorrect. Although using testing techniques is allowed, it is not that we *must* use them to derive test cases. Exploratory testers usually do not design test cases, but test the software "on-line," in an interactive way. Their future actions are usually based on the current program behavior, their intuition, and experience.

Question 20. (FL-1.2.3)

Correct answer: B

An error is a human action that produces an incorrect result. A person can make an error (mistake), which can lead to the introduction of a defect (fault, bug) in the software code or in some other related work product. If a defect in the code is executed, this may cause a failure. Failures can also be caused by environmental conditions.

A is incorrect, because this is an example of a defect in the code, not a (human) error.

C is incorrect, because this is an example of a failure due to environmental conditions.

D is incorrect, because this is an example of a failure: a system does not perform a required function.

Question 21. (FL-3.2.1)

Correct answer: C

A and D are incorrect, because they are part of the planning activities.

B is incorrect, because metrics are gathered for more formal review types within the "fixing and reporting" activity.

Question 22. (FL-6.2.2)

Correct answer: A

As per syllabus, after the tool acquisition, a pilot project should be performed. Hence, A is correct.

B is incorrect (see A).

C and D are incorrect, as these activities are done during the test selection process.

Question 23. (FL-5.1.1)

Correct answer: B

Independent testers see other and different defects, and are unbiased, since they do not test their own products. Hence, B is correct.

A is incorrect, because isolation from the development team is a drawback, not a benefit.

C is incorrect, because this is just one of the organizational ways of working and does not explain directly any benefit or drawback.

D is incorrect. Although independent testing *may* be cheaper, usually it is not. Nevertheless, the cost is not the main reason of why independent testing is used.

Question 24. (FL-1.4.3)

Correct answer: B

Per syllabus, test cases are designed and executed to exercise test conditions defined in test analysis. Hence, B is correct.

A is incorrect, because test conditions may be derived from the risk item, not exercised.

C is incorrect, because requirements may be used to derive test conditions, not to exercise them.

D is incorrect, because test data is just a part of a test case, which exercises test conditions.

Question 25. (FL-4.2.5)

Correct answer: C

From the question stem we know that the exceptions may occur in the following steps:

Step 3—exceptions E2 and E3
Step 4—exceptions E1, E2 and E3
Step 8—exceptions E1 and E3
Step 9—exceptions E1 and E3.

Therefore, we need 1 test case for the main scenario (use case flow with no exceptions) and 9 test cases for testing each of the 9 occurrences of the exceptions E1, E2, and E3. Altogether, we need 1+9=10 test cases. Hence, C is correct and A, B, D are incorrect.

Question 26. (FL-3.2.3)
Correct answer: D

Walkthroughs may take form of a dry run, so that the review team will gain understanding about the way the software works. Hence, D is correct and A, B, C are incorrect.

Question 27. (FL-2.2.1)
Correct answer: D

Defect 1—unreachable code—is most likely to be discovered during the component testing, as in this phase we have access to the code. During higher-level testing we usually don't have this access, and since code is unreachable, we will never detect this fact.

Failure 2 describes some data flow between two components, so this is a communication issue. Hence, Failure 2 will be most likely detected during the integration testing, as this type of testing focuses solely on the integration and communication issues, not the components themselves.

Failure 3 describes a problem with wrong realization of a functional requirement. These kinds of failures are usually discovered during the system testing. At this level, the software is fully integrated, so we are able to perform tests that check functional and nonfunctional requirements.

Hence, D is correct and A, B, C are incorrect.

Question 28. (FL-1.4.1)
Correct answer: B

ISO/IEC/IEEE 29119—"Software Testing Standard" is a standard which—in its second part—describes the software testing process as a multi-layer model that consists of three layers: Organizational test process, Test management processes and Dynamic test processes. Hence, B is correct.

A is incorrect, because IEEE 829 is a test documentation standard.

C and D are incorrect, because ISO 9126 and ISO/IEC/IEEE 25000 (which replaced ISO 9126) are the standards for software quality, not for testing processes.

Question 29. (FL-4.4.3)
Correct answer: D

A checklist in a checklist-based approach should contain a list of test conditions, that is, the things that may be verified by a tester. Usability characteristics are a good example of such the test conditions. Such the checklist could be used during the usability testing.

A is incorrect, because information about test levels and test types is useless for a tester in this moment.

B is incorrect, because lists of defects are used in a fault attack technique, which is a structured approach to the error-guessing technique, not a checklist-based approach.

C is incorrect, because such checklist may be helpful as an organizational tool in a test automation project, but not in checklist-based testing. It does not inform us what should be tested.

Question 30. (Chapter 4 Keywords)

Correct answer: A

Test technique is a procedure to derive and/or select test cases. Test cases are derived from test conditions and contain test data. Hence, test technique must be able to identify test conditions, test cases, and test data (see Syllabus, Sect.4.1.). Hence, A is correct.

B, C, and D are incorrect—see above.

Question 31. (FL-3.2.4)

Correct answer: A

With scenario-based reviewing, reviewers are provided with structured guidelines on how to read through the work product. Where requirements, designs, or tests are documented in a suitable format (e.g., use cases, as in our scenario), a scenario-based approach supports reviewers in performing "dry runs" on the work product based on expected usage of the work product. These scenarios provide reviewers with better guidelines on how to identify specific defect types than simple checklist entries. This makes the option A most reasonable.

B is incorrect, because there are no checklists mentioned in the scenario.

C and D are incorrect, because they focus on roles and perspectives—they are not based on the use cases.

Question 32. (FL-1.2.4)

Correct answer: B

B is correct, because incorrect calculation is a failure, which may result from the low quality of the requirement specification (e.g., specification may be unclear or wrong about the rules for interest rate calculation).

A is incorrect, because every document can be reviewed. Besides, this is not an example of a failure.

C is incorrect, because this failure is more due to some problems with the nonfunctional requirements.

D is incorrect, because—although the root cause can result in this situation—wrong document's id is an example of a defect, not a failure.

Question 33. (FL-5.3.1)

Correct answer: C

Defect density is the number of defects per software volume. Hence, C is correct. B is a defect frequency. A and D have no reasonable meaning.

Question 34. (FL-4.2.2)

Correct answer: C

This is a tricky question. It is impossible to achieve full BVA coverage, because there are an infinite number of equivalence classes: $\{1, 2, 3\}$, $\{4\}$, $\{5, 6, 7\}$, $\{8\}$, $\{9, 10, 11\}$, $\{12\}$, and so on. To cover all the boundary values with the 2-point BVA, we would have to test the values 1, 3, 4, 5, 7, 8, 9, 11, and so on. Hence, C is correct and A, B, D are incorrect.

It is an interesting example of a problem for which in order to apply the BVA analysis, we need to reformulate it in terms of the standard equivalence partitioning technique. The natural test idea here is to check the behavior of the isLeapYear on the different types of boundaries. Let A, B, C, D denote respectively:

- A = a year not divisible by 4 (non-leap year)
- B = a year divisible by 4 and not divisible by 100 (leap year),
- C = a year divisible by 4 and 100, but not by 400 (non-leap year),
- D = a year divisible by 4, 100 and 400 (leap year).

The different "boundaries" to check are as follows:

- Two consecutive years of types A and A (e.g., 2001 and 2002)
- Two consecutive years of types A and B (e.g., 2003 and 2004)
- Two consecutive years of types A and C (e.g., 2099 and 2100)
- Two consecutive years of types A and D (e.g., 2399 and 2400)
- Two consecutive years of types B and A (e.g., 2004 and 2005)
- Two consecutive years of types C and A (e.g., 2100 and 2101)
- Two consecutive years of types D and A (e.g., 2400 and 2401)

Notice that there are no other possible sequences of types for two consecutive years. Now, we can partition the set of all possible years into seven equivalence partitions, reflecting the above mentioned "boundaries":

1. Years of type A such that their successors are of type A
2. Years of type A such that their successors are of type B
3. Years of type A such that their successors are of type C
4. Years of type A such that their successors are of type D
5. Years of type B such that their successors are of type A
6. Years of type C such that their successors are of type A
7. Years of type D such that their successors are of type A

Now we can apply the equivalence partitioning for this partition. In this way, we can check all possible "boundaries," that is, all possible sequences of the types of two consecutive years. The seven example years may be: 2001, 2003, 2099, 2399, 2004, 2100, 2400.

Question 35. (FL-1.1.1)
Correct answer: A
    Testing objectives are not "carved in stone" for every possible project. As testing is context dependent, its objectives vary depending upon the context. B is incorrect, because correcting defects is a debugging, not testing activity. C and D are incorrect, because we cannot say in general what is the main objective of a given test phase—it

always depends on the context, stakeholders, project constraints, and many other factors.

Question 36. (FL-4.2.2)
Correct answer: C

The equivalence partitioning for X is as follows:

- {1, 2, ..., 49, 50} for the output "student failed"
- {51, 52, ..., 89, 90} for the output "student passed"
- {91, 92, ..., 99, 100} for the output "student passed with distinctions"

As we already have the tests that cover all the boundary values for the 2-point boundary value analysis, we know that these values must be 1, 50, 51, 90, 91, and 100. To cover the boundary values for the 3-point boundary value analysis, we need to take both neighbors for each boundary. These are:

- 1 and 2 for boundary value 1
- 49, 50, 51 for boundary value 50
- 50, 51, 52 for boundary value 51
- 89, 90, 91 for boundary value 90
- 90, 91, 92 for boundary value 91
- 99, 100 for boundary value 100

Notice that we do not consider values like 0 or 101, because from the specification, we know that it is impossible to force inputs that lie outside the set {1, 2, ..., 99, 100}. So, in 3-point boundary value analysis, we need to cover points 1, 2, 49, 50, 51, 52, 89, 90, 91, 92, 99, 100. We have already covered 1, 50, 51, 90, 91, and 100. Hence, the missing test cases are for the values 2, 49, 52, 89, 92, and 99, so we need 6 more test cases. Hence, C is correct and A, B, and D are incorrect.

Question 37. (FL-5.2.2)
Correct answer: D

A state machine is a model that describes some aspect of the product under test. The coverage criterion drives the tester in designing the test cases from this model. Hence, this is a typical model-based approach and D is correct.

A is incorrect, because in the analytical approach, the test strategy is based on an analysis of some factor, for example, risk or requirements.

B is incorrect, because in the methodical approach, a tester uses some predefined set of tests or test conditions, such as a methodical checklist of common or likely types of failure, or a standard set of tests.

C is incorrect, because in the process-complaint strategy a tester follows some external standard.

Question 38. (FL-5.6.1)

Correct answer: C

Analyzing the trend of number of defects raised in time allows us to track the progress in system quality. If the testing process works correctly, the number of defects should decrease in time. The decrease rate may be an indicator when it is reasonable to stop testing and release the product. Hence, C is correct.

A is incorrect, because bug classification will not help us in tracking the system quality.

B is incorrect, because it is usually impossible to analyze all the bug descriptions; besides, the whole point of using a reporting system is the ability to create the summative, aggregated reports that can show us interesting trends or statistics.

D is incorrect, because this information says nothing about the quality itself. Rather it is some information related to the individual testers.

Question 39. (FL-1.2.2)

Correct answer: A

Quality assurance, in general, is a set of activities that *prevent* bugs from occurrence in the product. Therefore, quality assurance usually focuses on process elements of an organization. One example of such activity is defining a proper process for requirements definition, so that they are defined at the proper level of detail. This will reduce the risk that the bugs occur due to low quality of the requirement specification. Hence, A is correct.

B is incorrect, because measuring the process is a typical control activity, belonging to the testing process—so it is part of a quality control.

C is incorrect, because inspections are the static testing techniques, so inspections are also a typical part of quality control activities.

D is incorrect, because raising a defect report is a typical tester's task, related to the result of the control process. Hence, as B and C, this is also the part of quality control activities.

Question 40. (FL-5.5.2)

Correct answer: B

Quality risk is a product risk that is associated with specific quality characteristics of a product. A poor performance is a typical risk related to the quality characteristic, hence B is true.

A is incorrect, because this is an example of a project risk, not a product risk (hence, not a quality risk).

C and D are incorrect, because they are the examples of the functional risks, so these are not the quality issues.

Chapter 16
Answers to Question Set 5

Question 1. (Chapter 1 Keywords)

Correct answer: A

Traceability is defined as the degree to which a relationship can be established between two or more work products. In the figure, two types of such relations are presented: the relation between particular components and test conditions, and between the test conditions and the test cases. Thanks to traceability, we are able to trace back from the test case to the component(s), which it is related with.

B is incorrect, because a test suite is a set of test cases organized with a common purpose or test objective. The picture presents not only the test cases, but also components and test conditions.

C is incorrect, because impact analysis identifies all work products affected by a change, including an estimate of the resources needed to accomplish the change. The picture presents only the traceability between some work products. The traceability is used by the impact analysis, but it is not this analysis itself.

D is incorrect, because test basis is used as the basis for test analysis and design. In the picture, the products of test design (test cases) are already presented.

Question 2. (FL-3.1.2)

Correct answer: A

Only A refers to an example of static technique such as review. This is an example of detecting defects that might be hard to detect in dynamic testing.

B is incorrect, because test execution is an example of dynamic testing, not static technique.

C is incorrect, because planning is not a type of static technique—we do not really test anything in this process.

D is incorrect, because test automation is not an example of static technique.

© Springer Nature Switzerland AG 2018
A. Roman, *A Study Guide to the ISTQB® Foundation Level 2018 Syllabus*,
https://doi.org/10.1007/978-3-319-98740-8_16

Question 3. (FL-4.1.1)

Correct answer: A

The test cases were designed on the analysis of the test basis, without the knowledge on how the processing occurs. Then, a state transition technique was used. This is clearly an example of a black-box (or specification-based) technique.

B is incorrect, as we do not have any knowledge about the internal structure of the software. User stories are not a white-box model of a system.

C is incorrect, as experience-based testing uses knowledge, intuition, and experience of a tester and does not really rely on a formal test basis.

D is incorrect, as risk analysis is not a test technique.

Question 4. (FL-5.2.3)

Correct answer: A

Entry criteria allow us to verify, if we are well prepared for the forthcoming task in our project. Hence, A is correct.

B is incorrect, as this is the definition of the exit criteria.

C is incorrect, because entry criteria can be defined for any type of task.

D is incorrect, because entry criteria are internal, technical conditions used by team members for verification rather than validation.

Question 5. (FL-3.2.4)

Correct answer: A

First possible operation is CREATE, so every PUSH and POP are done after the stack is created. Hence, 1 is always fulfilled.

After CREATE we can immediately invoke POP, so we may try to pop the element from an empty stack. Hence, 2 may not be fulfilled.

If we PUSH an element and proceed one of the two loops, we will always perform the corresponding POP operation, so before reaching DELETE we will push and pop the same number of elements. Hence, 3 is always fulfilled.

If we PUSH an element, the next operation will always be POP, so the maximal stack size is 1. Hence, 4 is always fulfilled.

This means that A is correct and B, C, D are incorrect.

Question 6. (FL-5.1.2)

Correct answer: A

Depending on the test level and the risks related to the product and the project, different people may take over the role of tester, keeping some degree of independence. Hence, A is correct.

B is incorrect (see A)—we should not confuse the job position with the role in the project. A person can act in different roles holding the same job position.

C is incorrect, because the tester was moved from X to Y to support testing, because Y is short on testing stuff, so it makes no sense to take back another tester from Y to X.

D is incorrect. It is true that the manager is responsible for the success of the project, but he needs to act in a rational, reasonable, and optimal way. He cannot do

Table 16.1 Behavior of the machine with events, actions, and conditions (Exam set 5, question 7)

Step	State	Actual x value	Event	Transition covered	New x value	New state
1	S1	0	Inc	(S1, Inc/x := x + 1, S2)	1	S2
2	S2	1	Inc	(S2, Inc/x := x + 1, S2)	2	S2
3	S2	2	Dec	(S2, Dec/x := x − 1, S2)	1	S2
4	S2	1	Inc	(S2, Inc/x := x + 1, S2)	2	S2
5	S2	2	Inc	(S2, Inc/x := x + 1, S2)	3	S2
6	S2	3	Fire	(S2, Fire [x > 2]/x := 0, S3)	0	S3
7	S3	0	Inc	(S3, Inc/x := x + 1, S3)	1	S3
8	S3	1	Fire	(S3, Fire [x < 2], S4)	1	S4

whatever he wants, because bad decisions may harm the project. Hence, even if the first part of the sentence is true, the explanation is incorrect.

Question 7. (FL-4.2.4)

Correct answer: D

Consider the sequence Inc, Inc, Dec, Inc, Inc, Fire, Inc, Fire of events from answer D and let's see what happens in the machine. The machine behavior is presented in Table 16.1. The consecutive columns represent: step number, current state, the x value before invoking the event, invoked event, transition executed (and, at the same time, covered), the value of x after executing the transition, and the new state after transition execution.

In the first step, we invoke an event Inc going from S1 to S2 and increasing x by 1. In steps 2, 3, 4, 5 we resp. increase, decrease, increase, and decrease by 1 the x value, so after these steps $x = 3$. In step 6 we have an event Fire, which can be executed, since the condition $x > 2$ is true. Notice that the action $x := 0$ zeros the value of x. Hence, after moving to state S3 in step 6, $x = 0$. In step 7, we invoke Inc, increase x by 1, and stay in S3. Now $x = 1$, and in the last step we invoke Fire, which moves us to S4—again, this transition is possible, because the condition $x < 2$ is true. Notice that in these 8 steps, we covered all six different transitions in the state machine. Hence, D is correct.

A is incorrect, because in the sequence Inc, Dec, Dec, Inc, Inc, Inc, Inc, Fire, Inc, Inc, Fire after the 8-th event (Fire) we are in S3 and $x = 0$. Next two Inc increase x to 2, so the last sequence—Fire—is impossible to be executed, as the condition related with it ($x < 2$) is not true.

B is incorrect, because after first four transitions, we are in S2 and $x = 2$, so it is impossible to execute the Fire transition now, as the related condition ($x > 2$) is not fulfilled.

C is incorrect—although the sequence gives the correct behavior, we did not cover the transition (S2, Dec/x := x − 1, S2), so we did not achieve the 0-switch coverage.

Question 8. (FL-5.2.4)

Correct answer: A

Logical dependencies are the most important criterion: if a test case A can be executed only after the execution of a test case B, irrespective of the priorities, B must be executed first in order to run A. When we arrange test cases regarding the logical dependencies, we should first execute the ones with the highest priority. Test execution time is usually not an important criterion, but even if it is used, priority— according to the syllabus—is much more important criterion. Hence, A is correct and B, C, D are incorrect.

Question 9. (FL-1.4.3)

Correct answer: C

Test conditions, identified as part of test analysis, are the detailed measurable criteria that are used to validate the test basis (see also FL-1.4.2). For example, a test condition for a loan-granting system could be "check that a loan is granted for a customer who fulfills all the criteria defined in the requirements." Hence, C is correct and A, B, D are incorrect.

Question 10. (FL-2.1.2)

Correct answer: B

According to syllabus, not only software development life cycle models must be selected and adapted to the context of project and product characteristics, but also, depending on the context of the project, it may be necessary to combine or reorganize test levels and/or test activities. The syllabus gives exactly the example of integrating some COTS into an existing system. This requires integration testing on higher (system, acceptance) levels. Hence, B is correct.

A is incorrect, because we should expect that COTS is already tested at all possible levels.

C is incorrect, because our intention is to test the *integration* between two systems—this is our context of testing.

D is incorrect from the same reasons as A.

Question 11. (FL-6.1.1)

Correct answer: D

All test activities can be supported with the tools. The most trivial example is using a word processor, spreadsheet, or e-mail client to communicate with other stakeholders during any testing activity. Hence, D is correct.

A is incorrect, because in fact, usability testing can use very sophisticated tools, like eye-ball tracking systems, cameras, and so on.

B is incorrect, because test design can be supported by tool. In fact, it is a must in a model-based testing, where test cases are automatically derived (designed) from the models.

C is incorrect, because reports can be generated automatically. Of course, humans can interpret them and add some "creative" information, but the sole generation can be definitely supported by the tools.

Question 12. (FL-2.3.1)
Correct answer: D
D is a typical example of a nonfunctional testing. This is a performance test that checks "how" system works.

A and C check "what" the system does—so these are the examples of the functional testing.

B is an example of a white-box (structural), not nonfunctional test.

Question 13. (FL-4.2.2)
Correct answer: A
We are interested in achieving boundary value coverage only for the weight constraint. It says that the total weight of the ordered products cannot exceed 10 kg. This means that we need to test two boundary values: 10.0 kg (for the valid equivalence class; this is the maximal weight allowed) and 10.1 kg (for the invalid equivalence class; this is the lowest weight not allowed).

A is correct, because TC1 consists of four products whose total weight is $1.5 + 6.8 + 1.4 + 0.3 = 10.0$ and TC2 consists also of four products whose total weight is $1.5 + 6.8 + 1.4 + 0.4 = 10.1$. These two tests cover all the required boundary values.

B, C, and D are incorrect, because, as we saw in A, two tests are enough. Notice, that in case of D, we also cover the boundary value 5 for number of items, which is not covered in A. But we are not asked to cover these values.

Question 14. (FL-2.1.1)
Correct answer: D
Iterative models are best in situation, where the requirements are not well defined at the beginning, when we know in advance that the client may change her mind, etc. Iterative SDLC model allows us to be agile, when there is a need to change a requirement or to add a completely new one. Hence, D is correct.

A is incorrect, because sequential models work best in situation, where requirements are stable and well defined in the initial phase.

B is incorrect, because incremental models usually work with prototypes, so at least at some point, we should have the idea of the software as a whole.

C is incorrect, because—as can be seen from above—the SDLC model should be carefully chosen, as each model works well in certain circumstances. Adoption of a model that does not fit the project context may be very harmful to the project itself and to the product quality.

Question 15. (FL-3.1.3)
Correct answer: C
Dynamic testing finds failures during the execution. Static testing finds defects without executing the code. The typical defects that are easier and cheaper to find and fix through static testing include requirement defects, design defects, coding defects, deviations from standards, incorrect interface specifications, security vulnerabilities, test basis traceability or coverage gaps or inaccuracies, and maintainability defects.

A is incorrect, because this is an example of a requirement defect (requirement ambiguity).

B is incorrect, because this is an example of a maintainability defect.

D is incorrect, because this is an example of a deviation from standards.

Checking that the system allows to obtain the admin rights by an unauthorized user is possible by executing the software, so through the dynamic testing. Hence, C is correct.

Question 16. (FL-3.2.2)

Correct answer: D

After the review process, an author is responsible for fixing defects in the work product under review. Hence, D is correct.

A is incorrect, as mediating between the various points of view is the responsibility of a facilitator (moderator).

B is incorrect, as identifying potential defects in the work product under review is the responsibility of a reviewer. Of course, an author may also be a reviewer, but the question asks about the typical responsibility specific to the role of an author.

C is incorrect, as collecting potential defects found during the individual review activity is the responsibility of a scribe (recorder).

Question 17. (FL-4.3.1)

Correct answer: B

100% statement coverage requires that each statement should be executed in at least one test. The statement coverage is calculated as the number of different statements executed in tests divided by the total number of statements in the code.

In our code there are eight statements. The test 1, 3, 4, 3, 5, 6, 8 executes six statements: 1, 3, 4, 5, 6, 8. Hence, the coverage level achieved by this test is $6/8 = 75\%$. Notice that the fact, that we executed statement 3 twice, does not increase the coverage.

Question 18. (FL-4.4.2)

Correct answer: B

Exploratory testing is most useful when

- There are few or inadequate specifications.
- There is severe time pressure.
- Testers are experienced, and they have knowledge about the tested product.
- We want to augment or complement other, more formal, testing techniques.
- We want to verify the test process by helping to ensure that the most serious defects are found.

Hence, A, C, and D are incorrect. B is correct, because inexperienced testers will not be as effective in exploratory testing as experienced ones.

Question 19. (Chapter 4 Keywords)

Correct answer: D

Error guessing is a technique used to anticipate the occurrence of failures, based on the tester's knowledge, including:

- How the application has worked in the past
- What type of mistakes the developers tend to make
- Failures that have occurred in other applications

Hence, D is correct.

A is incorrect. In exploratory testing, informal (not predefined) tests are designed, executed, logged, and evaluated dynamically during test execution. Exploratory testing is therefore a "dynamic" approach—the tester's each next step depends on what has just happened in the current step.

B is incorrect. In the checklist-based testing, the tester uses an existing checklist (if available) or creates a list of test conditions and then design tests to exercise them. The checklists can be built based on experience, defect, and failure data, knowledge about what is important for the user, etc., but still the most important characteristic of this approach is the checklist created in advance, before the tests are designed and executed.

C is incorrect. Use case testing is based on the use cases, not on anticipating the occurrence of failures based on the tester's knowledge.

Question 20. (FL-3.2.5)
Correct answer: C

Training in review techniques is one of the success factors for a review. Hence, C is correct.

A is incorrect, because the main objective of inspection is to find defects. Evaluating alternatives is a good objective for technical reviews.

B is incorrect, because inspections are usually performed by peers. If a manager attends the review meeting, he may misunderstand the inspection's objective and may try to evaluate people based on their behavior during the meeting. This is a very bad and definitely not recommended practice.

D is incorrect, because collecting metrics helps in proceeding with a review and in improving the inspection process.

Question 21. (FL-1.1.2)
Correct answer: B

A developer found and fixed a code after a tester raised a bug. This is a classical example of debugging. Hence, B is correct.

A is incorrect, because during the inspection, the defects are not fixed—this is done later, during the debugging process. Besides, the inspection is a formal process involving many different roles like moderator etc.—this is not the case.

C is incorrect, because the testing activity was done by a tester. This resulted in a defect report. Now, the developer's task is to analyze this report and remove the bug that caused the failure.

D is incorrect from the similar reasons as A.

Question 22. (FL-1.3.1)
Correct answer: C

Undecidability of halting problem means that in general, we cannot determine if the system under test will finish its running. So we cannot say that this defect is not present in the code. Hence, this theorem justifies the testing principle saying that testing shows presence of defects, but cannot prove that there are no defects. We cannot, in particular, prove the halting property.

A is incorrect, because this rule is related to the validation process and client-centered view on a software quality. It says that the program can be perfectly OK, but it does not fulfill the client's needs. This principle cannot be really "proved."

B is incorrect, because the fact that we cannot decide if the software has the halting property does not prove that we cannot perform the exhaustive testing. If we would like to formally prove this principle, we could do it for example by showing that when there's a loop in the code, we are not able to test all possible control flow paths, because there are an infinite number of them.

D is incorrect, because pesticide paradox says that test effectiveness decreases in time, when the defects detected by this test are corrected. In fact, this is an obvious observation and it is no paradox, as the Syllabus claims (sic!). There's no need to formally prove this fact.

Question 23. (FL-6.2.3)
Correct answer: B

After tool acquisition we should perform a pilot project and after that, roll out the tool to the rest of the organization incrementally. Hence, B is correct.

A, C, and D are incorrect, because, as per syllabus, these are the success factors for tool introduction project.

Question 24. (FL-2.4.2)
Correct answer: C

Per syllabus, doing an impact analysis can be difficult if:

- Specifications are out of date or missing.
- Test cases are not documented or out of date.
- Bidirectional traceability between tests and the test basis has not been maintained.
- Tool support is weak or nonexistent.
- The people involved do not have domain and/or system knowledge.
- Insufficient attention has been paid to the software's maintainability during development.

Hence, C is correct.

A is incorrect, because requirement analysis in most part is done at the beginning of the project and software specification is built upon the requirements.

B is incorrect, because it is quite opposite: exploratory testing is useful in case of unclear of out-of-date requirements. Also, exploratory testing does not need any test cases to be performed.

D is incorrect, because specification review is simply a good idea to perform, in order to increase the specification quality.

Question 25. (FL-4.2.2)
Correct answer: D

The boundary has the form $w > 280$, where w denotes the total weight. Hence, we have only two equivalence classes: $\{\ldots, 279, 280\}$ and $\{281, 282, \ldots\}$. Their boundary values are 280 and 281, and since we use the 2-point boundary value

Table 16.2 Decision table built from specification (Exam set 5, question 26)

	1	2	3	4	5	6	7
Conditions							
Condition 1: Match result	Win	Win	Draw	Draw	Draw	Loss	Loss
Condition 2: Championships?	YES	NO	YES	YES	NO	YES	NO
Condition 3: Penalty kicks result	N/A	N/A	Win	Loss	N/A	N/A	N/A
Action							
Points assigned	3	3	2	1	1	0	0

analysis, these are at the same time the values that need to be tested in order to achieve the 100% coverage. Hence D is correct.

A and B are not true, since we have no information about the lower (resp. upper) boundary value for the first (resp. second) class. The only boundary that needs to be checked is $w > 280$.

C is not true. It would be true if we apply the 3-point boundary value analysis.

Question 26. (FL-4.2.3)
Correct answer: A

For each combination of the conditions there is a well-defined action. The decision table is shown in the table. N/A denotes the fact that this condition is not applicable in a given situation. For example, if a team wins, there will be no penalty kicks (they will hold only when there's a draw in a match during the championships) (Table 16.2).

For each of the 7 combinations of conditions, we were able to calculate the number of assigned points, according to the specification. Hence, A is correct.

B is incorrect, because if action depends on some condition, it is not a contradiction—this is a normal situation for which the decision tables are designed for.

C is incorrect, because no requirement is missing. Notice that the penalty kicks cannot end with a draw. The specification says that in case of penalty kicks only one out of two options is possible—either the team wins, or losses.

D is incorrect, because both conditions and actions can accept not only logical, but in fact *any* values.

Question 27. (FL-5.5.2)
Correct answer: C

Product characteristics are related to product risks. Hence, C is correct.

A, B, and D are incorrect, as these are the examples of project risks.

Question 28. (FL-4.3.3)
Correct answer: D

50% decision coverage means that there is at least one decision in a code and that we covered exactly half of the all possible decision outcomes. This means that we had to execute a statement that checks this decision outcome. Hence, D is correct.

A is incorrect—achieving 50% decision coverage does not mean that our tests executed all possible decisions. Look at Fig. 16.1a). There are three decisions in

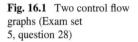

Fig. 16.1 Two control flow graphs (Exam set 5, question 28)

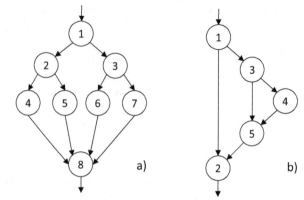

nodes 1, 2 and 3, with total of six possible outcomes. Two tests: (1, 2, 4, 8), (1, 2, 5, 8) evaluate decision 1 to one possible outcome and decision 2 to two possible outcomes. Hence, we covered three different outcomes out of six possible. We achieved 50% decision coverage, but no test covered decision 3.

B is incorrect. Look at Fig. 16.1b). There are two decisions in nodes 1 and 3, with four possible outcomes in total. A test (1, 3, 4, 5, 2) covers one outcome of decision 1 and one of decision 3, so the decision coverage is exactly 50%. On the other hand, this test covers all statements, so the statement coverage is 100%— greater than 50%.

C is incorrect. Look again at Fig. 16.1b) and suppose that decision outcomes (1, 3) and (3, 4) are TRUE outcomes. A test (1, 3, 4, 5, 2) exercises these two outcomes. We achieved 50% decision coverage, but no decision was evaluated to FALSE.

Question 29. (FL-4.4.3)
Correct answer: A

Checklist-based testing can provide guidelines and some degree of consistency. With a checklist, testing is more consistent, and there is no need to "reinvent the wheel" every time. Hence, A is correct.

B is incorrect, because exploratory testing by its nature has low repeatability— even the same tester, who has to execute the same exploratory session, will do it in a different way than during a previous session.

C and D are incorrect, because these are test types, not test techniques. Regression testing, although repeatable by its nature, may not be consistent when the tests are executed manually.

Question 30. (FL-5.5.1)
Correct answer: A

Risk level is determined by risk likelihood and risk impact. These two categories are independent: the likelihood tells us how often the risk may occur. The impact (usually measured in terms of money) tells us how severe will be the consequences of the risk occurrence. Hence, A is correct.

B and C are incorrect (see A).

D is incorrect, because both likelihood and impact are estimated during the risk analysis, so before the risk has a chance to occur. The whole point in estimating these parameters is to prepare the contingency plans and risk mitigation activities.

Question 31. (FL-4.2.1)
Correct answer: B

There are two valid equivalence classes for the variable representing the number of shopping sessions—one contains all positive integers divided by 5 (5, 10, 15, 20 and so on), and the other—all other positive integers (1, 2, 3, 4, 6, 7, 8, 9, 11, 12, 13, 14 and so on). Hence, the minimal set of test values would be: one positive integer value that is divisible by 5 and one that is not. Hence, B is correct, since 55 is divisible by 5 and 89 is not.

A is incorrect, because 0 is a value from the invalid equivalence class.

C is incorrect, because 1 and 6 are from the same equivalence class, so these tests are redundant from the equivalence partitioning point of view.

D is incorrect, because this set contains only the numbers divided by 5. Moreover, this set of test cases is infinite, which makes this "test suite" impossible to execute.

Question 32. (FL-5.1.1)
Correct answer: A

Operational acceptance testing is a type of an acceptance testing conducted by a user (operator of the system). The user is outside of the development team, while both developers and testers in this scenario are a part of the team. Hence, A is correct and B, C, D are incorrect.

Notice that in this scenario, the *role* of a tester was performed by a user, who may not be a professional tester, but still, when she does the testing, she is put in the role of a tester.

Question 33. (FL-2.3.3)
Correct answer: B

According to syllabus, after a defect is fixed, the software may be tested with all the test cases that *failed due to the defect*, which should be *re-executed* on the new software version. The purpose of this kind of tests is to confirm that the original defect has been successfully fixed. In the scenario, test 001 failed and was re-executed after the fix has been made. Hence, executing the test case 1 in step 5 is the confirmation test. No other test is the confirmation test, since no other test was re-executed after failure.

Regression testing involves executing tests to detect the unintended side-effects in *other* parts of the software than the one in which a change (or fix) has been done. Executing the test case 003 in step 6 is an example of a regression test, since it is a test case regarding module Y, which is rerunning after a fix has been made in other module (X).

Hence, B is correct.

A is incorrect, because test case 003 is not rerun after its failure—in step 3, it passed.

C is incorrect, because surely test case in step 5 is a confirmation test.

D is incorrect, because surely test case in step 6 is a regression test.

Question 34. (FL-5.2.1)
Correct answer: D

Selecting metrics for test monitoring and control is a typical activity documented in a test plan, hence D is correct.

A is incorrect, because test policy is a general document that does not go into details on metrics.

B and C are incorrect, because metrics have nothing to do neither with the test design nor with the test procedure.

Question 35. (FL-1.5.2)
Correct answer: B

A tester's primary goal is to verify that the product meets the organization's needs, so as to provide information about the product quality. A developer's primary goal is to design and build the product. Hence, B is correct.

A is incorrect, because, although the tester's and developer's mindsets are different, it is not true that the primary goal of a tester is to raise bugs—she does many other important tasks. Also, the developer's primary goal is to develop the product rather than fixing defects.

C is incorrect—although it is true that every team member must be responsible for the product quality, this does not explain the differences between the developer's and tester's mindsets. They have the common goal, but they realize it through completely different activities.

D is incorrect, because in reality, it is usually uncommon that every team member can fulfill any role in the project.

Question 36. (FL-1.2.2)
Correct answer: B

Quality control activities verify if there exist some problems in any of the SDLC artifacts. Hence, they are more related to testing than to quality assurance. Code reviews are typical static techniques for doing that, hence B is correct.

A and D are incorrect, because changing or improving the processes has a preventive role—we do it not with the intention of detecting some problems in the software, but in order to reduce the risk of further occurrence of bugs in future. Hence, these are the quality assurance activities.

C is incorrect, because the intention of organizing a training for developers is to increase their programming skills, so that they will make less errors in the future—like A and D, this is also a preventive measure, so a quality assurance activity, not a testing activity.

Question 37. (FL-1.5.1)
Correct answer: B

Alleged criticism against the product may be perceived as a destructive activity. Developers may feel that their constructive work (building the software) is diminished by testers, who raise bugs in this software. Hence, B is correct.

A is incorrect—although testing is expensive, it is not a reason that it can be perceived as a destructive activity—rather, as an expensive or ineffective one.

C is incorrect, because it refers to the alleged inefficiency, not destructiveness of the test process.

D is incorrect from the same reason as A and C.

Question 38. (FL-5.6.1)
Correct answer: D

Severity is one of the most important information in the defect report, as it allows the developers to prioritize their debug activities. From the scenario we know that the defects should be fixed starting from the most important ones. Hence, D is correct.

A is incorrect. The defect status is important, but in our case, a developer would benefit more from the information about severity. Besides, from the report, it can be deduced that this is a new defect.

B is incorrect, because expected and actual results are included in the report. Expected result is put in the "What is the expected behavior?" box. Actual result is described in the 5th step of the "Steps to reproduce" section.

C is incorrect, because the tester's name is not as important for the developer as bug severity in this scenario. Besides, the defect management applications usually automatically identify authors of the documents, because in order to use such the systems, users should usually be logged in.

Question 39. (FL-1.4.2)
Correct answer: A

Entry and exit criteria are defined during the planning activities (see also FL-5.2.3). Hence, A is true.

Question 40. (FL-5.4.1)
Correct answer: B

Requirement 2 is tested only by TC001, so we do not need to use TC002. The client's build is in version 1.1.002, which was tested with TC001 ver. 001.2.0. Hence, to reproduce the failure in this build, we need to use TC001 ver. 001.2.0. Therefore, B is correct.

A and D are incorrect, because the failure is related to Requirement 2, and TC002 does not test this requirement.

C is incorrect, because TC001 ver. 001.2.1 was not used for the client's build. It may be even impossible to run this test on the older version of the system.

Appendix A Glossary

Foundation Syllabus Glossary Terms

In tune with the new syllabus, significant changes to many glossary terms have been made. In this chapter, we give the definitions of all the terms that occur in the new Foundation syllabus, and this has been rephrased in simple language. Most of the definitions are based on the following standards, methods, and approaches:

- CMMI—Capability Maturity Model Integration
- IEEE 730—Standard for Software Quality Assurance Processes
- IEEE 1028—Standard for Software Reviews and Audits
- IEEE 1044—Standard Classification for Software Anomalies
- ISO/IEC 2382—Information Technology—Vocabulary
- ISO/IEC 14764—Software Engineering—Software Life Cycle Processes—Maintenance
- ISO/IEC 19506—Information Technology—Object Management Group Architecture-Driven Modernization (ADM)—Knowledge Discovery Meta-Model (KDM)
- ISO/IEC 20246—Software and Systems Engineering—Work Product Reviews
- ISO/IEC/IEEE 24765—Systems and Software Engineering—Vocabulary
- ISO/IEC 25010—Systems and Software Engineering—Systems and Software Quality Requirements and Evaluation (SQuaRE)—System and Software Quality Models
- ISO/IEC 25040—Systems and Software Engineering—Systems and Software Quality Requirements and Evaluation (SQuare)—Evaluation Process
- ISO/IEC/IEEE 29119-1—Software Testing Standard—Concepts and Definitions
- ISO 31000—Risk Management
- PMBOK—Project Management Body of Knowledge
- TMap—Test Management Approach

© Springer Nature Switzerland AG 2018
A. Roman, *A Study Guide to the ISTQB® Foundation Level 2018 Syllabus*,
https://doi.org/10.1007/978-3-319-98740-8

Acceptance Criteria *Ref: ISO 24765.* The criteria that a component or system must satisfy in order to be accepted by a user, customer, or other authorized entity.

Acceptance Testing *Ref: After ISO 24765. See also: user acceptance testing.* Formal testing with respect to user needs, requirements, and business processes conducted to determine whether or not a system satisfies the acceptance criteria and to enable the user, customers, or other authorized entity to determine whether or not to accept the system.

Accessibility *Ref: After ISO 25010.* The degree to which a component or system can be used by people with the widest range of characteristics and capabilities to achieve a specified goal in a specified context of use.

Accessibility Testing Testing to determine the ease by which users with disabilities can use a component or system.

Actual Result *Synonym: actual outcome.* The behavior produced/observed when a component or system is tested.

Ad Hoc Reviewing *Ref: After ISO 20246.* A review technique carried out by independent reviewers informally, without a structured process.

Alpha Testing Simulated or actual operational testing conducted in the developer's test environment, by roles outside the development organization.

Anomaly *Ref: IEEE 1044. See also: defect, error, fault, failure, incident, problem.* Any condition that deviates from expectation based on requirements specifications, design documents, user documents, standards, etc., or from someone's perception or experience. Anomalies may be found during, but not limited to, reviewing, testing, analysis, compilation, or use of software products or applicable documentation.

Audit *Ref: After IEEE 1028.* An independent examination of a work product, process, or set of processes that is performed by a third party to assess compliance with specifications, standards, contractual agreements, or other criteria.

Availability *Ref: After ISO 25010.* The degree to which a component or system is operational and accessible when required for use.

Behavior The response of a component or system to a set of input values and preconditions.

Beta Testing *Synonym: field testing.* Simulated or actual operational testing conducted at an external site, by roles outside the development organization.

Black-Box Test Technique *Synonyms: black-box technique, specification-based technique, specification-based test technique.* A procedure to derive and/or select test cases based on an analysis of the specification, either functional or nonfunctional, of a component or system without reference to its internal structure.

Boundary Value A minimum or maximum value of an ordered equivalence partition.

Boundary Value Analysis *See also: boundary value.* A black-box test technique in which test cases are designed based on boundary values.

Burndown Chart A publicly displayed chart that depicts the outstanding effort versus time in an iteration. It shows the status and trend of completing the tasks of the iteration. The X-axis typically represents days in the sprint, while the Y-axis is the remaining effort (usually either in ideal engineering hours or story points).

Checklist-Based Reviewing *Ref: ISO 20246.* A review technique guided by a list of questions or required attributes.

Checklist-Based Testing An experience-based test technique whereby the experienced tester uses a high-level list of items to be noted, checked, or remembered, or a set of rules or criteria against which a product has to be verified.

Code Coverage An analysis method that determines which parts of the software have been executed (covered) by the test suite and which parts have not been executed, e.g., statement coverage, decision coverage, or condition coverage.

Commercial Off-the-shelf (COTS) *Synonym: off-the-shelf software.* A software product that is developed for the general market, i.e., for a large number of customers, and that is delivered to many customers in identical format.

Compatibility The degree to which a component or system can exchange information with other components or systems.

Complexity *See also: cyclomatic complexity.* The degree to which a component or system has a design and/or internal structure that is difficult to understand, maintain, and verify.

Compliance *Ref: IEEE 730.* The capability of the software product to adhere to standards, conventions, or regulations in laws and similar prescriptions.

Component *Synonyms: module, unit.* A minimal part of a system that can be tested in isolation.

Component Integration Testing *Synonym: link testing.* Testing performed to expose defects in the interfaces and interactions between integrated components.

Component Specification A description of a component's function in terms of its output values for specified input values under specified conditions, and required nofunctional behavior (e.g., resource utilization).

Component Testing *Ref: ISO 24765. Synonyms: module testing, unit testing.* The testing of individual hardware or software components.

Condition *See also: condition testing.* Synonyms: branch condition. A logical expression that can be evaluated as True or False, e.g., $A > B$.

Configuration The composition of a component or system as defined by the number, nature, and interconnections of its constituent parts.

Configuration Item *Ref: ISO 24765.* An aggregation of work products that is designated for configuration management and treated as a single entity in the configuration management process.

Configuration Management *Ref: ISO 24765.* A discipline applying technical and administrative direction and surveillance to identify and document the functional and physical characteristics of a configuration item, control changes to those characteristics, record and report change processing and implementation status, and verify compliance with specified requirements.

Configuration Management Tool A tool that provides support for the identification and control of configuration items, their status over changes and versions, and the release of baselines consisting of configuration items.

Confirmation Testing *Synonym: retesting.* Dynamic testing conducted after fixing defects with the objective to confirm that failures caused by those defects do not occur anymore.

Contractual Acceptance Testing Acceptance testing conducted to verify whether a system satisfies its contractual requirements.

Control Flow *Ref: ISO 29119.* The sequence in which operations are performed during the execution of a test item.

Cost of Quality The total costs incurred on quality activities and issues and often split into prevention costs, appraisal costs, internal failure costs, and external failure costs.

Coverage *Ref: After ISO 29119. Synonym: test coverage.* The degree to which specified coverage items have been determined or have been exercised by a test suite expressed as a percentage.

Coverage Item *Ref: ISO 29119.* An attribute or combination of attributes that is derived from one or more test conditions by using a test technique that enables the measurement of the thoroughness of the test execution.

Coverage Tool *Synonym: coverage measurement tool.* A tool that provides objective measures of what structural elements, e.g., statements, branches have been exercised by a test suite.

Data Flow An abstract representation of the sequence and possible changes of the state of data objects, where the state of an object is any of creation, usage, or destruction.

Data-Driven Testing *See also: keyword-driven testing.* A scripting technique that stores test input and expected results in a table or spreadsheet, so that a single control script can execute all of the tests in the table. Data-driven testing is often used to support the application of test execution tools such as capture/playback tools.

Debugging The process of finding, analyzing, and removing the causes of failures in software.

Decision *Ref: ISO 29119.* A type of statement in which a choice between two or more possible outcomes controls which set of actions will result.

Decision Coverage The coverage of decision outcomes.

Decision Outcome The result of a decision that determines the next statement to be executed.

Decision Table *Ref: ISO 24765. Synonym: cause–effect decision table.* A table used to show sets of conditions and the actions resulting from them.

Decision Table Testing *See also: decision table.* A black-box test technique in which test cases are designed to execute the combinations of inputs and/or stimuli (causes) shown in a decision table.

Decision Testing A white-box test technique in which test cases are designed to execute decision outcomes.

Defect *Ref: After IEEE 1044. Synonyms: bug, fault.* An imperfection or deficiency in a work product where it does not meet its requirements or specifications.

Defect Density *Ref: After ISO 24765. Synonym: fault density.* The number of defects per unit size of a work product.

Defect Management *See also: incident management.* The process of recognizing and recording defects, classifying them, investigating them, taking action to resolve them, and disposing of them when resolved.

Defect Management Tool *See also: incident management tool. Synonyms: bug tracking tool, defect-tracking tool.* A tool that facilitates the recording and status tracking of defects.

Defect Report *See also: incident report. Synonym: bug report.* Documentation of the occurrence, nature, and status of a defect.

Driver *Ref: After TMap. Synonym: test driver.* A software component or test tool that replaces a component that takes care of the control and/or the calling of a component or system.

Dynamic Analysis *Ref: After IEEE 610.* The process of evaluating behavior, e.g., memory performance, CPU usage of a system or component during execution.

Dynamic Analysis Tool A tool that provides run-time information on the state of the software code. These tools are most commonly used to identify unassigned pointers, check pointer arithmetic, to monitor the allocation, use, and de-allocation of memory, and to flag memory leaks.

Dynamic Testing Testing that involves the execution of the software of a component or system.

Effectiveness *Ref: ISO 9241. See also: efficiency.* Extent to which correct and complete goals are achieved.

Efficiency *Ref: ISO 9241. See also: effectiveness.* Resources expended in relation to the extent with which users achieve specified goals.

Entry Criteria *Synonym: definition of ready.* The set of conditions for officially starting a defined task.

Equivalence Partition *Synonym: equivalence class.* A portion of the value domain of a data element related to the test object for which all values are expected to be treated the same based on the specification.

Equivalence Partitioning *Ref: After ISO 29119. Synonym: partition testing.* A black-box test technique in which test cases are designed to exercise equivalence partitions by using one representative member of each partition.

Error *Ref: ISO 24765. Synonym: mistake.* A human action that produces an incorrect result.

Error Guessing *Ref: ISO 29119.* A test technique in which tests are derived on the basis of the tester's knowledge of past failures, or general knowledge of failure modes.

Executable Statement A statement which, when compiled, is translated into object code, and which will be executed procedurally when the program is running and may perform an action on data.

Exercised A program element is said to be exercised by a test case when the input value causes the execution of that element, such as a statement, decision, or other structural element.

Exhaustive Testing *Synonym: complete testing.* A test approach in which the test suite comprises all combinations of input values and preconditions.

Exit Criteria *Synonyms: completion criteria, test completion criteria, definition of done.* The set of conditions for officially completing a defined task.

Expected Result *Ref: After ISO 29119. Synonyms: expected outcome, predicted outcome*The predicted observable behavior of a component or system executing under specified conditions, based on its specification or another source.

Experience-Based Test Technique *Synonym: experience-based technique.* A procedure to derive and/or select test cases based on the tester's experience, knowledge, and intuition.

Experience-Based Testing Testing based on the tester's experience, knowledge, and intuition.

Exploratory Testing *Ref: After ISO 29119.* An approach to testing whereby the testers dynamically design and execute tests based on their knowledge, exploration of the test item, and the results of previous tests.

Extreme Programming (XP) *See also: Agile software development.* A software engineering methodology used within Agile software development whereby core practices are programming in pairs, doing extensive code review, unit testing of all code, and simplicity and clarity in code.

Facilitator *Ref: After IEEE 1028. See also: moderator.* The leader and main person responsible for an inspection or review process.

Fail A test is deemed to fail if its actual result does not match its expected result.

Failure *Ref: After ISO 24765.* An event in which a component or system does not perform a required function within specified limits.

Failure Rate *Ref: ISO 24765.* The ratio of the number of failures of a given category to a given unit of measure.

Feature *Ref: After IEEE 1008. Synonym: software feature.* An attribute of a component or system specified or implied by requirements documentation (e.g., reliability, usability, or design constraints).

Finding A result of an evaluation that identifies some important issue, problem, or opportunity.

Formal Review *Ref: ISO 20246.* A form of review that follows a defined process with a formally documented output.

Functional Integration *See also: integration testing.* An integration approach that combines the components or systems for the purpose of getting a basic functionality working early.

Functional Requirement *Ref: ISO 24765.* A requirement that specifies a function that a component or system must be able to perform.

Functional Suitability *Ref: After ISO 25010. Synonym: functionality.* The degree to which a component or system provides functions that meet stated and implied needs when used under specified conditions.

Functional Testing *Ref: ISO 24765. See also: black-box testing.* Testing conducted to evaluate the compliance of a component or system with functional requirements.

GUI Acronym for Graphical User Interface.

High-Level Test Case *See also: low-level test case. Synonyms: abstract test case, logical test case.* A test case without concrete values for input data and expected results.

IDEAL An organizational improvement model that serves as a roadmap for initiating, planning, and implementing improvement actions. The IDEAL model is named for the five phases it describes: initiating, diagnosing, establishing, acting, and learning.

Impact Analysis *Ref: After ISO 24765.* The identification of all work products affected by a change, including an estimate of the resources needed to accomplish the change.

Incident Report *Ref: ISO 29119. Synonyms: deviation report, software test incident report, test incident report.* Documentation of the occurrence, nature, and status of an incident.

Incremental Development Model *Ref: After PMBOK. See also: iterative development model.* A development life cycle model in which the project scope is generally determined early in the project life cycle, but time and cost estimates are routinely modified as the project team's understanding of the product increases. The product is developed through a series of repeated cycles, each delivering an increment, which successively adds to the functionality of the product.

Independence of Testing *Ref: After DO-178b.* Separation of responsibilities, which encourages the accomplishment of objective testing.

Informal Group Review *Ref: ISO 20246. See also: informal review.* An informal review performed by three or more persons.

Informal Review *Ref: ISO 20246.* A type of review without a formal (documented) procedure.

Input *Ref: ISO 24765.* Data received by a component or system from an external source.

Inspection *Ref: After ISO 20246.* A type of formal review to identify issues in a work product, which provides measurement to improve the review process and the software development process.

Installation Guide Supplied instructions on any suitable media, which guides the installer through the installation process. This may be a manual guide, step-by-step procedure, installation wizard, or any other similar process description.

Integration The process of combining components or systems into larger assemblies.

Integration Testing *See also: component integration testing, system integration testing.* Testing performed to expose defects in the interfaces and in the interactions between integrated components or systems.

Interoperability *Ref: After ISO 25010.* The degree to which two or more components or systems can exchange information and use the information that has been exchanged.

Interoperability Testing *See also: functionality testing. Synonym: compatibility testing.* Testing to determine the interoperability of a software product.

Iterative Development Model A development life cycle where a project is broken into a usually large number of iterations. An iteration is a complete development loop resulting in a release (internal or external) of an executable product, a subset of the final product under development, which grows from iteration to iteration to become the final product.

Keyword-Driven Testing *See also: data-driven testing. Synonym: action word-driven testing.* A scripting technique that uses data files to contain not only test data and expected results, but also keywords related to the application being tested. The keywords are interpreted by special supporting scripts that are called by the control script for the test.

Life Cycle Model *Ref: CMMI. See also: software life cycle.* A description of the processes, workflows, and activities used in the development, delivery, maintenance, and retirement of a system.

Load Testing *Ref: After ISO 29119. See also: performance testing, stress testing.* A type of performance testing conducted to evaluate the behavior of a component or system under varying loads, usually between anticipated conditions of low, typical, and peak usage.

Low-Level Test Case *See also: high-level test case. Synonym: concrete test case.* A test case with concrete values for input data and expected results.

Maintainability *Ref: After ISO 25010.* The degree to which a component or system can be modified by the intended maintainers.

Maintenance *Ref: After ISO 14764.* The process of modifying a component or system after delivery to correct defects, improve quality attributes, or adapt to a changed environment.

Maintenance Testing Testing the changes to an operational system or the impact of a changed environment to an operational system.

Master Test Plan *See also: test plan.* A test plan that is used to coordinate multiple test levels or test types.

Maturity *Ref: ISO 25010.* (1) The capability of an organization with respect to the effectiveness and efficiency of its processes and work practices. (2) The degree to which a component or system meets needs for reliability under normal operation.

Measure *Ref: After ISO 25040.* The number or category assigned to an attribute of an entity by making a measurement.

Measurement *Ref: After ISO 25040.* The process of assigning a number or category to an entity to describe an attribute of that entity.

Memory Leak A memory access failure due to a defect in a program's dynamic store allocation logic that causes it to fail to release memory after it has finished using it, eventually causing the program and/or other concurrent processes to fail due to lack of memory.

Metric A measurement scale and the method used for measurement.

Milestone A point in time in a project at which defined (intermediate) deliverables and results should be ready.

Model-Based Testing (MBT) Testing based on or involving models.

Moderator *See also: facilitator. Synonym: inspection leader.* A neutral person who conducts a usability test session.

Monitoring Tool *Ref: ISO 24765. See also: dynamic analysis tool.* A software tool or hardware device that runs concurrently with the component or system under test and supervises, records, and/or analyzes the behavior of the component or system.

Nonfunctional Requirement *Ref: After ISO 24765.* A requirement that describes how the component or system will do what it is intended to do.

Nonfunctional Testing Testing conducted to evaluate the compliance of a component or system with nonfunctional requirements.

Operational Acceptance Testing *See also: operational testing. Synonym: production acceptance testing.* Operational testing in the acceptance test phase, typically performed in a (simulated) operational environment by operations and/or systems administration staff focusing on operational aspects, e.g., recoverability, resource-behavior, installability, and technical compliance.

Operational Environment Hardware and software products installed at users' or customers' sites where the component or system under test will be used. The software may include operating systems, database management systems, and other applications.

Output *Ref: After ISO 24765.* Data transmitted by a component or system to an external destination.

Pass A test is deemed to pass if its actual result matches its expected result.

Path *Synonym: control flow path.* A sequence of events, e.g., executable statements, of a component or system from an entry point to an exit point.

Peer Review *Ref: After ISO 20246.* A form of review of work products performed by others qualified to do the same work.

Performance Efficiency *Ref: After ISO 25010. Synonyms: time behavior, performance.* The degree to which a component or system uses time, resources, and capacity when accomplishing its designated functions.

Performance Indicator *Ref: CMMI. Synonym: key performance indicator.* A high-level metric of effectiveness and/or efficiency used to guide and control progressive development, e.g., lead-time slip for software development.

Performance Testing *See also: efficiency testing.* Testing to determine the performance of a software product.

Performance Testing Tool A test tool that generates load for a designated test item and that measures and records its performance during test execution.

Perspective-Based Reading *Ref: After ISO 20246. Synonym: perspective-based reviewing.* A review technique whereby reviewers evaluate the work product from different viewpoints.

Planning Poker *See also: Agile software development, Wideband Delphi.* A consensus-based estimation technique, mostly used to estimate effort or relative size of user stories in Agile software development. It is a variation of the Wideband Delphi method using a deck of cards with values representing the units in which the team estimates.

Portability *Ref: ISO 9126.* The ease with which the software product can be transferred from one hardware or software environment to another.

Portability Testing *Synonym: configuration testing.* Testing to determine the portability of a software product.

Postcondition The expected state of a test item and its environment at the end of test case execution.

Precondition The required state of a test item and its environment prior to test case execution.

Priority The level of (business) importance assigned to an item, e.g., defect.

Probe Effect The effect on the component or system by the measurement instrument when the component or system is being measured, e.g., by a performance testing tool or monitor. For example performance may be slightly worse when performance testing tools are being used.

Problem *Ref: ISO 24765.* An unknown underlying cause of one or more incidents.

Process *Ref: ISO 12207.* A set of interrelated activities, which transform inputs into outputs.

Process Improvement *Ref: CMMI.* A program of activities designed to improve the performance and maturity of the organization's processes, and the result of such a program.

Product Risk *See also: risk.* A risk impacting the quality of a product.

Project *Ref: ISO 9000.* A project is a unique set of coordinated and controlled activities with start and finish dates undertaken to achieve an objective conforming to specific requirements, including the constraints of time, cost, and resources.

Project Risk *See also: risk.* A risk that impacts project success.

Quality *Ref: ISO 24765.* The degree to which a component, system or process meets specified requirements and/or user/customer needs and expectations.

Quality Assurance *Ref: ISO 9000.* Part of quality management focused on providing confidence that quality requirements will be fulfilled.

Quality Characteristic *Ref: ISO 24765. Synonyms: quality characteristic, software product characteristic, software quality characteristic, quality attribute.* A category of product attributes that bears on quality.

Quality Control *Ref: after ISO 8402.* The operational techniques and activities, part of quality management, that are focused on fulfilling quality requirements.

Quality Management *Ref: ISO 9000.* Coordinated activities to direct and control an organization with regard to quality. Direction and control with regard to quality generally includes the establishment of the quality policy and quality objectives, quality planning, quality control, quality assurance and quality improvement.

Quality Risk *See also: quality characteristic, product risk.* A product risk related to a quality characteristic.

Rational Unified Process (RUP) A proprietary adaptable iterative software development process framework consisting of four project life cycle phases: inception, elaboration, construction and transition.

Regression A degradation in the quality of a component or system due to a change.

Regression Testing Testing of a previously tested component or system following modification to ensure that defects have not been introduced or have been uncovered in unchanged areas of the software, as a result of the changes made.

Regulatory Acceptance Testing Acceptance testing conducted to verify whether a system conforms to relevant laws, policies and regulations.

Reliability *Ref: After ISO 25010.* The degree to which a component or system performs specified functions under specified conditions for a specified period of time.

Reliability Growth Model A model that shows the growth in reliability over time during continuous testing of a component or system as a result of the removal of defects that result in reliability failures.

Requirement *Ref: ISO 24765.* A provision that contains criteria to be fulfilled.

Requirements Management Tool A tool that supports the recording of requirements, requirements attributes (e.g., priority, knowledge responsible) and annotation, and facilitates traceability through layers of requirements and requirements change management. Some requirements management tools also provide facilities for static analysis, such as consistency checking and violations to predefined requirements rules.

Result *See also: actual result, expected result. Synonyms: outcome, test outcome, test result.* The consequence/outcome of the execution of a test. It includes outputs to screens, changes to data, reports, and communication messages sent out.

Retrospective Meeting *Synonym: post-project meeting.* A meeting at the end of a project during which the project team members evaluate the project and learn lessons that can be applied to the next project.

Review *Ref: After IEEE 1028.* A type of static testing during which a work product or process is evaluated by one or more individuals to detect issues and to provide improvements.

Review Plan A document describing the approach, resources, and schedule of intended review activities. It identifies, among others, documents and code to be reviewed, review types to be used, participants, as well as entry and exit criteria to be applied in case of formal reviews, and the rationale for their choice. It is a record of the review planning process.

Reviewer *Ref: After ISO 20246. Synonyms: checker, inspector.* A participant in a review, who identifies issues in the work product.

Risk A factor that could result in future negative consequences.

Risk Analysis The overall process of risk identification and risk assessment.

Risk Level *Synonym: risk exposure.* The qualitative or quantitative measure of a risk defined by impact and likelihood.

Risk Management *Ref: ISO 31000.* The coordinated activities to direct and control an organization with regard to risk.

Risk Mitigation *Synonym: risk control.* The process through which decisions are reached and protective measures are implemented for reducing or maintaining risks to specified levels.

Risk Type *Synonym: risk category.* A set of risks grouped by one or more common factors.

Risk-Based Testing *Ref: After ISO 29119.* Testing in which the management, selection, prioritization, and use of testing activities and resources are based on corresponding risk types and risk levels.

Robustness *Ref: ISO 24765. See also: error-tolerance, fault-tolerance.* The degree to which a component or system can function correctly in the presence of invalid inputs or stressful environmental conditions.

Role-Based Reviewing *Ref: After ISO 20246.* A review technique where reviewers evaluate a work product from the perspective of different stakeholder roles.

Root Cause *Ref: CMMI.* A source of a defect such that if it is removed, the occurrence of the defect type is decreased or removed.

Root Cause Analysis *Synonym: causal analysis.* An analysis technique aimed at identifying the root causes of defects. By directing corrective measures at root causes, it is hoped that the likelihood of defect recurrence will be minimized.

Safety *Ref: After ISO 24765.* The capability that a system will not, under defined conditions, lead to a state in which human life, health, property, or the environment is endangered.

Scenario-Based Reviewing *Ref: ISO 20246.* A review technique where the review is guided by determining the ability of the work product to address specific scenarios.

Scribe *Ref: After IEEE 1028. Synonym: recorder.* A person who records information during the review meetings.

Scrum *See also: Agile software development.* An iterative incremental framework for managing projects commonly used with Agile software development.

SDLC *See: software development life cycle*

Security *Ref: After ISO 25010.* The degree to which a component or system protects information and data so that persons or other components or systems have the degree of access appropriate to their types and levels of authorization.

Security Testing *See also: functionality testing.* Testing to determine the security of the software product.

Sequential Development Model A type of development life cycle model in which a complete system is developed in a linear way of several discrete and successive phases with no overlap between them.

Session-Based Testing An approach to testing in which test activities are planned as uninterrupted sessions of test design and execution, often used in conjunction with exploratory testing.

Severity The degree of impact that a defect has on the development or operation of a component or system.

Simulation *Ref: ISO 2382.* The representation of selected behavioral characteristics of one physical or abstract system by another system.

Simulator *Ref: ISO 24765. See also: emulator.* A device, computer program, or system used during testing, which behaves or operates like a given system when provided with a set of controlled inputs.

Software *Ref: ISO 24765.* Computer programs, procedures, and possibly associated documentation and data pertaining to the operation of a computer system.

Software Development Life cycle The activities performed at each stage in software development, and how they relate to one another logically and chronologically.

Software Life cycle The period of time that begins when a software product is conceived and ends when the software is no longer available for use. The software life cycle typically includes a concept phase, requirements phase, design phase, implementation phase, test phase, installation and checkout phase, operation and maintenance phase, and, sometimes, retirement phase. Note these phases may overlap or be performed iteratively.

Software Quality *Ref: After ISO 9126. See also: quality.* The totality of functionality and features of a software product that bear on its ability to satisfy stated or implied needs.

Specification *Ref: After IEEE 610.* A document that specifies, ideally in a complete, precise and verifiable manner, the requirements, design, behavior, or other characteristics of a component or system, and, often, the procedures for determining whether these provisions have been satisfied.

Stability *Ref: ISO 25010.* The degree to which a component or system can be effectively and efficiently modified without introducing defects or degrading existing product quality.

Standard *Ref: After CMMI.* Formal, possibly mandatory, set of requirements developed and used to prescribe consistent approaches to the way of working or to provide guidelines (e.g., ISO/IEC standards, IEEE standards, and organizational standards).

State Diagram *Ref: After ISO 24765. Synonym: state transition diagram.* A diagram that depicts the states that a component or system can assume, and shows the events or circumstances that cause and/or result from a change from one state to another.

State Transition A transition between two states of a component or system.

State Transition Testing *See also: N-switch testing. Synonym: finite state testing.* A black-box test technique using a state transition diagram or state table to derive test cases to evaluate whether the test item successfully executes valid transitions and blocks invalid transitions.

Statement *Synonym: source statement.* An entity in a programming language, which is typically the smallest indivisible unit of execution.

Statement Coverage The percentage of executable statements that have been exercised by a test suite.

Statement Testing A white-box test technique in which test cases are designed to execute statements.

Static Analysis *Ref: After ISO 24765.* The process of evaluating a component or system without executing it, based on its form, structure, content, or documentation.

Static Testing Testing a work product without code being executed.

Structural Coverage Coverage measures based on the internal structure of a component or system.

Stub *Ref: After IEEE 610.* A skeletal or special-purpose implementation of a software component, used to develop or test a component that calls or is otherwise dependent on it. It replaces a called component.

System *Ref: After ISO 24765.* A collection of interacting elements organized to accomplish a specific function or set of functions.

System Integration Testing Testing the combination and interaction of systems.

System Testing Testing an integrated system to verify that it meets specified requirements.

System Under Test (SUT) A type of test object that is a system.

Technical Review *Ref: IEEE 1028.* A formal review type by a team of technically-qualified personnel that examines the suitability of a work product for its intended use and identifies discrepancies from specifications and standards.

Test A set of one or more test cases.

Test Analysis The activity that identifies test conditions by analyzing the test basis.

Test Approach The implementation of the test strategy for a specific project.

Test Automation The use of software to perform or support test activities, e.g., test management, test design, test execution, and results checking.

Test Basis *Ref: After TMap.* The body of knowledge used as the basis for test analysis and design.

Test Case *Ref: After ISO 29119.* A set of preconditions, inputs, actions (where applicable), expected results, and postconditions, developed based on test conditions.

Test Case Specification *Ref: ISO 29119. See also: test specification.* Documentation of a set of one or more test cases.

Test Charter *See also: exploratory testing. Synonym: charter.* Documentation of test activities in session-based exploratory testing.

Test Completion *Ref: After ISO 29119.* The activity that makes test assets available for later use, leaves test environments in a satisfactory condition and communicates the results of testing to relevant stakeholders.

Test Condition *Synonyms: test requirement, test situation.* An aspect of the test basis that is relevant in order to achieve specific test objectives.

Test Control *See also: test management.* A test management task that deals with developing and applying a set of corrective actions to get a test project on track when monitoring shows a deviation from what was planned.

Test Cycle Execution of the test process against a single identifiable release of the test object.

Test Data *Ref: After ISO 29119.* Data created or selected to satisfy the execution preconditions and inputs to execute one or more test cases.

Test Data Preparation Tool *Synonym: test generator.* A type of test tool that enables data to be selected from existing databases or created, generated, manipulated and edited for use in testing.

Test Design *Ref: After ISO 29119. See also: test design specification.* The activity of deriving and specifying test cases from test conditions.

Test Design Tool A tool that supports the test design activity by generating test inputs from a specification that may be held in a CASE tool repository, e.g., requirements management tool, from specified test conditions held in the tool itself, or from code.

Test Environment *Ref: ISO 24765. Synonyms: test bed, test rig.* An environment containing hardware, instrumentation, simulators, software tools, and other support elements needed to conduct a test.

Test Estimation The calculated approximation of a result related to various aspects of testing (e.g., effort spent, completion date, costs involved, number of test cases, etc.) which is usable even if input data may be incomplete, uncertain, or noisy.

Test Execution The process of running a test on the component or system under test, producing actual result(s).

Test Execution Schedule A schedule for the execution of test suites within a test cycle.

Test Execution Tool A test tool that executes tests against a designated test item and evaluates the outcomes against expected results and postconditions.

Test Harness A test environment comprised of stubs and drivers needed to execute a test.

Test Implementation The activity that prepares the testware needed for test execution based on test analysis and design.

Test Infrastructure The organizational artifacts needed to perform testing, consisting of test environments, test tools, office environment, and procedures.

Test Input The data received from an external source by the test object during test execution. The external source can be hardware, software, or human.

Test Item *See also: test object.* A part of a test object used in the test process.

Test Leader *See also: test manager. Synonym: lead tester.* On large projects, the person who reports to the test manager and is responsible for project management of a particular test level or a particular set of testing activities.

Test Level *Ref: After ISO 29119. Synonym: test stage.* A specific instantiation of a test process.

Test Management *Ref: ISO 29119.* The planning, scheduling, estimating, monitoring, reporting, control and completion of test activities.

Test Management Tool A tool that provides support to the test management and control part of a test process. It often has several capabilities, such as testware management, scheduling of tests, the logging of results, progress tracking, incident management and test reporting.

Test Manager The person responsible for project management of testing activities and resources, and evaluation of a test object. The individual who directs, controls, administers, plans, and regulates the evaluation of a test object.

Test Monitoring *See also: test management.* A test management activity that involves checking the status of testing activities, identifying any variances from the planned or expected status, and reporting status to stakeholders.

Test Object *See also: test item.* The component or system to be tested.

Test Objective A reason or purpose for designing and executing a test.

Test Oracle *Synonym: oracle.* A source to determine expected results to compare with the actual result of the system under test.

Test Plan *Ref: After ISO 29119.* Documentation describing the test objectives to be achieved and the means and the schedule for achieving them, organized to coordinate testing activities.

Test Planning The activity of establishing or updating a test plan.

Test Policy *Synonym: organizational test policy.* A high-level document describing the principles, approach and major objectives of the organization regarding testing.

Test Procedure *Ref: ISO 29119. See also: test script.* A sequence of test cases in execution order, and any associated actions that may be required to set up the initial preconditions and any wrap up activities post execution.

Test Process The set of interrelated activities comprising of test planning, test monitoring and control, test analysis, test design, test implementation, test execution, and test completion.

Test Process Improvement *Ref: After CMMI.* A program of activities designed to improve the performance and maturity of the organization's test processes and the results of such a program.

Test Progress Report *Synonym: test status report.* A test report produced at regular intervals about the progress of test activities against a baseline, risks, and alternatives requiring a decision.

Test Report Documentation summarizing test activities and results.

Test Reporting *See also: test process.* Collecting and analyzing data from testing activities and subsequently consolidating the data in a report to inform stakeholders.

Test Schedule A list of activities, tasks or events of the test process, identifying their intended start and finish dates and/or times, and interdependencies.

Test Script *See also: test procedure.* A sequence of instructions for the execution of a test.

Test Session *See also: exploratory testing.* An uninterrupted period of time spent in executing tests. In exploratory testing, each test session is focused on a charter, but testers can also explore new opportunities or issues during a session. The tester creates and executes on the fly and records their progress.

Test Strategy *Ref: After ISO 29119. Synonym: organizational test strategy.* Documentation that expresses the generic requirements for testing one or more projects run within an organization, providing detail on how testing is to be performed, and is aligned with the test policy.

Test Suite *Synonyms: test case suite, test set.* A set of test cases or test procedures to be executed in a specific test cycle.

Test Summary Report *Ref: ISO 29119. Synonym: test report.* A test report that provides an evaluation of the corresponding test items against exit criteria.

Test Technique *Synonyms: test case design technique, test specification technique, test technique, test design technique.* A procedure used to derive and/or select test cases.

Test Tool *Ref: TMap. See also: CAST.* A software product that supports one or more test activities, such as planning and control, specification, building initial files and data, test execution and test analysis.

Test Type *Ref: After TMap.* A group of test activities based on specific test objectives aimed at specific characteristics of a component or system.

Testability *Ref: After ISO 25010.* The degree of effectiveness and efficiency with which tests can be designed and executed for a component or system.

Testable Requirement *Ref: After IEEE 610.* A requirements that is stated in terms that permit establishment of test designs (and subsequently test cases) and execution of tests to determine whether the requirement has been met.

Tester A skilled professional who is involved in the testing of a component or system.

Testing The process consisting of all life cycle activities, both static and dynamic, concerned with planning, preparation and evaluation of software products and related work products to determine that they satisfy specified requirements, to demonstrate that they are fit for purpose and to detect defects.

Testware *Ref: After ISO 29119.* Work products produced during the test process for use in planning, designing, executing, evaluating and reporting on testing.

Traceability *Ref: After ISO 19506. See also: horizontal traceability, vertical traceability.* The degree to which a relationship can be established between two or more work products.

Understandability *Ref: ISO 9126. See also: usability.* The capability of the software product to enable the user to understand whether the software is suitable, and how it can be used for particular tasks and conditions of use.

Unit Test Framework A tool that provides an environment for unit or component testing in which a component can be tested in isolation or with suitable stubs and drivers. It also provides other support for the developer, such as debugging capabilities.

Unreachable Code *Synonym: dead code.* Code that cannot be reached and therefore is impossible to execute.

Usability *Ref: After ISO 25010.* The degree to which a component or system can be used by specified users to achieve specified goals in a specified context of use.

Usability Testing *Ref: After ISO 25010.* Testing to evaluate the degree to which the system can be used by specified users with effectiveness, efficiency, and satisfaction in a specified context of use.

Use Case A sequence of transactions in a dialogue between an actor and a component or system with a tangible result, where an actor can be a user or anything that can exchange information with the system.

Use Case Testing *Synonyms: scenario testing, user scenario testing.* A black-box test technique in which test cases are designed to execute scenarios of use cases.

User Acceptance Testing *See also: acceptance testing.* Acceptance testing conducted in a real or simulated operational environment by intended users focusing their needs, requirements, and business processes.

User Interface All components of a system that provide information and controls for the user to accomplish specific tasks with the system.

User Story *See also: Agile software development, requirement.* A high-level user or business requirement commonly used in Agile software development, typically consisting of one sentence in the everyday or business language capturing what functionality a user needs and the reason behind this, any nonfunctional criteria, and also includes acceptance criteria.

V-model A sequential development life cycle model describing a one-for-one relationship between major phases of software development from business requirements specification to delivery, and corresponding test levels from acceptance testing to component testing.

Validation *Ref: ISO 9000.* Confirmation by examination and through provision of objective evidence that the requirements for a specific intended use or application have been fulfilled.

Variable An element of storage in a computer that is accessible by a software program by referring to it by a name.

Verification *Ref: ISO 9000.* Confirmation by examination and through provision of objective evidence that specified requirements have been fulfilled.

Walkthrough *Ref: After ISO 20246. See also: peer review. Synonym: structured walkthrough.* A type of review in which an author leads members of the review through a work product and the members ask questions and make comments about possible issues.

White-Box Test Technique *Synonyms: structural test technique, structure-based test technique, structure-based technique, white-box technique.* A procedure to derive and/or select test cases based on an analysis of the internal structure of a component or system.

White-Box Testing *Synonyms: clear-box testing, code-based testing, glass-box testing, logic-coverage testing, logic-driven testing, structural testing, structure-based testing.* Testing based on an analysis of the internal structure of the component or system.

Wideband Delphi An expert-based test estimation technique that aims at making an accurate estimation using the collective wisdom of the team members.

Appendix B Questions Distribution by Learning Objectives

Table B.1 shows the question numbers in all five exam sets, sorted by Learning Objectives. This table is helpful if you want to assess your knowledge related to a specific Learning Objective. For example, if you are interested in questions related to the boundary value analysis (FL-4.2.2), you should look up in the row corresponding to this Learning Objective and you will find that the questions on this topic are:

- Question number 35 in the Exam Set 1
- Question number 35 in the Exam Set 2
- Question number 2 in the Exam Set 3
- Questions number 34 and 36 in the Exam Set 4
- Questions number 13 and 25 in the Exam Set 5

© Springer Nature Switzerland AG 2018

A. Roman, *A Study Guide to the ISTQB® Foundation Level 2018 Syllabus*,
https://doi.org/10.1007/978-3-319-98740-8

Table B.1 Questions distribution by Learning Objectives

Learning Objective	Exam set 1	Exam set 2	Exam set 3	Exam set 4	Exam set 5
Chapter 1: Fundamentals of Testing					
Chapter 1 keywords	5	9	6	8	1
FL-1.1.1	2		13	35	
FL-1.1.2	12			11	21
FL-1.2.1		40	3		
FL-1.2.2	26			39	36
FL-1.2.3		3	15	20	
FL-1.2.4	24	29		32	
FL-1.3.1		2	39		22
FL-1.4.1	7			28	
FL-1.4.2		33	38		39
FL-1.4.3	33			24	9
FL-1.4.4		5	21		
FL-1.5.1		17			37
FL-1.5.2	32		31		35
Chapter 2: Testing Throughout the Software Development Life Cycle					
FL-2.1.1	20	11	4		14
FL-2.1.2	21			2	10
FL-2.2.1	4	31		27	
FL-2.3.1			36	17	12
FL-2.3.2		22	20		
FL-2.3.3		7		5	33
FL-2.4.1	1		18	18	
FL-2.4.2	15	21	35		24
Chapter 3: Static Testing					
FL-3.1.1	27	13		13	
FL-3.1.2	36		11		2
FL-3.1.3			28	14	15
FL-3.2.1	11	36		21	
FL-3.2.2			8		16
FL-3.2.3		34	22	26	
FL-3.2.4	34	19	24	31	5
FL-3.2.5	17	20			20
Chapter 4: Test Techniques					
Chapter 4 keywords	19	23	26	30	19
FL-4.1.1		6	1		3
FL-4.2.1	6, 22	16, 24	12, 27	4	31
FL-4.2.2	35	35	2	34, 36	13, 25
FL-4.2.3	9	25	9	6	26
FL-4.2.4	30	12	25	9	7
FL-4.2.5	38	15	34	25	
FL-4.3.1		38	16		17
FL-4.3.2	13		19	12	

(continued)

Table B.1 (continued)

Learning Objective	Exam set 1	Exam set 2	Exam set 3	Exam set 4	Exam set 5
FL-4.3.3	3	39		3	28
FL-4.4.1	18		17		
FL-4.4.2		18		19	18
FL-4.4.3	28			29	29
Chapter 5: Test Management					
FL-5.1.1	23			23	32
FL-5.1.2		8	5		6
FL-5.2.1		1		1	34
FL-5.2.2	25		30	37	
FL-5.2.3		4			4
FL-5.2.4	8	10	7	7	8
FL-5.2.5	16		14	16	
FL-5.2.6	31	27	32		
FL-5.3.1		32		33	
FL-5.3.2	14		33	15	
FL-5.4.1	39		40		40
FL-5.5.1	29				30
FL-5.5.2		26		40	27
FL-5.5.3		28	23		
FL-5.6.1	37	37	37	38	38
Chapter 6: Tool Support for Testing					
FL-6.1.1	10	14	10	10	11
FL-6.1.2			29		
FL-6.1.3		30			
FL-6.2.1	40				
FL-6.2.2				22	
FL-6.2.3					23

CPSIA information can be obtained
at www.ICGtesting.com
Printed in the USA
LVHW020007071118
596187LV00007B/120/P